Junges Digitales Recht | Young Digital Law

Hamburg 2022

Simone Kuhlmann | Fabrizio De Gregorio | Martin Fertmann
Hannah Ofterdinger | Anton Sefkow [Eds.]

Transparency or Opacity

A Legal Analysis of the Organization
of Information in the Digital World

 Nomos    MANZ    DIKE

© Coverpicture: Who is Danny – stock.adobe.com

Die Deutsche Nationalbibliothek verzeichnet diese Publikation in
der Deutschen Nationalbibliografie; detaillierte bibliografische
Daten sind im Internet über http://dnb.d-nb.de abrufbar.

The Deutsche Nationalbibliothek lists this publication in the
Deutsche Nationalbibliografie; detailed bibliographic data
are available on the Internet at http://dnb.d-nb.de

ISBN (Print) 978-3-7560-0027-2 (Nomos Verlagsgesellschaft mbH & Co. KG, Baden-Baden)
ISBN (ePDF) 978-3-7489-3606-0 (Nomos Verlagsgesellschaft mbH & Co. KG, Baden-Baden)
ISBN (Print) 978-3-03891-588-1 (Dike Verlag, Zürich/St. Gallen)
ISBN (Print) 978-3-214-25099-7 (MANZ'sche Verlags- u. Universitätsbuchhandlung GmbH, Wien)

British Library Cataloguing-in-Publication Data
A catalogue record for this book is available from the British Library.

ISBN (Print) 978-3-7560-0027-2 (Nomos Verlagsgesellschaft mbH & Co. KG, Baden-Baden)
ISBN (ePDF) 978-3-7489-3606-0 (Nomos Verlagsgesellschaft mbH & Co. KG, Baden-Baden)
ISBN (Print) 978-3-03891-588-1 (Dike Verlag, Zürich/St. Gallen)
ISBN (Print) 978-3-214-25099-7 (MANZ'sche Verlags- u. Universitätsbuchhandlung GmbH, Wien)

Library of Congress Cataloging-in-Publication Data
Kuhlmann, Simone | De Gregorio, Fabrizio | Fertmann, Martin
Ofterdinger, Hannah | Sefkow, Anton
Transparency or Opacity
A Legal Analysis of the Organization of Information in the Digital World
Simone Kuhlmann | Fabrizio De Gregorio | Martin Fertmann
Hannah Ofterdinger | Anton Sefkow (Eds.)
251 pp.
Includes bibliographic references and index.

ISBN (Print) 978-3-7560-0027-2 (Nomos Verlagsgesellschaft mbH & Co. KG, Baden-Baden)
ISBN (ePDF) 978-3-7489-3606-0 (Nomos Verlagsgesellschaft mbH & Co. KG, Baden-Baden)
ISBN (Print) 978-3-03891-588-1 (Dike Verlag, Zürich/St. Gallen)
ISBN (Print) 978-3-214-25099-7 (MANZ'sche Verlags- u. Universitätsbuchhandlung GmbH, Wien)

1. Auflage 2023 | 1st Edition 2023
© The Authors

Published by
Nomos Verlagsgesellschaft mbH & Co. KG
Waldseestraße 3–5 | 76530 Baden-Baden
www.nomos.de

Production of the printed version:
Nomos Verlagsgesellschaft mbH & Co. KG
Waldseestraße 3–5 | 76530 Baden-Baden

Onlineversion
Nomos eLibrary

ISBN (Print) 978-3-7560-0027-2 (Nomos Verlagsgesellschaft mbH & Co. KG, Baden-Baden)
ISBN (ePDF) 978-3-7489-3606-0 (Nomos Verlagsgesellschaft mbH & Co. KG, Baden-Baden)
ISBN (Print) 978-3-03891-588-1 (Dike Verlag, Zürich/St. Gallen)
ISBN (Print) 978-3-214-25099-7 (MANZ'sche Verlags- u. Universitätsbuchhandlung GmbH, Wien)
DOI https://doi.org/10.5771/9783748936060

Foreword

This volume collects the contributions to the second conference of the research network Young Digital Law (Junges Digitales Recht), which took place at the University of Hamburg on 22 and 23 July 2022. The conference was held in a hybrid format, in person and online. In the pursuit of fostering a broad, international debate, presentations were held either in German or in English by contributors who come from two continents and eight countries.

The conference theme for 2022 was "Transparency or Opacity". While this dichotomy in itself predates the legal debates stirred by the digital transformation, recent technological and legal innovations invite us to revisit it: If knowledge is power, the question of who gets to know what is inherently political, even more so in the age of the infosphere, where hopes of an egalitarian access to information for all have been frustrated by the recognition that actionable knowledge requires organization. The technical and business architecture that empowers the infosphere – and the organization of said knowledge – is thus one of fundamental informational asymmetries. These asymmetries are neither inherently good nor bad, but: influential.

The contributions of this volume join the larger debate among legal scholars on how transparency shall be understood, whether it shall be granted, under which conditions and with which modalities. To find answers to the debate topics the contributors take into account to which extent existing concepts are applicable to new technologies and functions and if needed suggest new approaches to fill in observed blank spaces or inadequacies. What (and whose) purpose does transparency serve? In which constellations does opacity actually hold value – for example by protecting data, by preventing an informational overload, structuring interactions, enabling intra-institutional functioning or ensuring due process? The instrumental nature of transparency to enable potential actions, means that our allocations of it reflect notions of individual and collective agency and rationality that otherwise often remain implicit in legal discourse. It enables us to question which actor is presumed when knowledge is made accessible.

Given the conference series' goal to enable exchanges on the law of digital transformation across the traditional dividing lines between the different fields and sub-disciplines of the law, the contributions in this volume cover a wide range of subject areas. Across them, the concept of transparency rises as independent from the ones of information accessibility or explainability, and yet with them deeply intertwined; it emerges as inherently contextual, and yet universally necessary to foster trust and allocate responsibilities among the stakeholders of the digital world.

The relation between transparency and opacity is addressed in four sections: (i) state, regulation, and administration; (ii) algorithms and automation; (iii) transparency in health care; and (iv) transparency in the financial system. In the first section, Prof. Dr. Thomas Wischmeyer investigates the nature of the relation between transparency and opacity in the realm of state secrecy; Dr. Jonas Botta and Dr. Gordian Ebner complete the discourse of the role of transparency in the public sector by focusing on, respectively, the digitalisation of public administration and data protection. In the second section, Jun.-Prof. Dr. Elena Freisinger and Jun.-Prof. Dr. Juliane Mendelsohn explore the interplay between algorithms and consumer protection; Marco Billi and Alessandro Parenti offer a case-study to enhance transparency in Smart Legal Contracts; Kostina Prifti, Joris Krijger, Tamara Thuis, and Prof. Dr. Evert Stamhuis analyze the transparency obligations set out by the GDPR in the context of the digital ecosystem of trust; while Dr. Tobias Mast closes the section weighting the differences between machine and human decision-making. In the third section, transparency in healthcare, both authors focus on the practitioner-patient relationship: Paul Nolan discusses the function of transparency, and David Schneeberger tackles the role of AI. Finally, in the fourth section, the two contributions by Dr. Christopher Rennig, and Patrick Raschner demystify the transparency of two modern financial tools: respectively, decentralized finance and robo-investing.

Believing in the utter importance of the topic, we organized the conference and edited this volume. The insights of the contributions exceeded our most optimistic hope and we are humbled to host such an interesting debate: thus, we would like to sincerely thank all contributors. Our deep gratitude goes to Centre of Law in Digital Transformation (ZeRdiT) and the Project "The Law and its Teaching in Digital Transformation" as well as the Leibniz-Institute for Media Research | Hans-Bredow-Institut (HBI), whose support was indispensable for the conference, and there especially to Prof. Dr. Hans-Heinrich Trute and Prof. Dr. Wolfgang Schulz. We also thank Nomos and in particular Dr. Marco Ganzhorn for their support in putting the conference on track and publishing this volume. Lastly, we owe a great thanks to the staff of University of Hamburg, including the academic personnel, the professors and the students, who showed unwavering support to YDL 2022, both intellectual and practical. More specifically, thanks to Hauke Varoga and Florian Lucks, without whom this conference would not have been possible.

Hamburg, October 2022

Dr. Simone Kuhlmann
Fabrizio De Gregorio
Martin Fertmann
Hannah Ofterdinger
Anton Sefkow

Table of Content

Table of Content

I. State, Regulation and Administration

Why do States Keep Secrets?[1]

Thomas Wischmeyer

A. Introduction

The idea of the organizers to start this conference on digital law with a keynote on state secrecy – a decidedly pre-digital topic – resonated with me, because the discourse on digital law oftentimes suffers from a lack of history and context. This is not particularly surprising given that the object of our studies, digital tech, "moves fast and breaks things." And legislators try to keep up and fix things with a tsunami of new regulations covering almost all parts of the digital society. For legal academia, this poses a huge intellectual challenge: It has become so hard to even keep track of the regulatory developments that it is almost impossible to find time for contextualization. However, all big ideas that drive and structure digital law have a history. And from time to time, it may be helpful to step back and reflect on these concepts, their origins, the way they developed – and then also the way they are transformed under the conditions of a digital lifeworld. Such theoretical and historical reflections are more than a source for "back in the day" anecdotes. Instead, they protect against tendencies in contemporary research that feast on the supposed uniqueness of the digital age and its ideas. The main themes of this conference – secrecy/opacity and transparency/openness – are promising starting points for such a type of reflection.

The appropriate preface in this regard is offered by *Humphrey Appleby*, Permanent Secretary in the British TV classic "Yes, Minister" – still the best introductory course to political science and administrative law: "Open government is a contradiction in terms: you can be open or you can have government."[2] This sounds irritating: Isn't openness a value, something we should strive for, rather than a type of order or rather of dis-order

---

1 The presentation character of the keynote was preserved. The author would like to thank Torben Klausa for support in the preparation of the final manuscript. Parts of this paper are based on *T. Wischmeyer*, Formen und Funktionen des exekutiven Geheimnisschutzes, DV 2018, 393.
2 Yes, Minister, Season 1, Episode 1 "Open Government."

as Appleby suggests? And isn't public government *per se* something that is or at least should be open, considering that the very term "public" originates with Latin *publicus/populus*, suggesting a minimum of openness towards the people? And hasn't, e.g., the German Federal Constitutional Court therefore held that all executive decision-making be "visible and understandable?"[3] In other words: Is Appleby just a cynic or does he have a point?

To find out, we need to explore the complex relationship between public government and secrecy. I start with a very quick dip into constitutional history. Here, I want to show you that the concept of state secrecy is intimately connected to the very idea of modern statehood (B.). In a second step, I switch to constitutional theory and try to justify why even in a democratic constitutional state such as Germany transparency is not always a good thing. Instead, I will argue that under certain conditions there are reasons to justify state secrecy. Like *Hans Christian Andersen's* Emperor, a completely transparent state would also be a naked state and a helpless state in every respect (C.). Thirdly and finally, I look at the regulatory framework by which states try to create and enforce state secrecy (D.). This final step links my topic to many papers presented at this conference. But while in digital law we typically think about how to foster transparency through regulation, for states, the challenge is exactly the opposite: How to stop the leaks?

B. *History: The common tradition of state secrecy and transparency*

Many historians have observed that secrecy was a key element in forming the modern state.[4] In the medieval system of government, secrets played an important role in legitimizing power, too, but they were still closely

---

3 BVerfGE 89, 155 (185); 97, 350 (369). Similarly already BVerfGE 40, 296 (327): "Parliamentary democracy is based on the trust of the people; trust without transparency, which allows to follow what is happening politically, is not possible." (Translated by the author).

4 From the very rich literature on this subject see especially *L. Hölscher*, Öffentlichkeit und Geheimnis, Stuttgart 1979; *M. Stolleis*, Arcana imperii und Ratio status, Göttingen 1980; *B. W. Wegener*, Der geheime Staat, Göttingen 2006; *E. Horn*, Der geheime Krieg, Frankfurt a. M. 2007; *E. Horn*, Logics of Political Secrecy, Theory, Culture & Society 2012, 103; *L. Quill*, Secrets and Democracy, Basingstoke 2014; *R. Voigt* (ed.), Staatsgeheimnisse, Wiesbaden 2017.

related to the realm of religion.[5] Around 1500, secrecy was then seculari-zed and became part of the idea of the modern state. In the context of the so-called *arcana imperii* (arcane politics), a veritable cult of secrecy developed, most prominently in the writings of *Niccolò Machiavelli* and *Giovanni Botero*: "Secrecy is of great importance to a prince, because it makes him similar to God, so that people are in tense anticipation of his plans because they do not know his thoughts."[6] With this little phrase – "similar to God" – Botero transfers the legitimizing power of the secret from the sphere of religion to the state.

Machiavelli and his fellow early modernists had recognized the emin-ently political dimension of government information flows – and the power that lay within designing these flows. Much later, sociology would spell this out in detail. *Max Weber* devoted many pages is his sociology of domination (*Herrschaftssoziologie*) to describe how power is distributed both within the state as well as between the state and society through the design of the informational architectures.[7] And *Michel Foucault* recog-nized that there is no power relation without a corresponding field of knowledge being constituted – and that there is no knowledge that does not simultaneously presuppose and constitute power relations.[8] But from an early modernist's perspective, later sociological approaches only devel-oped in theory what absolutist rulers had already figured out in practice: that "knowledge is power" (*Francis Bacon*) and that rulers needed to create an arcane realm in order to legitimize their rule and to secure it.

Similarly, when enlightenment revolutionized political thought, its theory of information flows was not revolutionary at all. To the political philosophers of the new era, knowledge was power as much as it used to be for *Botero* and his colleagues. The enlightened liberals now simply used the logic and grammar of absolutism for their own ends. When the new theorists devoted their analyses to state secrecy, it was not to praise but to denounce it. But at the same time, they recognized that if they wanted to change the design and purpose of the state, they needed to transform its informational architecture. The existing structure of informa-tion flows had to be broken up and replaced with a new structure which

---

5 R. *Otto*, Das Heilige, München 1917 (on the *mysterium tremendum et fascinans*); *Horn*, Logics of Political Secrecy (n. 4), p. 103 et seqq.

6 G. *Botero*, Della ragion di stato libri dieci, Venice 1606, p. 77.

7 M. *Weber*, Wirtschaft und Gesellschaft, Tübingen 1980, p. 548; M. *Weber*, Gesam-melte politische Schriften, Tübingen 1988, p. 351 et seqq.

8 Cf. for his take on the *acrana imperii*: M. *Foucault*, Geschichte der Gouvernementa-lität I, Frankfurt a. M. 2004, p. 396 et seqq.

they called "open" or "public." It was during the same eighteenth century that the concept of "public opinion," rarely used until then, became a central concept of the political discourse[9] and contributed to the process that has famously been described as the "structural transformation of the public sphere." But although the new approach to secrecy and information appeared as a counter-concept to despotism, criticizing its arcane politics and non-publicity of the legal sphere,[10] liberalism was and is still indebted to the insight: Knowledge is power, and the way knowledge is distributed matters politically.

Against this backdrop, *Hannah Arendt's* famous "Real power begins where secrecy begins" – a quote missing in hardly any paper on secrecy – appears incomplete.[11] Rather, as the enlightenment philosophers recognized, the call for transparency is also always a demand for real power and its redistribution. Transparency is thus neither a neutral category nor the natural way information is distributed. It is instead a distinct form of organizing information and thus of designing institutions, which in itself needs to be justified. In other words, *Humphrey Appleby* has a point.

To sum this up: Historically, secrecy and transparency are not at all fundamentally different ideas. Rather, both concepts were used to structure the flow of information and communication within and between organizations. Against this backdrop, rules on state secrecy can be understood as attempts to stabilize two types of boundaries: those between the state and society on the one hand and those between institutions within the state on the other.[12]

---

9 Cf. *Hölscher*, Öffentlichkeit und Geheimnis (n. 4); *H. Hofmann*, Öffentlich/privat, in: J. Ritter/K. Gründer (eds.), Historisches Wörterbuch der Philosophie, Vol. 6, Darmstadt 1984, col. 1131; *L. Hölscher*, Öffentlichkeit, in: J. Ritter/K. Gründer (eds.), Historisches Wörterbuch der Philosophie, Vol. 6, Darmstadt 1984, col. 1134 (1135, 1136).

10 Cf. *H.-J. Lüsebrink*, in: A. Assmann/J. Assmann (eds.), Schleier und Schwelle, Vol. 1, München 1997, p. 111 (111).

11 *H. Arendt*, The Burden of Our Time, London 1951, p. 386, as cited in *Horn*, Logics of Political Secrecy (n. 4), p. 103.

12 Cf. the characterization of rules on secrecy as "ultimate sociological form for the regulation of the flow and distribution of information" by *L. E. Hazelrigg*, A Reexamination of Simmel's "The Secret and the Secret Society": Nine Propositions, Social Forces 1969, 323 (324).

C. Theory: Justifying state secrets in constitutional democracies

As much as state secrecy is not a prerogative of autocracies but instead an inevitable feature of all forms of organized statehood, this does not mean that constitutional democracies always take a rational approach towards state secrecy. Rather, even in democracies, state secrecy is abused – think of the Pentagon Papers, WikiLeaks, the NSA and the like. But not only these highly prominent cases demonstrate that many government officials are probably still a bit too fond of the idea of *arcana imperii*. If you look at the case law of German administrative courts, you will find many cases in which it is difficult to understand why information is (still) kept secret. One example is the case of a journalist who requested access to specific archival documents on the Adolf Eichmann case which was denied by the government – more than 50 years after the documents were filed.[13] In this case, there are no plausible grounds to refuse access. Not only are the documents so old that any detrimental consequences for the national interest are extremely unlikely. But even if the documents would unveil objectionable practice of the German intelligence agencies back in the 1960s and 70s, this would not necessarily harm the institutions today. As shown by the work of the Independent Commission of Historians for Research into the History of Germany's Foreign Intelligence Service, the uncovering of Nazi continuities in the services does not negatively affect today's trust in the institutions; on the contrary, it is viewed positively as evidence of appropriate dealing with the past.[14] Nevertheless, in a similar case from 2014, the government denied Members of Parliament access to information about the right-wing terrorist attack on the Oktoberfest, which took place in 1980 (!) – and the courts accepted it.[15]

The fact that even democracies sometimes fall back on patterns of arcane politics, however, does not refute the fact that they are generally a "government of visible power" as the Italian legal philosopher *Noberto Bobbio* has called them.[16] His assessment is based on the fact that democracies

---

13 On the restrictive handling of these norms by the intelligence services see the facts in BVerwGE 136, 345; BVerwG, order of January 10, 2012, 20 F 1/11; BVerwG, order of December 20, 2016, 20 F 10/15.

14 Several studies have emerged from the Commissions's work; see the references at http://www.uhk-bnd.de/?page_id=340 (last access: 20.09.2022). Respectively on the Federal Office for the Protection of the Constitution (BfV): C. *Goschler/M. Wala*, „Keine Neue Gestapo", Darmstadt 2015.

15 BVerfGE 146, 1.

16 *N. Bobbio*, Die Zukunft der Demokratie, Berlin 1988, p. 86.

have broken with the *natural* relationship between state power and the arcane. In a democracy, secrecy shields no longer any higher truths.[17] State secrets therefore need to be rationalized and justified. But under which conditions is this possible?

I. Strategic Secrecy

Secrecy creates information asymmetries – and information asymmetries enable strategic action. For private actors, this is probably the main reason for keeping information secret: to preserve a competitive edge. But from time to time, public authorities must act strategically, too. The ends to a state's strategic means, however, are always bound to its constitutional mission. Using information strategically is not only common practice in foreign policy vis-à-vis other states, but also within the national borders, where the state acts as an "organized unit for taking and enforcing decisions",[18] which is dependent on informational advantages over its legal subjects – in the fight against crime, the enforcement of tax and competition law, and financial market regulation, to give just a few examples.

However, before we can declare a specific strategic secret to be *legitimate*, we always need to balance the state's interest in secrecy with the conflicting interests in making the information public. And even if the latter turns out to be very weak, strategic secrecy is never self-serving: As soon as the state's need for strategic advantage vanishes, the information must be made accessible. Thus, the value of strategic secrecy decreases over time, while the burden of justification increases.

II. Institutional Secrecy

Social psychology tells us that persons who share secrets are more closely connected by this very fact. In this sense (shared) secrets generate and deepen communicative relationships.[19] Institutional secrecy differs from strategic-operational secrecy protection in that it is not related to a specific

---

17 *Assmann/Assmann*, Schleier und Schwelle (n. 10), p. 7 (9).
18 *H. Heller*, Staatslehre, Leiden 1934, p. 228 et seqq.
19 *Bohn*, in: Schleier und Schwelle (n. 10), p. 41 (48); *J. Westerbarkey*, Das Geheimnis, 1991, p. 115 (141 et seqq.) with further references.

temporal situation. In a constitutional democracy, institutional secrets can be legitimate in three constellations.

a) Secrecy enables organizational units to form a communicative identity and thereby stabilizes organizational differentiations: "The open word is only spoken behind closed doors."[20] Conversely, transparency obligations relativize the informational autonomy of an organization and impair its social cohesion, which is also based on shared secrets. Where strong social cohesion already exists, new transparency obligations can thus have the undesirable side-effect of increasing decentralization. They can also lead to decision-making processes being shifted from formal to informal fora.[21] Institutional secrecy can thus safeguard institutional differentiation and formal organizational structures and protect the separation of powers. This sociological observation is reflected in the constitutional doctrine of *"Kernbereichsschutz"* – the idea of each state power having a protected institutional "core" of activities to which other powers do not have any right to access.[22]

b) In institutions which decide by majority, the secrecy of deliberations can help to facilitate decision-making. This is because majority decisions are regularly based on compromises, which require a tactical approach, both within the group and in dealings with the public. It is easier to find common ground with your adversary if you do not have to publicly justify every position that you might adopt for mere tactical reasons. Conversely, transparency increases the political costs for those involved in negotiations and thus makes compromises more challenging. Even parliamentary work, guided by the ideal of representation, is not organized in a completely transparent manner for precisely these reasons.[23]

c) If we consider that too much transparency corrodes social cohesion within an institution and erodes public trust in it, it seems plausible

---

20 *M. Jestaedt*, Das Geheimnis im Staat der Öffentlichkeit, AöR 2001, 204 (230).

21 In detail on such costs of transparency *H. Tsoukas*, The tyranny of light: The temptations and the paradoxes of the information society, Futures 1997, 827; *Jestaedt*, Geheimnis (n. 20), 233; *J. Costas/C. Grey*, Secrecy at Work, Stanford 2016, p. 52 with further references; *M. Fenster*, The Transparency Fix. Secrets, Leaks, and Uncontrollable Government Information, Stanford 2017.

22 Seminal BVerfGE 67, 100 (139); on the development of the respective jurisdiction *P. Cancik*, Der „Kernbereich exekutiver Eigenverantwortung" – zur Relativität eines suggestiven Topos, ZParl 2014, 885 (892 et seqq.).

23 See only BVerfGE 120, 56 (74); 125, 104 (122 et seqq.); 140, 115 (150 et seq., 156)

to assume that shielding an institution from the strict scrutiny of the public eye both strengthens the acceptance of decisions of this institution and generates systemic trust. We should, however, be very careful with this argument, because systemic trust presupposes a high degree of openness in the first place.[24] Therefore, in a democracy institutional secrecy must never be used to obscure potentially irrational decision-making practices. Secrecy can be permitted in special cases but must be accompanied by compensatory transparency requirements at the same time. This is especially the case in situations where there is a high degree of discretion for a decision, but the result of the decision claims to be highly binding as it is the case with judicial deliberations, which are to be kept secret under all circumstances.[25] Such a rule is justified only in the context of a procedural law that is otherwise fully committed to the idea of transparency.[26]

It is important to highlight that institutional secrecy can only be justified where the positive effects described here actually materialize. The trust argument in particular is based on empirical assumptions; if it cannot be proven that informational secrecy increases trust in an institution, transparency takes precedence. In any case, as with strategic secrecy, the consequences of secrecy depend on an appropriate design of access rights and barriers.

III. Fiduciary Secrecy

In social interactions, individuals regularly exchange information that they do not want to disclose to third parties. As we have seen, such shared secrets enable deeper cooperation, facilitate coordinated strategic behavior, and stabilize trust between the actors. Regardless of potential strategic and institutional effects, however, secrecy may also be justified if and to the extent that the *specific relationship* on which the information sharing is

---

24 Trust arises "between knowledge and ignorance," as German sociologist Georg Simmel has put it. Simmel, Soziologie, Gesamtausgabe Vol. 11, Frankfurt a. M. 2016, p. 393.

25 Cf. sec. 43 Deutsches Richtergesetz (German Judiciary Act): "Judges are to preserve secrecy regarding the course of deliberations and voting even after their service has ended."

26 Cf. sec. 169 (1) Gerichtsverfassungsgesetz (Court Constitution Act): "Hearings before the adjudicating court, including the pronouncement of judgments and rulings, shall be public."

based enjoys legal protection. The legal system recognizes numerous such fiduciary relationships among private individuals and protects them, inter alia, by imposing penalties for breaches of secrecy.[27]

The state, too, can be the recipient of such fiduciary secrets. This is the case when, e.g., a person submits a request to a public authority and communicates facts that, in the applicant's view, require secrecy. In addition, government agencies have the power to – openly or secretly – collect personal information which then must be protected from disclosure to third parties. Here, too, the state becomes a trustee of secrets and is thus responsible for protecting the integrity and confidentiality of the information.

As all other types of secrets, fiduciary secrets guarded by the state need to be balanced with conflicting transparency interests. To conduct a proper proportionality test, courts must not only analyze the normative weight of the competing legal interests. They also need to be aware of the different ways secrets can be protected. This brings me to the final section of my paper: How do states enforce state secrecy?

D. Practice: Implementing State Secrecy

It is once again Sir Humphrey who offers a guiding preface for the practice of state secrecy: "The Official Secrets Act is not to protect secrets, it is to protect officials."[28] And once again, there is more to this quip than meets the eye. Law cannot change technology, let alone the world, and it certainly cannot keep information secret. What law can do, however, is to attribute responsibility to someone for something, or to release someone from responsibility. In this sense, legal rules concerned with state secrecy assign responsibilities to government officials on how to organize information flows. They put transparency and secrecy as complementary modes of the governmental information regime into practice. (Not only) German law has a complex regulatory regime for this purpose, which includes procedural, organizational, and technical norms.

---

27 Sec. 203 Strafgesetzbuch (German Criminal Code) for example punishes the violation of certain private secrets.

28 Yes, Prime Minister, Season 2, Episode 2 "Official Secrets."

I. Defining state secrets

Legal cornerstone of administrative secrecy in Germany is the *Sicher-heitsüberprüfungsgesetz* (SÜG – Security Clearance Act).[29] The SÜG is a risk-based regulation which contains precise instructions on how state secrets need to be handled. Paradoxically, the main effect of the SÜG is that it safeguards transparency: By defining under which conditions which types of information can be classified as what kind of secret (cf. sec. 4 SÜG), the law prevents the establishment of informational "black holes" within the administration that are fully exempt from any kind of control. Instead of giving a carte blanche to handlers of certain documents, the SÜG puts a justificatory burden on every act of classifying government information. Thus, the legal formalization of what constitutes state secrecy contributes to its limitation – not only by defining what a secret *is*, but even more so by declaring what *is not*.

II. Defining role-based criteria for information access

A secret is not a secret, if nobody gets to know about it. Secrets are not simply non-communication. Rather, as we have seen, secrets are a form of privileged communication that specifically excludes third parties. Accordingly, the laws on state secrecy do not simply ban the disclosure of information. Rather, they regulate – explicitly or implicitly – who is part of the communicative relationship constituting the secret. Legal academia has so far paid comparatively little attention to this institutional dimension of secrecy. This may be partly because the discourse on open government is focused on granting public access to government information. However, even where the general public remains excluded from a state secret, legitimacy and accountability concerns can at least partly be addressed by granting privileged third parties – independent authorities, external experts, parliamentary subcommittees, judges, etc. – access. Such

---

29 Further details are regulated by the "Allgemeine Verwaltungsvorschrift des Bundesministerium des Innern zum materiellen und organisatorischen Schutz von Verschlusssachen" ("General Administrative Regulation of the Federal Ministry of the Interior on the Material and Organizational Protection of Classified Information"). Corresponding regulations exist for other authorities. For the EU perspective, see *D. Curtin*, Overseeing Secrets in the EU: A Democratic Perspective, JCMS 2014, 684.

differentiated access rights, which are well-known from intelligence law, can have significant control effects.

In addition, increasing the number of participants in a state secret also offers indirect protection against the dangers of over-classification, because it increases the probability that relevant information will indirectly reach the public – be it by accident, negligence, or deliberate disclosure. The major "leaks" of the past few years show that in complex bureaucracies information flows can never be controlled completely.[30] Such whistle-blowing might (still) be illegal, yet it is a helpful corrective against pathologies of state secrecy.[31]

III. Defining the substantive scope of information access

Information requiring secrecy can often be disclosed to the public in a way that does not undermine the purposes of secrecy protection. Think of statistical information on wire-tapping, that does not allow conclusions to be drawn about individual cases but enables an overall assessment of government activities and thus helps to create transparency. Tweaking the scope of transparency obligations in similar ways helps to protect classified information, but at the same time ensures that supervisory bodies – e.g. parliaments, courts, committees – know that there is something in which they might have an information interest and can exercise their specific control rights.

Various options for structuring the protection of secrets in such a transparency-sensitive manner exist. At the most abstract level, the publication of laws, administrative regulations and guidelines already contributes to transparency and allows the public to get a more precise picture of the information that the state is allowed to withhold from them. Similarly, on a purely individual level, the need to formally deny an information access request can be transparency-enhancing, if the executive needs to justify its decision with a substantive legal statement (see sec. 39 of the German Administrative Procedures Act).

---

30 *M. L. Sifry*, WikiLeaks and the Age of Transparency, Berkeley 2011.

31 From an administrative science perspective, whistleblowing is an example of "useful illegality" in the sense of *N. Luhmann*, Funktionen und Folgen formaler Organisation, Berlin 1999, p. 304 et seqq. See, however, the Directive (EU) 2019/1937 of the European Parliament and of the Council of 23 October 2019 on the protection of persons who report breaches of Union law, Official Journal of the European Union 2019, 17–56.

IV. Defining temporal criteria for information access

From a functional point of view, democratic secrets are always "temporal," as we have seen. Unlimited restrictions on access to information cannot be justified. But again, the legal system can provide for very different temporal access regimes. Rigid time limits or flexible models can be chosen, combined with fixed expiry dates where appropriate.

The periods of protection required differ depending on the type of secrets. Strategic secrets lose their need for protection when their strategic advantage is gone. Institutional secrets might require a longer period of protection to prevent protected interests, such as the impartiality of judicial decision-making or the possibility of compromise. Similar reasoning applies to the handling of fiduciary secrets. Here too, however, the interests of those affected by the disclosure of information to third parties lose weight over time.[32] Given the general precedence of transparency and publicity – "delaying access is denying access" –, it appears sensible to keep mandatory protection periods short, and to provide for a possibilities of extension, if needed.

In the end, a combination of different access restrictions will offer the most comprehensive approach, as time limits can be combined with substantive and personal restrictions. This makes it possible to, e.g., give a small group such as a parliamentary subcommittee comprehensive and immediate access, while the public is only informed in general or statistical terms, until the full set of facts can safely be openly disclosed after a fixed time limit has expired.

E. Outlook

Since *Machiavelli* and his colleagues left their footprint in political theory, the democratic state has sobered up from the *arcana imperii* and the protection of classified information no longer provokes goosebumps. Instead of shielding power, today's rules on secrecy need to be carefully designed and must be justified within a functionally differentiated constitutional system.

---

32 The limits of post-mortem protection of fundamental rights (BVerfGE 30, 173 (196)) have also influenced the most recent reform of the Bundesarchivgesetz (German Federal Archives Act – BArchG), as shown by the shortened period of protection from 30 to 10 years after the death of the person concerned compared with the old version of the law. Cf. also the exception in Section 11 (4) BArchG.

But what sounds like a loss of power or a missing source of authority for the state has instead become a new toolkit in its informational relations. Not having secrets for their own sake ties the means back to their ends: to the welfare of a society as well as its individual members.

This development has taken centuries to unfold, but it can offer orientation for present regulatory initiatives, as well. In view of warnings against digital companies creating a modern arcane realm of technology,[33] knowledge about the historic bond of secrecy and transparency can immunize against a one-sided regulatory approach focusing on transparency only. Hence, the question might not only be how the new actors can be made more transparent – but also what the intended effect of such transparency is. In this regard, as we have seen, *Sir Humphrey's* criticism against open government contains a plausible core that could be paraphrased to suit the current discussions on digital regulation: Ripping off all covers does not make you transparent, but naked. And such a state of affairs suits neither governments nor (reputable) businesses.

---

33 *T. Barczak*, Algorithmus als Arkanum, DÖV 2020, 997 (1000 et seq.).

Der digitale Staat als gläserner Staat. Transparenz als Bedingung verfassungskonformer Registermodernisierung

Jonas Botta

A. Auf dem Weg zum digitalen Staat

Deutschland befindet sich bereits seit mehr als zwei Jahrzehnten auf dem Weg, ein digitaler Staat zu werden. Als E-Government-Vorreiter gilt die Bundesrepublik bis heute gleichwohl nicht.[1] Spätestens die globale COVID-19-Pandemie hat den politischen Verantwortungsträgern jedoch nachdrücklich vor Augen geführt, dass eine digitale Verwaltung entscheidend dafür ist, die Herausforderungen des 21. Jahrhunderts bewältigen zu können. Folgerichtig entschied sich die schwarz-rote Bundesregierung 2020 dafür, als „Digitalisierungsbooster" zusätzliche drei Milliarden Euro für die Umsetzung des Onlinezugangsgesetzes (OZG) in ihrem Corona-Konjunkturpaket vorzusehen.[2]

I. Elektronische Verwaltungsleistungen

Das OZG ist seit seinem Inkrafttreten 2017 das zentrale Gesetz für die Verwaltungsdigitalisierung in Deutschland. Sein verfassungsrechtliches Fundament ist der Art. 91c Abs. 5 GG, der den Bundesgesetzgeber ermächtigt, den übergreifenden informationstechnischen Zugang zu den Verwaltungsleistungen von Bund und Ländern zu regeln. Demgemäß verpflichtet § 1 OZG beide Staatsebenen, ihre Verwaltungsleistungen bis Ende 2022 auch elektronisch anzubieten und über eine Verknüpfung ihrer Verwaltungsportale (Portalverbund) zugänglich zu machen. Eine Frist, die Bund

---

1 In internationalen E-Government-Rankings belegte Deutschland bislang keine Spitzenplätze. Siehe EU-Kommission, Index für die digitale Wirtschaft und Gesellschaft 2022, Länderbericht Deutschland (englischsprachige Fassung), Brüssel 2022, S. 15; United Nations, Department of Economic and Social Affairs, E-Government Survey 2020, Digital Government in the Decade of Action for Sustainable Development, New York 2020, S. 51.
2 S. E. *Schulz*, Der elektronische Zugang zur Verwaltung, RDi 2021, 377 (378).

und Länder trotz der coronabedingten „Finanzspritze" nicht einhalten konnten.[3] Nun soll das „OZG 2.0" den bestehenden Rechtsrahmen weiterentwickeln und zum einen Antworten auf Fragen der föderalen Zusammenarbeit und der End-to-End-Digitalisierung finden und zum anderen das Once-Only-Prinzip endlich Wirklichkeit werden lassen.[4]

II. Once-Only-Prinzip

Das Once-Only-Prinzip verspricht eine erhebliche Entlastung für Bürger und Unternehmen. Perspektivisch soll ihnen nicht nur der „Gang aufs Amt" erspart bleiben, sondern es soll ihnen auch offenstehen, der Verwaltung ihre Daten und Nachweise nur noch einmalig zu übermitteln.[5] Benötigt eine Behörde anschließend Informationen, die bereits (bei einer anderen Behörde) vorliegen, kann sie zukünftig auf diese elektronisch zugreifen, anstatt sie erneut erheben zu müssen. Dadurch sollen Bürger 84 Mio. und die Verwaltung 64 Mio. Zeitstunden jährlich einsparen können, was eine Aufwandsreduzierung um 47 % bzw. 60 % bedeutete.[6] Als Pilotprojekt lassen sich die Namensbestimmung, die Geburtsurkundenbestellung sowie das Kinder- und Elterngeld in Bremen seit dem 1.7.2022 gebündelt online beantragen („Einfach Leistungen für Eltern", kurz ELFE).[7] Um Once-Only für alle (geeigneten) Verwaltungsleistungen bundesweit anbieten zu können, müssen jedoch noch erhebliche rechtliche und technische Hürden genommen werden. Der behördliche Datenaustausch setzt insbesondere eine Reform der Registerlandschaft voraus.

---

3 O. *Voß/L. Rusch*, Digitalisierung in der Warteschleife: „Ein bisschen Veränderung hier, ein wenig dort – so kommen wir nicht weiter", Tagesspiegel.de v. 9.12.2022, https://www.tagesspiegel.de/politik/verheerende-bilanz-digitalgipfel-in-krisenzeiten -9003220.html (zuletzt abgerufen: 11.12.2022).

4 M. *Punz*, OZG: Was ein Folgegesetz bringen soll, Tagesspiegel Background v. 8.2.2022, abrufbar unter https://background.tagesspiegel.de/smart-city/ozg-was-ein -folgegesetz-bringen-soll (zuletzt abgerufen: 11.12.2022).

5 H. P. *Bull*, Die Nummerierung der Bürger und die Angst vor dem Überwachungsstaat, DÖV 2022, 261 (265); M. *Martini/M. Wenzel*, »Once only« versus »only once«: Das Prinzip einmaliger Erfassung zwischen Zweckbindungsgrundsatz und Bürgerfreundlichkeit, DVBl. 2017, 749.

6 Nationaler Normenkontrollrat, Mehr Leistung für Bürger und Unternehmen: Verwaltung digitalisieren. Register modernisieren., Berlin 2017, S. 55.

7 M. *Klein*, Per Once-Only zu Kinder- und Elterngeld, eGovernment Computing v. 25.3.2022, abrufbar unter https://www.egovernment-computing.de/per-once-onl y-zu-kinder-und-elterngeld-a-1105530/ (zuletzt abgerufen: 11.12.2022).

III. Registermodernisierung

Unter den (uneinheitlich definierten) Registerbegriff fallen in erster Linie alle (elektronischen) Datenbestände, die Informationen enthalten, die für ein Verwaltungsverfahren erforderlich sind, die als staatliche Entscheidungsgrundlage dienen oder die für die amtliche Statistik genutzt werden sollen.[8] Aktuell gibt es in Deutschland über 375 zentrale und dezentrale Registertypen.[9] Die Gesamtzahl der einzelnen Register ist zudem noch viel höher. So existieren bundesweit über 5000 kommunale Melderegister. Register sind somit die „Datenschätze" der öffentlichen Verwaltung. Sie zu „bergen", kann sich bislang als schwieriges bis unmögliches Unterfangen erweisen. Auf die Register können im Regelfall nur die registerführenden Stellen selbst zugreifen. Zwischenbehördliche Austauschmöglichkeiten sind die Ausnahme. Die Register beinhalten daher zumeist alle Daten, die für ihren Anwendungsbereich notwendig sind. Dies führt einerseits zu Mehrfacherhebungen derselben Datenkategorien (z.B. Name, Geburtsdatum und Anschrift) und andererseits aufgrund von unterschiedlichen Aktualisierungsfrequenzen sowie Transkriptionsfehlern zu uneinheitlichen Datenbeständen für dieselbe Person. Unter diesen Bedingungen lässt sich Once-Only nur sehr eingeschränkt umsetzen.

Mit dem Registermodernisierungsgesetz (RegMoG) verfolgt der Bundesgesetzgeber nunmehr das Ziel, zumindest die wichtigsten Register(typen) bis 2025 zu verknüpfen, um Informationen registerübergreifend übermitteln und medienbruchfreie E-Government-Angebote gewährleisten zu können. Außerdem sollen perspektivisch neue Register geschaffen (z.B. ein Gebäude- und Wohnungsregister) und analog geführte Register digitalisiert werden. Die föderale Registerarchitektur lässt der Gesetzgeber indes grundsätzlich unangetastet.[10]

---

8 Nationaler Normenkontrollrat, Mehr Leistung für Bürger und Unternehmen (Fn. 6), S. 13; *E. Peuker*, Registermodernisierung und Datenschutz, NVwZ 2021, 1167 (1168). Weiterführend zum Registerbegriff *F. Wollenschläger*, Register als Instrument der Wirtschaftsverwaltung, ZHR 186 (2022), 474 (477 ff.).

9 IT-Planungsrat, Registermodernisierung: Zielbild und Umsetzungsplanung, 2021, S. 12.

10 *A. Guckelberger/G. Starosta*, Die Fortentwicklung des Onlinezugangsgesetzes, NVwZ 2021, 1161 (1165).

B. Risiko der gläsernen Bürger

Kernstück des RegMoG ist das Identifikationsnummerngesetz (IDNrG). Es führt ein Identitätsmanagement ein, um bei den registerübergreifenden Datenübermittlungen Personenverwechselungen zu verhindern (§ 1 Nr. 1 IDNrG) und die unterschiedlichen Register miteinander zu synchronisieren. Dadurch soll die Datenqualität erhöht (§ 1 Nr. 2 IDNrG) und Once-Only ermöglicht (§ 1 Nr. 3 IDNrG) werden. Seine Vorschriften treten überwiegend erst an dem Tag in Kraft, an dem das Bundesministerium des Innern (BMI) im Bundesgesetzblatt bekannt gibt, dass die technischen Voraussetzungen für das IDNrG vorliegen (Art. 22 S. 2 RegMoG).

I. Einführung einer Identifikationsnummer

Für das registerübergreifende Identitätsmanagement soll ein zusätzliches Ordnungsmerkmal in die 51 Register(typen) eingefügt werden, die in der Anlage zu § 1 IDNrG aufgelistet sind. Der Bundesgesetzgeber hat darauf verzichtet, ein neues Ordnungsmerkmal zu schaffen und hat stattdessen bestimmt, dass die Identifikationsnummer nach § 139b Abgabenordnung als Ordnungsmerkmal fungieren soll (§ 1 IDNrG).

Durch das „Upgrade" der Steuer-ID erhält das Bundeszentralamt für Steuern eine Schlüsselposition im Rahmen der Registermodernisierung.[11] Es ist fortan dafür zuständig, die Qualität der sogenannten Basisdaten nach § 4 Abs. 2 und 3 IDNrG (neben der Steuer-ID insbesondere Name, Geburtsdatum und -ort, Geschlecht, Staatsangehörigkeit, Anschrift und Datum des letzten Verwaltungskontakts) zu überwachen (§ 10 Abs. 1 IDNrG). Die registerführenden Stellen des Bundes und der Länder fügen die Steuer-ID in ihre Datenbestände ein und passen die Informationen, die den Basisdaten entsprechen, an diese an (§ 2 Nr. 1 und 2 IDNrG). Die Übermittlung der Basisdaten erfolgt dabei nicht unmittelbar zwischen den Behörden, sondern über das Bundesverwaltungsamt als Registermodernisierungsbehörde i.S.d. § 3 IDNrG (§ 6 Abs. 1 S. 1 Hs. 1 IDNrG).[12] Die Behörden können die Basisdaten auch bei der Registermodernisierungsbehörde abrufen, wenn sie eine OZG-Leistung erbringen (§ 6 Abs. 2 S. 1 IDNrG). Nach dem Übermittlungsvorgang löscht die Registermodernisierungsbehörde die Daten unver-

---

11 *M. Knauff/L. Lehmann*, Das Registermodernisierungsgesetz, DÖV 2022, 159 (160).

12 Mit Ausnahme des Datenabrufs bei den Meldebehörden (§ 6 Abs. 1 S. 1 Hs. 2 IDNrG).

züglich (§ 11 IDNrG). Dadurch ist sichergestellt, dass kein zusätzliches Basisdatenregister entsteht.

Die Nutzung der Steuer-ID als Ordnungsmerkmal wird sich nicht auf die Basisdaten beschränken. Vielmehr können öffentliche (und nicht-öffentliche) Stellen auch weitergehende Informationen und Nachweise unter Verwendung der Steuer-ID miteinander austauschen. Dies setzt voraus, dass eine Einwilligung vorliegt (§ 5 Abs. 1 S. 2 Var. 2 IDNrG) oder die Datenverarbeitung einem der abschließend aufgezählten Zwecke dient. Zulässige Verarbeitungszwecke sind – abgesehen vom Abgleich der Basisdaten (§ 5 Abs. 1 S. 1 Nr. 2 IDNrG) – die Zuordnung der Datensätze zur richtigen Person (§ 5 Abs. 1 S. 1 Nr. 1 IDNrG), die Erbringung von OZG-Leistungen auf Grundlage von Rechtsvorschriften (§ 5 Abs. 1 S. 2 Var. 1 IDNrG) und ein registerbasierter Zensus (§ 5 Abs. 1 S. 2 Var. 3 IDNrG). Wenn die übermittelnden Behörden unterschiedlichen Bereichen[13] angehören, ist ihnen kein direkter Datenaustausch erlaubt, sondern nur eine verschlüsselte Übermittlung über sogenannte Vermittlungsstellen (§ 7 Abs. 2 S. 1 IDNrG). Dieser Übertragungsweg wird als 4-Corner-Modell (Behörde A ↔ Vermittlungsstelle 1 ↔ Vermittlungsstelle 2 ↔ Behörde B) bezeichnet.[14]

II. Unions- und verfassungsrechtliche Zulässigkeit

Die Einführung der Identifikationsnummer nach § 1 IDNrG ist äußerst umstritten. Ihre Kritiker fürchten, dass sie einer panoptischen Gesellschaftsordnung den Weg bereitet, in der der Staat immer umfassendere Einblicke in das Leben seiner Bürger erhält. Ob sie rechtlich zulässig ist, bemisst sich nach den Vorgaben des Unions- und Verfassungsrechts.

1. Öffnungsklausel für nationale Kennziffern (Art. 87 DSGVO)

Das Recht der digitalen Verwaltung ist keineswegs eine rein nationale Materie. Mit der „Single Digital Gateway"-Verordnung (EU) 2018/1724 verpflichtet die Union ihre Mitgliedstaaten, ausgewählte Verwaltungsleistun-

---

13 Die Behörden sollen bundesweit in mindestens sechs unterschiedliche Bereiche aufgeteilt werden (§ 7 Abs. 2 S. 2 IDNrG), z.B. in Inneres (1), Justiz (2), Wirtschaft und Finanzen (3), Arbeit und Soziales (4), Gesundheit (5) und Statistik (6). Siehe BT-Drs. 19/24226, S. 74.

14 *Knauff/Lehmann*, Registermodernisierungsgesetz (Fn. 11), 161; *Peuker*, Registermodernisierung (Fn. 8), 1171.

gen bis Ende 2023 online anzubieten und dabei das Once-Only-Prinzip zu beachten (Art. 6 i.V.m. Anhang II sowie Art. 13 und 14 SDG-VO).[15] Zur Verwendung einer Identifikationsnummer schweigt sich die SDG-VO indes aus.[16] Ihre Rechtmäßigkeit richtet sich vielmehr nach dem geltenden Datenschutzrecht. Denn die behördliche Verarbeitung personenbezogener Daten ruft grundsätzlich die Datenschutz-Grundverordnung auf den Plan (Art. 2 Abs. 1 DSGVO). Ihr weiter Anwendungsbereich und das Erfordernis, jeden Verarbeitungsvorgang auf einen Erlaubnistatbestand stützen zu können (Art. 6 Abs. 1 UAbs. 1 DSGVO), haben der Verordnung den Ruf eines „Digitalisierungsverhinderungsrechts" eingebracht.

Die DSGVO stellt es den nationalen Gesetzgebern indes frei, ob sie eine Identifikationsnummer für ihre Bürger verwenden wollen. Die Öffnungsklausel des Art. 87 S. 1 DSGVO erlaubt es ihnen, näher zu bestimmen, unter welchen spezifischen Bedingungen eine nationale Kennziffer oder ein Kennzeichen von allgemeiner Bedeutung Gegenstand einer Verarbeitung sein dürfen.[17] Voraussetzung ist, dass geeignete Garantien für die Rechte und Freiheiten der betroffenen Personen die Verarbeitung flankieren (Art. 87 S. 2 DSGVO). Die Verordnung konkretisiert diese geeigneten Garantien zwar nicht, sie müssen aber jedenfalls das Schutzniveau der allgemeinen Datenschutzgrundsätze wahren (vgl. ErwGr. 156 DSGVO): in erster Linie die Grundsätze der Transparenz (Art. 5 Abs. 1 lit. a Var. 3 DSGVO), der Zweckbindung (Art. 5 Abs. 1 lit. b Hs. 1 DSGVO) und der Datenminimierung (Art. 5 Abs. 1 lit. c DSGVO).[18] Unter Beachtung

---

15 Dazu *M. Martini*, Digitalisierung der Verwaltung, in: W. Kahl/M. Ludwigs (Hrsg.), Handbuch des Verwaltungsrechts, Heidelberg 2021, Rn. 33 f.; *T. Siegel*, Der Europäische Portalverbund – Frischer Digitalisierungswind durch das einheitliche digitale Zugangstor („Single Digital Gateway"), NVwZ 2019, 905 ff.

16 Der EU-Kommissionsvorschlag einer Verordnung über die europäische digitale Identität (EUid) sieht hingegen eine eindeutige und dauerhafte Kennung zur Identifizierung vor (COM(2021) 281 final, S. 32). Von dieser Regelung ist die EU-Kommission jedoch zwischenzeitlich abgerückt (*S. Krempl*, EU-weite Online-Ausweise: Lebenslange Identifikationsnummer vorerst vom Tisch, heise online v. 12.7.2022, abrufbar unter https://www.heise.de/news/EU-weite-Online-Ausweis e-Dauerhafte-Identifikationsnummer-vorerst-vom-Tisch-7177700.html [zuletzt abgerufen: 11.12.2022]).

17 Obwohl die Identifikationsnummer zunächst „nur" in 51 Register eingeführt werden soll, ist sie aufgrund ihres weiten Anwendungsbereichs als nationale Kennziffer anzusehen (a.A.: *E. Ehmann*, Registermodernisierung in Deutschland, ZD 2021, 509 (511); *K. von Lewinski*, in: H. A. Wolff/S. Brink (Hrsg.), BeckOK DatenschutzR, 40. Ed. (Stand: 1.5.2022), München, Art. 87 Rn. 28.1.

18 *M. Hansen*, in: S. Simitis/G. Hornung/I. Spiecker gen. Döhmann (Hrsg.), DSGVO, Baden-Baden 2019, Art. 87 Rn. 24; *M. Martini/D. Wagner/M. Wenzel*,

dieser Vorgaben lässt sich eine Identifikationsnummer somit unionskonform einführen.

2. Recht auf informationelle Selbstbestimmung (Art. 2 Abs. 1 i.V.m. Art. 1 Abs. 1 GG)

Da der Unionsgesetzgeber die Verwendung einer nationalen Kennziffer nicht abschließend geregelt hat, ist ihre Zulässigkeit in Deutschland insbesondere anhand der Vorschriften des Grundgesetzes zu überprüfen.[19] Einschlägig ist das Recht auf informationelle Selbstbestimmung, das das BVerfG aus Art. 2 Abs. 1 i.V.m. Art. 1 Abs. 1 GG abgeleitet hat. Es schützt die Befugnis des Einzelnen, grundsätzlich selbst über die Preisgabe und Verwendung seiner persönlichen Daten zu bestimmen.[20] In dieses Grundrecht greifen das Vorhaben der Registermodernisierung im Allgemeinen und das IDNrG im Besonderen ein. Bereits die bloße Verknüpfungsmöglichkeit personenbezogener Daten stellt eine Persönlichkeitsgefährdung dar, die als Eingriff zu werten ist.[21] Daher ist es unerheblich, dass der Einzelne grundsätzlich darauf verzichten kann, seine Daten nach dem Once-Only-Prinzip an den Staat zu übermitteln. Jedenfalls kann er sich nicht der anlasslosen Vergabe einer Identifikationsnummer und deren Implementierung in die Fachregister entziehen.

Die aus dem RegMoG erfolgenden Eingriffe könnten sogar derart intensiv sein, dass sie nicht mehr zu rechtfertigen sind. Denn nach der Rechtsprechung des BVerfG ist es grundrechtswidrig, den Menschen zwangsweise in seiner ganzen Persönlichkeit zu registrieren und zu katalogisieren.[22] „[D]ie Einführung eines einheitlichen, für alle Register und Dateien geltenden Personenkennzeichens […] wäre aber gerade ein entscheidender Schritt, den einzelnen Bürger in seiner ganzen Persönlichkeit zu registrieren und zu katalogisieren".[23] Bei der Identifikationsnummer nach § 1 IDNrG handelt es sich um ein solches einheitliches Personenkennzei-

---

Rechtliche Grenzen einer Personen- bzw. Unternehmenskennziffer in staatlichen Registern, Speyer 2017, S. 7; vgl. auch *T. Weichert*, in: J. Kühling/B. Buchner (Hrsg.), DSGVO/BDSG, 3. Aufl., München 2020, Art. 87 Rn. 15.

19 Vgl. BVerfGE 152, 216 (229); *J. Botta*, „Digital First" und „Digital Only" in der öffentlichen Verwaltung, NVwZ 2022, 1247 (1249 f.).

20 BVerfGE 65, 1 (43).

21 BVerfGE 65, 1 (45).

22 BVerfGE 27, 1 (6).

23 BVerfGE 65, 1 (57).

chen[24] – ein Novum in der deutschen Rechtsordnung unter Geltung des Grundgesetzes.[25] Dem steht nicht entgegen, dass sie zunächst nicht in alle Register Einzug hält und das IDNrG sie (im Gegensatz zur Gesetzesbegründung)[26] als bereichsspezifisches Kennzeichen ausweist (vgl. § 16 Abs. 2 S. 2 Nr. 1 Alt. 1 IDNrG). Denn schon durch die *de lege lata* getroffene Registerauswahl ließen sich umfassende Persönlichkeitsprofile erstellen, da sie wesentliche Lebensbereiche abdeckt. Insoweit unterscheidet sich die Identifikationsnummer nach § 1 IDNrG von der bloßen Steuer-ID, die nur zu Besteuerungszwecken dient (auch wenn das Steuerrecht ebenfalls sehr tiefe Einblicke in das Leben der Steuerpflichtigen ermöglicht).[27] Zudem hat sich der Bundesgesetzgeber offengehalten, die Identifikationsnummer zukünftig in alle Register einzufügen (vgl. § 16 Abs. 2 S. 2 Nr. 1 Alt. 2 IDNrG). Während die Steuer-ID als verfassungsgemäß erachtet worden ist,[28] könnte ihre modifizierte Verwendung somit per se verfassungswidrig sein.

Aus dem zitierten Volkszählungsurteil das absolute Verbot einer einheitlichen Identifikationsnummer zu folgern, schösse jedoch über den Schutz des Rechts auf informationelle Selbstbestimmung hinaus.[29] Das Kennzeichen selbst ist – zumal als sogenannte nicht-sprechende Nummer[30] – ungefährlich.[31] Erst seine konkrete Verwendungsmöglichkeit zur Erstellung umfassender Datensätze über den Einzelnen lässt es bedroh-

---

24 *C. Sorge/J. von Lucke/I. Spiecker gen. Döhmann*, Registermodernisierung, Potsdam 2021, S. 14 f.; a.A.: *Ehmann*, Registermodernisierung (Fn. 17), 512; *Peuker*, Registermodernisierung (Fn. 8), 1170.

25 Die DDR führte ab 1970 schrittweise eine Personenkennzahl (PKZ) für ihre Bürger ein. Siehe *T. Weichert*, in: J. Kühling/B. Buchner (Hrsg.), DSGVO/BDSG, 3. Aufl., München 2020, Art. 87 Rn. 13.

26 BT-Drs. 19/24226, S. 6.

27 FG Köln, Urt. v. 7.7.2010 – 2 K 2999/08, BeckRS 2010, 26030144, Rn. 136.

28 BFH, Urt. v. 18.1.2012 – II R 49/10, BeckRS 2012, 94274, Rn. 46; *Knauff/Lehmann*, Registermodernisierungsgesetz (Fn. 11), 162.

29 *Martini/Wagner/Wenzel*, Personen- bzw. Unternehmenskennziffer (Fn. 18), S. 31 f.; *Peuker*, Registermodernisierung (Fn. 8), 1170; a.A.: *M. Kleinert/M. Kuhn/C. Otte/R. Will*, Stellungnahme zum Referentenentwurf eines Gesetzes zur Einführung einer Identifikationsnummer in die öffentliche Verwaltung und zur Änderung weiterer Gesetze (Registermodernisierungsgesetz), vorgänge. Zeitschrift für Bürgerrechte und Gesellschaftspolitik 2020, Nr. 230, 125 (130 ff.).

30 Die Steuer-ID ist eine elfstellige Nummer, die zufällig erzeugt wird und keine Informationen über den Bürger enthält.

31 *K. von Lewinski/M. Gülker*, Europa-, verfassungs- und datenschutzrechtliche Grundfragen des Registermodernisierungsgesetzes (RegMoG), DVBl. 2021, 633 (634); *Peuker*, Registermodernisierung (Fn. 8), 1170.

lich werden. Für eine derartige Differenzierung spricht insbesondere, dass das BVerfG in seinem damaligen Urteil die Bedingungen der modernen Datenverarbeitung als die entscheidende Herausforderung benannt hat.[32] Schon 1983 stand damit das Gefährdungspotenzial neuer Verknüpfungsmöglichkeiten und nicht die Verarbeitung personenbezogener Daten schlechthin im Mittelpunkt der verfassungsrechtlichen Erwägungen. Angesichts der heute als modern geltenden Datenverarbeitung haben sich die Gefährdungslagen deutlich gegenüber dem Stand der Technik von vor 40 Jahren geändert. In Zeiten von Big-Data-Analysen und künstlicher Intelligenz bedarf es längst keines Personenkennzeichens mehr, um den Einzelnen zu durchleuchten. Ein derartiges Kennzeichen erleichtert eine Profilbildung lediglich.

Die Nutzung der Steuer-ID als registerübergreifendes Ordnungsmerkmal verstößt folglich nicht generell gegen geltendes Verfassungsrecht und ist damit rechtfertigungsfähig. Eingriffe in das Recht auf informationelle Selbstbestimmung sind indes nur im überwiegenden Allgemeininteresse gerechtfertigt.[33] Für das RegMoG ergibt sich ein derartiges Allgemeininteresse grundsätzlich aus der Sicherstellung einer zeitgemäßen und funktionierenden Verwaltung.[34] Denn ohne eine Reform der deutschen Registerlandschaft lassen sich die Effizienzpotenziale von Once-Only nicht entfalten.

Zudem muss das RegMoG den Grundsatz der Verhältnismäßigkeit wahren und der Bundesgesetzgeber Vorkehrungen getroffen haben, die der Gefahr einer Persönlichkeitsverletzung entgegenwirken.[35] Entscheidend für die Verfassungsmäßigkeit der einheitlichen Identifikationsnummer sind somit neben der Frage nach gleich geeigneten, aber milderen Mitteln,[36] bspw. der Kombination allgemeiner und bereichsspezifischer Perso-

---

32 BVerfGE 65, 1 (42, 43, 45, 46 und 48).
33 BVerfGE 65, 1 (44).
34 Vgl. *Botta*, „Digital First" und „Digital Only" in der Verwaltung (Fn. 19), 1250.
35 Vgl. BVerfGE 65, 1 (44).
36 Aufgrund der gesetzgeberischen Einschätzungsprärogative mehren sich im Schrifttum zwar die Stimmen, die die Identifikationsnummer als erforderlich ansehen (*Knauff/Lehmann*, Registermodernisierungsgesetz (Fn. 11), 162 f.; *von Lewinski/Gülker*, Registermodernisierungsgesetz (Fn. 31), 636 ff.; *Peuker*, Registermodernisierung (Fn. 8), 1171 f.), gegen diese Auffassung sind aber gewichtige Argumente vorgetragen worden (*Kleinert/Kuhn/Otte/Will*, Registermodernisierungsgesetz (Fn. 29), 129 f. und *Sorge/von Lucke/Spiecker gen. Döhmann*, Registermodernisierung (Fn. 24), S. 16 f.). Es kann daher zumindest als offen gelten, wie das BVerfG entscheiden wird, wenn es die Verfassungsmäßigkeit der einheitlichen Identifikationsnummer überprüfen muss.

nenkennzeichen („österreichisches Modell"),[37] die ergriffenen technischen, organisatorischen und rechtlichen Schutzmaßnahmen.[38]

C. *Chance des gläsernen Staates*

Das Unionsrecht und das deutsche Verfassungsrecht stehen einer einheitlichen Identifikationsnummer nicht unüberwindbar entgegen. Sowohl die Öffnungsklausel des Art. 87 DSGVO als auch das Recht auf informationelle Selbstbestimmung verlangen jedoch, dass der Staat den damit einhergehenden Datenschutzrisiken vorbeugt. Von Bedeutung sind dabei insbesondere die Transparenzmechanismen.[39] Dass der Staat grundsätzlich offen und nachvollziehbar handeln muss, war zwar bereits im analogen Zeitalter ein elementares Prinzip im demokratischen Rechtsstaat.[40] Aus der digitalen Transformation folgt nunmehr aber die Chance, dass der Staat für seine Bürger noch durchsichtiger wird.[41] Dieser Gewinn an Transparenz kann grundsätzlich einen (gewissen) Verlust an informationeller Selbstbe-

---

37 Dazu *Martini/Wagner/Wenzel*, Personen- bzw. Unternehmenskennziffer (Fn. 18), S. 36 ff.; *Sorge/von Lucke/Spiecker gen. Döhmann*, Registermodernisierung (Fn. 24), S. 16 f.

38 *Martini/Wagner/Wenzel*, Personen- bzw. Unternehmenskennziffer (Fn. 18), S. 33.

39 Vgl. *M. Martini*, Transformation der Verwaltung durch Digitalisierung, DÖV 2017, 443 (452); *I. Sommer*, Datenschutz – Betroffenenrechte: Transparenz als Werkzeug und Voraussetzung der informationellen Selbstbestimmung, in: H. Lühr/R. Jabkowski/S. Smentek (Hrsg.), Handbuch Digitale Verwaltung, Wiesbaden 2019, S. 233 (234).

40 Im Grundgesetz findet sich zwar im Gegensatz zum unionalen Primärrecht (z.B. in Art. 1 Abs. 2 EUV) kein ausdrückliches Transparenzprinzip, dieses lässt sich aber aus den Grundrechten (insbesondere der Informationsfreiheit nach Art. 5 Abs. 1 S. 1 Alt. 2 GG) sowie dem Demokratie- und Rechtsstaatsprinzip (Art. 20 Abs. 2 und 3 GG) ableiten (weiterführend *J. Bröhmer*, Transparenz als Verfassungsprinzip, Tübingen 2004, S. 33 ff.; *B. W. Wegener*, Der geheime Staat, Göttingen 2006, S. 394 ff.). Da die Transparenz staatlichen Handelns nicht unbeschränkt gilt, spricht *C. Gusy*, Der transparente Staat, DVBl. 2013, 941 (942) vom Grundsatz der limitierten Öffentlichkeit. Zur Bedeutung des staatlichen Geheimnisschutzes siehe *T. Wischmeyer*, Formen und Funktionen des exekutiven Geheimnisschutzes, Die Verwaltung 51 (2018), 393 ff. m.w.N.

41 *J. Fährmann*, Mehr Transparenz durch technische Innovationen?, MMR 2021, 775 ff.; *C. Fischer/S. Kraus*, Digitale Transparenz, in: T. Klenk/F. Nullmeier/G. Wewer (Hrsg.), Handbuch Digitalisierung in Staat und Verwaltung, Wiesbaden 2020, S. 159 ff.; *J. von Lucke*, Transparenz 2.0 – Transparenz durch E-Government, in: S. A. Jansen/E. Schröter/N. Stehr (Hrsg.), Transparenz, Wiesbaden 2010, S. 396 (398 ff.).

stimmung rechtfertigen, insoweit er es vermag, die informationellen Machtasymmetrien in der digitalen Verwaltung auszugleichen.

I. Verfassungsgerichtliche Transparenzanforderungen

Unter welchen Bedingungen die staatliche Datenverarbeitung als transparent anzusehen ist, hat das BVerfG in seiner Rechtsprechung niedergelegt.[42] Die Transparenzmechanismen des RegMoG müssen diesen Anforderungen genügen, um die angestrebte Reform tatsächlich verfassungsrechtlich absichern zu können.

Eine zentrale Transparenzanforderung ist der Grundsatz der Offenheit der Datenverarbeitung.[43] Zum einen muss der Person, die von der Datenverarbeitung betroffen ist, ein Auskunftsanspruch gegenüber den verarbeitenden Behörden zustehen.[44] Zum anderen müssen die verarbeitenden Behörden sie unabhängig von einem konkreten Auskunftsersuchen über die Datenverarbeitung informieren.[45] Dabei darf sich die Information nicht darauf beschränken, dass staatliche Stellen Daten verarbeiten, sondern muss insbesondere die konkreten Verarbeitungszwecke benennen.[46] Außerdem müssen die behördlichen Angaben hinreichend verständlich sein. Anderenfalls könnten die Bürger nicht wirklich wissen, wer was wann und bei welcher Gelegenheit über sie weiß.[47]

Dieses Wissen ist Voraussetzung dafür, dass die betroffene Person ihre Rechte – z.B. auf Löschung oder Berichtigung der personenbezogenen Daten – effektiv wahrnehmen kann.[48] Es ermöglicht ihr, die Datenverarbeitung in der Öffentlichkeit zu thematisieren und ihre etwaige Unrecht-

---

42 Das BVerfG entwickelt seine Transparenzanforderungen nicht nur aus dem Recht auf informationelle Selbstbestimmung, sondern auch aus dem Fernmeldegeheimnis (Art. 10 Abs. 1 Var. 3 GG) und dem Recht der Unverletzlichkeit der Wohnung (Art. 13 Abs. 1 GG). Sie stehen zudem in einem engen Zusammenhang zum Recht auf effektiven Rechtsschutz (Art. 19 Abs. 4 GG). Dazu ausführlich *B. Manthey*, Das datenschutzrechtliche Transparenzgebot, Baden-Baden 2020, S. 165 ff.

43 BVerfGE 125, 260 (335 f.).

44 BVerfGE 154, 152 (287).

45 BVerfGE 125, 260 (335); vgl. BVerfGE 100, 313 (361); 109, 279 (363 f.); 118, 168 (207 f.); 120, 351 (361 f.).

46 Vgl. BVerfGE 65, 1 (45).

47 Vgl. BVerfGE 65, 1 (43).

48 BVerfGE 125, 260 (335); vgl. BVerfGE 100, 313 (361); 109, 279 (363); 118, 168 (207 f.); 120, 351 (361).

mäßigkeit aufsichtsbehördlich oder gerichtlich überprüfen zu lassen.[49] Die Kenntnis von der Datenverarbeitung erlaubt der betroffenen Person darüber hinaus, ihr Verhalten anzupassen und z.B. bewusst auf Once-Only zu verzichten.[50] Das Erfordernis einer transparenten Datenverarbeitung verfolgt jedoch nicht nur einen individuellen, sondern auch einen gesamtgesellschaftlichen Zweck. Denn ist die Datenverarbeitung unter Nutzung der Identifikationsnummer hinreichend bekannt, beugt dies Spekulationen über eine heimliche Zusammenführung der Fachregister zu einer Art „Superregister" vor. So kann der Staat das Vertrauen seiner Bürger in den Prozess der Verwaltungsdigitalisierung stärken.[51]

Das Ausmaß der erforderlichen Transparenzmaßnahmen hängt vom Eingriffsgewicht der jeweiligen Verarbeitungsregelungen ab.[52] Auf den ersten Blick ließe sich annehmen, dass für die Registermodernisierung und die Einführung der Identifikationsnummer deutlich niedrigere Anforderungen als für die Antiterrordatei oder die Vorratsdatenspeicherung gelten, die den maßstabsetzenden Entscheidungen des BVerfG zugrunde lagen. Denn bislang stand mit der Leistungsverwaltung ein Bereich im Mittelpunkt der Verwaltungsdigitalisierung, in dem die Datenverarbeitung allgemein als nicht besonders grundrechtssensibel gilt, da sich Bürger ihr leichter entziehen können und aus ihr regelmäßig keine Eingriffe in die Freiheit der Person oder ihr Eigentum erfolgen.[53] Bei näherem Hinsehen erstreckt sich das RegMoG indes – im Gegensatz zum OZG[54] – auch auf die Eingriffsverwaltung. So soll die Identifikationsnummer bspw. in das Bundeszentralregister eingefügt werden (Nr. 27 Anlage zu § 1 IDNrG), aus dem u.a. strafrechtliche Verurteilungen oder gerichtliche Feststellungen zur Betäubungsmittelabhängigkeit hervorgehen. Die Verarbeitung und Verknüpfung derartig sensibler Daten gebietet ein hohes Transparenzniveau.

---

49 BVerfGE 125, 260 (335).
50 Vgl. BVerfGE 133, 277 (366).
51 Vgl. BVerfGE 133, 277 (366).
52 BVerfGE 156, 11 (46). Zur Eingriffsintensität staatlicher Datenverarbeitung siehe BVerfGE 115, 320 (347 ff.).
53 Vgl. *D. Caliebe*, Datenschutz – Allgemeines, in: H. Lühr/R. Jabkowski/S. Smentek (Hrsg.), Handbuch Digitale Verwaltung, Wiesbaden 2019, S. 226 (230 f.); *J. Masing*, Herausforderungen des Datenschutzes, NJW 2012, 2305 (2307); *M.-T. Tinnefeld/B. Buchner/T. Petri/H.-J. Hof*, Einführung in das Datenschutzrecht, 6. Aufl., Berlin 2018, S. 296 ff.
54 *M. Martini*, in: I. von Münch/P. Kunig (Hrsg.), GG, 7. Aufl., München 2021, Art. 91c Rn. 67.

II. Ausgestaltung des Datenschutzcockpits (§ 10 OZG)

Der zentrale Transparenzmechanismus des RegMoG ist das Datenschutz-cockpit (zunächst Datencockpit genannt).[55] Seine Rechtsgrundlage wurde als § 10 neu in das OZG eingefügt[56] und tritt ebenfalls erst in Zukunft in Kraft (Art. 22 S. 2 RegMoG). In Bremen wird gleichwohl schon jetzt ein

---

55 BT-Drs. 19/24226, S. 2; *Knauff/Lehmann*, Registermodernisierungsgesetz (Fn. 11), 163.

56 Wortlaut der Vorschrift in ihrer Fassung nach Änderung durch das Gesetz v. 28.6.2021, BGBl. I S. 2250 (2261):

§ 10 Datenschutzcockpit

(1) [1]Ein „Datenschutzcockpit" ist eine IT-Komponente im Portalverbund, mit der sich natürliche Personen Auskünfte zu Datenübermittlungen zwischen öffentlichen Stellen anzeigen lassen können. [2]Erfasst werden diejenigen Datenübermittlungen, bei denen eine Identifikationsnummer nach § 5 des Identifikationsnummerngesetzes zum Einsatz kommt.

(2) [1]Im Datenschutzcockpit werden nach Maßgabe von Absatz 4 Satz 3 ausschließlich Protokolldaten nach § 9 des Identifikationsnummerngesetzes einschließlich der dazu übermittelten Inhaltsdaten sowie die Bestandsdaten der Register angezeigt. [2]Diese Daten werden im Datenschutzcockpit nur für die Dauer des jeweiligen Nutzungsvorgangs ge-speichert; nach Beendigung des Nutzungsvorgangs sind sie unverzüglich zu löschen. [3]Der Auskunftsanspruch nach Artikel 15 der Verordnung (EU) 2016/679 des Europäischen Parlaments und des Rates vom 27. April 2016 zum Schutz natürlicher Personen bei der Verarbeitung personenbezogener Daten, zum freien Datenverkehr und zur Aufhebung der Richtlinie 95/46/EG (Datenschutz-Grundverordnung) (ABl. L 119 vom 4.5.2016, S. 1; L 314 vom 22.11.2016, S. 72; L 127 vom 23.5.2018, S. 2; L 74 vom 4.3.2021, S. 35) bleibt unberührt. [4]Das Datenschutzcockpit ist aus Sicht des Nutzers einfach und zweckmäßig auszugestalten. [5]Es sind technische und organisatorische Maßnahmen vor-zusehen, damit staatliche Eingriffe zum Nachteil des Nutzers nicht möglich sind

(3) [1]Jede natürliche Person kann sich bei der öffentlichen Stelle, die das Datenschutz-cockpit betreibt, für ein Datenschutzcockpit registrieren. [2]Sie hat sich bei der Regis-trierung und Nutzung des Datenschutzcockpits mit einem Identifizierungsmittel auf dem Vertrauensniveau hoch zu identifizieren. [3]Zur Feststellung der Identität darf bei Registrierung und Nutzung das dienste- und kartenspezifische Kennzeichen verarbeitet werden. [4]Im Übrigen kann sich der Nutzer auch mit einem Nutzerkonto des Portalver-bundes beim Datenschutzcockpit registrieren.

(4) [1]Das Datenschutzcockpit darf die Identifikationsnummer nach § 139b der Abgaben-ordnung als Identifikator für die Anfrage zur Erhebung und Anzeige der Daten nach Absatz 2 verarbeiten. [2]Zur Anfrage nach § 6 des Identifikationsnummerngesetzes erhebt das Datenschutzcockpit bei der Registrierung des Nutzers folgende Daten:

1. Namen,

2. Vornamen,

3. Anschrift,

4. Geburtsname und

5. Tag der Geburt.

Pilot des Cockpits für ELFE entwickelt, dessen Erprobung sich auf § 11 OZG und Art. 21 RegMoG stützen kann. Wann der Pilot in der Hansestadt einsetzbar sein wird und wann er bundesweit Anwendung finden kann, ist noch offen.

1. De lege lata

Das Datenschutzcockpit ist eine IT-Komponente[57] im Portalverbund, mit der sich natürliche Personen Auskünfte zu Datenübermittlungen zwischen öffentlichen Stellen anzeigen lassen können (§ 10 Abs. 1 S. 1 OZG). Dies soll sicherstellen, dass die behördliche Datenverarbeitung nicht heimlich erfolgt. Das BMI bestimmt durch Rechtsverordnung die öffentliche Stelle,[58] die das Cockpit errichtet und betreibt (§ 10 Abs. 5 S. 1 OZG). Damit wird auf die regionale Erprobung ein zentrales Cockpit folgen.

a) Zugang zum Datenschutzcockpit

Es steht jeder natürlichen Person frei, sich für das Datenschutzcockpit zu registrieren (§ 10 Abs. 3 S. 1 OZG). Dabei muss sie ein Identifizierungsmittel auf dem Vertrauensniveau hoch verwenden (§ 10 Abs. 3 S. 2 OZG), z.B. das Nutzerkonto des Portalverbundes (§ 10 Abs. 3 S. 4 OZG), soweit dieses

---

[3]*Der Nutzer legt fest, in welchem Umfang das Datenschutzcockpit Protokolldaten einschließlich der übermittelten Inhaltsdaten sowie die Bestandsdaten der Register nach Absatz 2 erheben und anzeigen darf.* [4]*Auf diese Daten hat nur der Nutzer Zugriff.* [5]*Der Nutzer muss sein Konto im Datenschutzcockpit jederzeit selbst löschen können.* [6]*Das Konto im Datenschutzcockpit wird automatisiert gelöscht, wenn es drei Jahre nicht verwendet wurde.*

(5) [1]*Das Datenschutzcockpit wird von einer öffentlichen Stelle errichtet und betrieben, die durch Rechtsverordnung des Bundesministeriums des Innern, für Bau und Heimat im Benehmen mit dem IT-Planungsrat mit Zustimmung des Bundesrates bestimmt wird.* [2]*Das Nähere zu den technischen Verfahren, den technischen Formaten der Datensätze und den Übertragungswegen legt das Bundesministerium des Innern, für Bau und Heimat im Benehmen mit dem IT-Planungsrat mit Zustimmung des Bundesrates durch Rechtsverordnung fest.*

57 „IT-Komponenten" sind IT-Anwendungen, Basisdienste und die elektronische Realisierung von Standards, Schnittstellen und Sicherheitsvorgaben, die für die Anbindung an den Portalverbund, für den Betrieb des Portalverbundes und für die Abwicklung der Verwaltungsleistungen im Portalverbund erforderlich sind (§ 2 Abs. 6 OZG).

58 Im Benehmen mit dem IT-Planungsrat und mit Zustimmung des Bundesrates.

auf einem entsprechenden Niveau eingerichtet worden ist.[59] Die Verwendung des Cockpits ist folglich fakultativ und insbesondere keine Voraussetzung, um digitale Verwaltungsleistungen beantragen zu können. Staatliche Stellen haben keinen Zugang zum Cockpit (vgl. § 10 Abs. 4 S. 4 OZG). Es sind vielmehr technische und organisatorische Maßnahmen vorzusehen, damit staatliche Eingriffe zum Nachteil der betroffenen Personen ausgeschlossen sind (§ 10 Abs. 2 S. 5 OZG).

b) Angezeigte Daten im Datenschutzcockpit

Im Datenschutzcockpit erhält die betroffene Person eine Übersicht über diejenigen Datenübermittlungen, bei denen ihre Identifikationsnummer zum Einsatz gekommen ist (§ 10 Abs. 1 S. 2 OZG). Damit beschränkt sich das Transparenzkonzept des § 10 OZG auf eine Ex-post-Kontrolle. Die betroffene Person erhält keine Benachrichtigung vor oder zeitgleich zu der Datenverarbeitung, sondern muss sich selbständig einen Kenntnisstand verschaffen. In welchem Umfang sie die Daten angezeigt bekommen will, legt sie ebenfalls individuell fest (§ 10 Abs. 4 S. 3 OZG).

Konkret kann sich die betroffene Person die Protokolldaten nach § 9 IDNrG einschließlich der dazu übermittelten Inhaltsdaten sowie die Bestandsdaten der Register anzeigen lassen (§ 10 Abs. 2 S. 1 OZG).[60] Die Daten stammen einerseits von allen öffentlichen Stellen, zwischen denen Datenübermittlungen unter Nutzung der Identifikationsnummer stattgefunden haben (§ 9 Abs. 1 S. 1 IDNrG).[61] Andererseits stammen sie von der Registermodernisierungsbehörde, die sowohl die bei ihr erfolgten Datenabrufe als auch die Datenübermittlungen zwischen ihr und dem Bundeszentralamt für Steuern erfasst (§ 9 Abs. 1 S. 2 IDNrG). Da das Cockpit nutzerzentriert ausgestaltet sein soll (§ 10 Abs. 2 S. 4 OZG), müssen diese Informationen verständlich aufbereitet sein. Der Datenbestand soll zudem

---

59 Das Nutzerkonto lässt sich auf einem oder mehreren Vertrauensniveaus einrichten und nutzen (Basisregistrierung/substantielles Vertrauensniveau/hohes Vertrauensniveau).

60 Ursprünglich sollten sich die betroffenen Personen nur die Protokolldaten anzeigen lassen können (BT-Drs. 19/24226, S. 80 f.).

61 Damit beschränken sich die angezeigten Datenübermittlungen nicht auf bereichsübergreifende Datenübermittlungen i.S.v. § 7 Abs. 2 IDNrG, was während des Gesetzgebungsverfahrens noch unklar gewesen war (BfDI, Stellungnahme zum Entwurf eines Gesetzes zur Einführung einer Identifikationsnummer in die öffentliche Verwaltung und zur Änderung weiterer Gesetze (Registermodernisierungsgesetz), Bonn 26.8.2020, S. 4).

in Echtzeit einsehbar sein, was sich infolge der Vielzahl an zu verknüpfenden Registern als technisch herausfordernd darstellen dürfte.[62]

c) Speicherort der angezeigten Daten

Für die Speicherung der Daten, die sich im Datenschutzcockpit anzeigen lassen, hat der Bundesgesetzgeber das sogenannte „Quellenmodell" gewählt. Die Daten sind grundsätzlich nur in den „Quellregistern" bei den öffentlichen Stellen und der Registermodernisierungsbehörde gespeichert. Im Cockpit werden die Daten nur für die Dauer des jeweiligen Nutzungsvorgangs gespeichert und anschließend wieder gelöscht (§ 10 Abs. 2 S. 2 OZG). Das Cockpit fungiert somit nicht als eine Art „Datentresor", in dem alle personenbezogenen Daten dauerhaft zentral gespeichert wären.[63] Eine derartige Funktion würde eine Vorratsdatenspeicherung durch die Hintertür einführen.

2. De lege ferenda

Um als Garant einer verfassungskonformen Registermodernisierung dienen zu können, bedarf § 10 OZG noch deutlicher Nachschärfungen.

a) Erweiterung des Anwendungsbereichs (bei gleichzeitiger Verhinderung eines „information overload")

Bislang beschränkt sich der Anwendungsbereich des Datenschutzcockpits darauf, der betroffenen Person die Datenverarbeitung öffentlicher Stellen anzuzeigen (vgl. § 10 Abs. 1 S. 1 OZG). Wie sich jedoch aus § 5 Abs. 1 S. 2 IDNrG und der Gesetzesbegründung[64] ergibt, sollen auch nicht-öffentliche Stellen die Identifikationsnummer verarbeiten dürfen. Dies führt gegenwärtig zu einer Regelungslücke, die es zu schließen gilt. Die Registermodernisierung darf weder in einer Profilbildung durch den Staat noch

---

62 BT-Drs. 19/24226, S. 80 f.

63 *Guckelberger/Starosta*, Onlinezugangsgesetz (Fn. 10), 1166; vgl. *A. Berger*, Onlinezugangsgesetz und Digitalisierungsprogramm – Auf die Kommunen kommt es an!, KommJur 2018, 441 (443).

64 BT-Drs. 19/24226, S. 36.

durch die Privatwirtschaft münden. Der Transparenzmechanismus muss daher auf nicht-öffentliche Stellen erweitert werden. Dies erfordert zugleich, dass nicht-öffentliche Stellen zukünftig ebenfalls an die Protokollierungspflicht des § 9 Abs. 1 S. 1 IDNrG gebunden sind.

Des Weiteren sollten sich die betroffenen Personen auch grenzüberschreitende Datenübermittlungen im Cockpit anzeigen lassen können.[65] Denn mit der Umsetzung der SDG-VO umfasst der behördliche Datenaustausch nach dem Once-Only-Prinzip potenziell die gesamte Europäische Union. Dies kann der Bundesgesetzgeber zwar nicht einseitig im OZG festlegen, er sollte sich dafür aber auf Unionsebene einsetzen und die notwendigen technischen Voraussetzungen schaffen.

Je mehr Informationen sich im Cockpit abrufen lassen, umso wahrscheinlicher wird indes ein „information overload", d.h. eine intellektuelle Überforderung durch zu viele (ungefilterte) Informationen.[66] Entscheidend für den tatsächlichen Einblick in die behördliche Datenverarbeitung ist daher die Informationsdarstellung. Ausschließlich textbasierte, seitenlange Ausführungen erschweren regelmäßig das Verständnis, was dem Transparenzziel des § 10 OZG zuwiderliefe. „Icons" könnten hingegen ein niedrigschwelliger Lösungsansatz sein, um die Komplexität der Informationen zu reduzieren. Das Cockpit sollte der betroffenen Person sowohl derartige Vereinfachungen als auch umfassende Informationen anzeigen können.

b) Erweiterung der Anwendungsmöglichkeiten

Über das Datenschutzcockpit sollten sich neben dem Auskunftsanspruch aus § 10 OZG auch die allgemeinen datenschutzrechtlichen Betroffenenrechte (Art. 12 ff. DSGVO) ausüben lassen. Es erleichterte den Individualrechtsschutz nachhaltig, wenn die betroffenen Personen mithilfe derselben Anwendung zugleich den umfassenderen Auskunftsanspruch aus Art. 15 DSGVO, der von der nationalen Regelung unberührt bleibt (§ 10

---

65 *P. Parycek/V. Huber/S. S. Hunt/A.-S. Novak/B. E. P. Thapa*, Analyse der rechtlich-technischen Gesamtarchitektur des Entwurfs des Registermodernisierungsgesetzes, BT-Ausschuss-Drs. 19(4)667D, Berlin 2020, S. 21.

66 Zum Phänomen des „information overload" siehe bspw. *G. K. Ebner*, Information Overload 2.0?, ZD 2022, 364 (365 f.) und *D. M. Levy*, Information Overload, in: K. E. Himma/H. T. Tavani (Hrsg.), The Handbook of Information and Computer Ethics, New York 2008, S. 497 ff.

Abs. 2 S. 3 OZG)[67] und z.B. auch das Löschungs-, Berichtigungs- und Widerspruchsrecht geltend machen könnten.

Ein integrierter Informationskanal zu den Datenschutzbehörden würde zusätzlich eine niedrigschwellige Unterstützung bei der Rechtsdurchsetzung ermöglichen. Betroffene Personen könnten ihr Beschwerderecht aus Art. 77 DSGVO mit wenigen Klicks ausüben, sobald sie Datenschutzverstöße vermuten. Außerdem sollten sie Informationen nicht nur zu dem Zeitpunkt erlangen können, in dem sie das Cockpit aktiv nutzen. Vielmehr sollte das Cockpit über eine Benachrichtigungsfunktion verfügen, um die betroffene Person in Echtzeit über solche Datenübermittlungen zu informieren, die sie vorher entsprechend ausgewählt hat.[68]

c) Einheitlicher Datenaustauschstandard

Für ein hohes Transparenzniveau müssen die im Datenschutzcockpit angezeigten Daten richtig und vollständig sein. Daher muss das Cockpit alle Datensätze ordnungsgemäß verarbeiten können. Dies stellt eine erhebliche Herausforderung dar, da grundsätzlich alle registerführenden Stellen (d.h. tausende Behörden unterschiedlicher Hoheitsträger) in der Lage sein müssen, ihre Daten an das Cockpit übermitteln zu können. Einen einheitlichen Datenaustauschstandard gibt es indes noch nicht.[69] Es existieren zwar bereits verschiedene Austauschstandards auf Grundlage des textbasierten Datenformats „XML in der öffentlichen Verwaltung" (XÖV). Diese kommen bislang aber nur für spezifische Fachverfahren innerhalb geschlossener Informationsverbünde zur Anwendung, etwa „XMeld" im Meldewesen.

Infolgedessen drohen fehlerhafte oder unvollständige Auskünfte im Cockpit. Der Bundesgesetzgeber hat auf diese Problematik noch nicht ausreichend reagiert. Während Datenabrufe bei der Registermodernisierungsbehörde nach einem einheitlichen Datenaustauschstandard erfolgen sollen (§ 7 Abs. 1 S. 1 IDNrG), fehlt eine entsprechende Vorgabe für die sonstigen Datenübermittlungen unter Nutzung der Identifikationsnummer. Es ist in erster Linie dem BMI überlassen, mittels Rechtsverordnung das Nähere zu

---

67 Zur notwendigen Unterscheidung der beiden Auskunftsansprüche siehe BfDI, Einführung einer Identifikationsnummer (Fn. 61), S. 12.
68 Vgl. *Martini*, Transformation der Verwaltung (Fn. 39), 452.
69 *M. Klein*, Gesucht wird ein übergreifender Standard, eGovernment Computing v. 12.4.2022, abrufbar unter https://www.egovernment-computing.de/gesucht-wird-ein-uebergreifender-standard-a-1110389/ (zuletzt abgerufen: 11.12.2022).

den technischen Verfahren, Datenformaten und Übertragungswegen zu regeln (§ 10 Abs. 5 S. 2 OZG). Bis es einen Standard für alle Übermittlungen gibt, sollte diese Rechtsverordnung vorsehen, dass das Cockpit über eine Komponente verfügen muss, die abweichende Standards übersetzen kann.[70]

d) Speicherdauer der Daten

Derzeit ist offen, über welchen Zeitraum sich die Daten im Datenschutzcockpit anzeigen lassen. Denn die Protokolldaten sind grundsätzlich nur zwei Jahre aufzubewahren und danach unverzüglich zu löschen (§ 9 Abs. 3 S. 1 Hs. 1 IDNrG). Zwar können die Daten auch länger gespeichert bleiben, um die Nutzung des Cockpits zu ermöglichen (§ 9 Abs. 3 S. 1 Hs. 2 i.V.m. Abs. 2 IDNrG). Eine konkrete Speicherdauer ist aber gesetzlich nicht vorgesehen.[71]

Aus dieser Regelungslücke erwachsen zwei Risiken. Auf der einen Seite könnten der betroffenen Person Verarbeitungsvorgänge verborgen bleiben, wenn sie das Cockpit nur selten nutzt[72] und ältere Datensätze bereits gelöscht sind. Auf der anderen Seite führte eine unbegrenzte Speicherdauer dazu, dass Dritte im Falle unberechtigter Datenzugriffe wesentlich umfangreichere Datensätze erlangen könnten. Angesichts dieses Spannungsfeldes zwischen Transparenz und Datenschutz wäre es vorzugswürdig, gesetzlich zu verankern, dass grundsätzlich der betroffenen Person die Entscheidung über die Speicherdauer zukommt. Nur wenn sie keine Entscheidung trifft, sollte eine gesetzliche Aufbewahrungs- bzw. Löschungsfrist greifen. Diese sollte der Bundesgesetzgeber präzise bestimmen, um die Rechtssicherheit zu erhöhen.

e) Datenschutzrechtliche Verantwortlichkeit

Damit das Datenschutzcockpit den betroffenen Personen Auskunft zu staatlichen Verarbeitungsvorgängen gewähren kann, ist es erforderlich,

---

70 *Parycek/Huber/Hunt/Novak/Thapa*, Registermodernisierungsgesetz (Fn. 65), S. 20.
71 Auch in dieser Hinsicht könnte die Rechtsverordnung nach § 10 Abs. 5 S. 2 OZG mehr Rechtsklarheit ermöglichen.
72 Nutzt die betroffene Person das Cockpit länger als drei Jahre nicht, wird es gelöscht (§ 10 Abs. 4 S. 6 OZG).

dass erneut personenbezogene Daten verarbeitet werden. Es muss daher Klarheit darüber bestehen, wer für diese Datenverarbeitung nach Art. 4 Nr. 7 Hs. 1 DSGVO verantwortlich ist. Denn der bzw. die Verantwortlichen haben die Einhaltung der datenschutzrechtlichen Pflichten sicherzustellen, d.h. insbesondere die Betroffenenrechte zu wahren. Die Verantwortlichkeit richtet sich nach den tatsächlichen Einflussnahmemöglichkeiten auf die Zwecke und Mittel der Datenverarbeitung.[73] Ist nur eine Stelle an der Datenverarbeitung beteiligt, liegt es mithin auf der Hand, dass sie verantwortlich ist.

Die Datenverarbeitung für die Auskunft im Cockpit zeichnet sich jedoch durch eine besondere Akteursvielfalt aus: Neben der Registermodernisierungsbehörde sind potenziell tausende Bundes-, Landes- und Kommunalbehörden an der Verarbeitung beteiligt. Deshalb muss der Bundesgesetzgeber einem Transparenz- und Datenschutzdefizit vorbeugen. § 10 OZG lässt die Verantwortlichkeit indes noch unerwähnt und § 8 IDNrG findet keine Anwendung, da er nur die Verantwortlichkeit für Datenabrufe bei der Registermodernisierungsbehörde regelt.[74] Allein aus der Gesetzesbegründung ergibt sich (wenn auch unverbindlich), dass die übermittelnden Stellen für die Richtigkeit der Auskunft verantwortlich sein sollen.[75] Gänzlich unbeantwortet bleibt demgegenüber die Frage, wer für die weitere Datenverarbeitung – insbesondere im Rahmen der Registrierung (vgl. § 10 Abs. 4 OZG) – verantwortlich ist.

Verantwortlicher könnte die Stelle sein, die das Cockpit betreibt (§ 10 Abs. 5 S. 1 OZG). Diese könnte aber auch nur als Auftragsverarbeiter (Art. 4 Nr. 8 DSGVO) derjenigen Stellen fungieren, die die Verwaltungsportale des Bundes und der Länder betreiben. Letztere wären dann allein verantwortlich. Denkbar wäre außerdem eine gemeinsame Verantwortlichkeit der genannten Stellen (Art. 26 Abs. 1 S. 1 DSGVO).[76] Ent-

---

73 *C. Böllhoff/J. Botta*, Das datenschutzrechtliche Verantwortlichkeitsprinzip als Herausforderung für die Verwaltungsdigitalisierung, NVwZ 2021, 425 (426); *K. Schreiber*, Gemeinsame Verantwortlichkeit gegenüber Betroffenen und Aufsichtsbehörden, ZD 2019, 55 (56).

74 Ebenfalls keine definitive Klärung bietet § 9c Abs. 2 EGovG Bund, der die Verantwortlichkeit für die Datenverarbeitung im Bundesverwaltungsportal grundsätzlich der Stelle zuordnet, die es betreibt. Wie sich diese Regelung zur Datenverarbeitung im Zusammenhang mit dem Cockpit verhält, bleibt fraglich, solange offen ist, auf welche Weise die IT-Komponente in den Portalverbund eingebunden sein wird.

75 BT-Drs. 19/24226, S. 80.

76 Der EuGH hat diese Rechtsfigur bislang sehr extensiv ausgelegt. Siehe seine st. Rspr.: Urt. v. 5.6.2018, Rs. C-210/16 (Wirtschaftsakademie SH), ECLI:EU:C:

scheidend ist letztendlich, wie die IT-Komponente in den Portalverbund eingebunden sein wird.[77] Um bei der technischen Entwicklung des Cockpits von Anfang an klare Verantwortungssphären sicherzustellen, sollte der Bundesgesetzgeber den oder die Verantwortlichen vorab gesetzlich bestimmen (Art. 4 Nr. 7 Hs. 2 DSGVO).[78] Dadurch lässt sich verhindern, dass die später als verantwortlich ausgewiesene Stelle und die datenschutzrechtlich tatsächlich (mit-)verantwortliche Stelle nicht übereinstimmen.

III. Notwendigkeit weiterer Schutzmechanismen

Auch wenn der Bundesgesetzgeber die vorgeschlagenen Ergänzungen des Datenschutzcockpits umsetzen sollte, der Transparenzmechanismus allein vermag es nicht, die Datenschutzrisiken der Registermodernisierung auf ein angemessenes Maß zu reduzieren.[79] Die bloße Ex-post-Kontrolle im Cockpit kann nicht verhindern, dass unrechtmäßige Datenverknüpfungen erfolgen, sondern hilft lediglich dabei, diese aufzuklären.

Es braucht daher auch ex ante wirkende Schutzmechanismen. Als ein solcher soll vorrangig das 4-Corner-Modell dienen. Kritisch ist indes zu sehen, dass es nur bei bereichsübergreifenden Datenübermittlungen zur Anwendung kommen soll.[80] Die in der Gesetzesbegründung genannten Bereiche sind vergleichsweise weit gefasst und es obliegt der Exekutive, die Bereiche festzulegen (§ 12 Abs. 1 S. 1 IDNrG). Dies birgt das Risiko, dass sehr viele Datenübermittlungen als bereichsintern gelten werden. Bei bereichsinternen Datenübermittlungen schützt jedoch allein das Cockpit die betroffenen Personen. Das ist unzureichend, da sich in diesen Fällen der Grundrechtsschutz de facto auf die Bürger verlagert. Die Nutzerakzeptanz des Cockpits ist zudem noch ungewiss.

2018:388, Rn. 25 ff.; Urt. v. 10.7.2018, Rs. C-25/17 (Jehovan todistajat), ECLI:EU: C:2018:551, Rn. 63 ff.; Urt. v. 29.7.2019, Rs. C-40/17 (Fashion ID), ECLI:EU:C: 2019:629, Rn. 64 ff. Kritisch dazu *Böllhoff/Botta*, Datenschutzrechtliches Verantwortlichkeitsprinzip (Fn. 73), 427.

77   BfDI, Einführung einer Identifikationsnummer (Fn. 61), S. 13.

78   Zu den Voraussetzungen einer mitgliedstaatlichen Festlegung der datenschutzrechtlichen Verantwortlichkeit siehe *Böllhoff/Botta*, Datenschutzrechtliches Verantwortlichkeitsprinzip (Fn. 73), 429 f.

79   *Sorge/von Lucke/Spiecker gen. Döhmann*, Registermodernisierung (Fn. 24), S. 24.

80   Darüber hinaus bietet das 4-Corner-Modell keinen Schutz vor unberechtigten Datenzugriffen. Siehe BfDI, Stellungnahme zum Entwurf eines Gesetzes zur Einführung einer Identifikationsnummer in die öffentliche Verwaltung und zur Änderung weiterer Gesetze (Registermodernisierungsgesetz), Bonn 21.10.2020, S. 5.

D. Fazit

Mit dem OZG und dem RegMoG hat der Bundesgesetzgeber die Weichen für die Zukunft der öffentlichen Verwaltung gestellt. Dafür greift er auch in die informationelle Selbstbestimmung ein. Die Registermodernisierung soll indes keine „gläsernen Bürger" hervorbringen, sondern vorrangig eine effizientere Verwaltungspraxis ermöglichen und zugleich den Staat selbst noch durchsichtiger werden lassen. Die Einlösung dieses Transparenzversprechens ist maßgebend für eine verfassungskonforme Registermodernisierung (wenn auch nicht ihre alleinige Garantie[81]).

Damit das Datenschutzcockpit aber seiner Bedeutung als zentraler Transparenzmechanismus gerecht werden kann, muss der Bundesgesetzgeber seine Potenziale voll ausschöpfen. Insbesondere ist sein Anwendungsbereich zu erweitern (ohne zugleich einen „information overload" zu bewirken). Außerdem bedarf es zusätzlicher Anwendungsmöglichkeiten, eines einheitlichen Datenaustauschstandards, einer grundsätzlichen Entscheidungsfreiheit über die Speicherdauer und der Klärung der datenschutzrechtlichen Verantwortlichkeit.

---

81 Siehe Fn. 36.

Weniger ist Mehr! Impulse für eine Neuregulierung der datenschutzrechtlichen Informationspflichten

Gordian Konstantin Ebner

A. Einleitung

Die Informationspflichten der DS-GVO sorgen nicht erst seit Inkrafttreten der Datenschutz-Grundverordnung für Aufsehen. Die auf ihnen beruhenden Datenschutzhinweise werden von einigen Menschen als lästig empfunden.[1] Der nachfolgende Beitrag illustriert knapp die den Normen zugrundeliegenden Hintergründe sowie die Kernpunkte der geäußerten Kritik. Um den identifizierten Nachteilen effektiv begegnen zu können, werden anschließend auch unter Berücksichtigung anderer Datenschutzrechtsordnungen Erwägungen für eine Novellierung der Transparenzpflichten diskutiert und darauf aufbauend konkrete Vorschläge zur Neuregulierung der Materie vorgestellt.

B. Hintergründe

Informationspflichten sind Normen, die bestimmte Stakeholder dazu verpflichten, einem bestimmten Personenkreis (typischerweise) vor einer anstehenden Entscheidung bestimmte Informationen zu vermitteln. Bei diesen Hinweisen handelt es sich um Modalitäten, die nach der Auffassung des Gesetzgebers für das Treffen einer rationalen Entscheidung über den Schluss eines Vertrages, die Nutzung eines Dienstes bzw. Produkts etc. relevant sind.

Diese Intention ist gerade im Daten(schutz)recht grundsätzlich sinnvoll. Denn die „Bedingungen der modernen Datenverarbeitung"[2], also die unternehmensseitigen Praktiken zur Nutzung personenbezogener Daten sowie drohende Risiken einer Datenpreisgabe sind betroffenen Personen

---

1 *A. Roßnagel*, Wie zukunftsfähig ist die Datenschutz-Grundverordnung? Welche Antworten bietet sie für die neuen Herausforderungen des Datenschutzrechts?, DuD 2016, 561 (563).
2 Vgl. bereits BVerfGE 65, 1.

ohne entsprechende Mitteilung weder abstrakt noch im konkreten Einzelfall bekannt.[3] Dementsprechend gibt ein Großteil der Europäerinnen und Europäer an, sich um die Verwendung „ihrer" personenbezogenen Daten zu sorgen.[4] Durch die Mitteilung der entsprechenden Details werden (zumindest in der Theorie) die hierfür relevanten Wissensdefizite sowie Informationsasymmetrien reduziert und mithin die Transparenz der anstehenden Datenverarbeitung zugunsten der Betroffenen gesteigert.[5] Zur (Wieder-)Herstellung bzw. Gewährleistung der datenbezogenen Selbstbestimmung sind Informationspflichten deshalb unerlässlich.[6] Nicht zuletzt deshalb scheinen Regelsetzer aktueller Datenschutzgesetze weltweit von der beschriebenen Wirkweise der Transparenzpflichten überzeugt zu sein.[7]

C. Kritik

Gleichwohl sind die Art. 12-14 DS-GVO immer wieder (zu Recht) Gegenstand teils harscher Kritik.[8] Denn trotz der grundsätzlichen Notwendigkeit der Informationspflichten gelingt es ihnen nicht, ihrem theoretischen Zweck der Transparenzgewährleistung gerecht zu werden („Informationspflichten-Dilemma").[9] Den auf ihnen beruhenden Datenschutzhinweisen

---

3 *A. Acquisti/L. Brandimarte/G. Loewenstein*, Privacy and human behavior in the age of information, Science 2015, 509 (509); *F. Kollmar/M. El-Auwad*, Grenzen der Einwilligung bei hochkomplexen und technisierten Datenverarbeitungen, K&R 2021, 73 (75).

4 *Europäische Kommission*, Special Eurobarometer 487a "The General Data Protection Regulation", 2019, S. 39.

5 *G. Ebner*, Information Overload 2.0?, ZD 2022, 364 (366).

6 *G. Ebner*, Weniger ist Mehr?, 2022, S. 89 f., 94.

7 Siehe etwa jüngst im Entwurf des American Data Privacy and Protection Act in Sec. 102; ausführlich zum American Data Privacy and Protection Act-Entwurf siehe *I. Marin/C. Spirkl/G. Ebner*, American Data Privacy and Protection Act: Der aktuelle Vorschlag für ein US-Bundesdatenschutzgesetz, MMR-Aktuell 2022, 449500.

8 Etwa bei *O. Vettermann*, Datenschutzrechtliche Informationspflichten zwischen Kreativität und Transparenz Urheberrechtlicher Schutz von Datenschutzerklärungen, ZD 2021, 257 (257); *L. Strassemeyer*, Die Transparenzvorgaben der DSGVO, K&R 2020, 176 (182); *J. Bunnenberg*, Privates Datenschutzrecht, Baden-Baden 2020, S. 107.

9 Vgl. *Ebner*, Information Overload (Fn. 5), 365.

wird schlicht zu wenig Beachtung geschenkt[10] - Tendenz steigend.[11] Das liegt vornehmlich an drei Gründen, die im Folgenden knapp dargestellt werden.

I. Länge der Datenschutzhinweise

Bei der Normierung der Informationspflichten hatte der europäische Gesetzgeber wohl das Ideal einer vorgebildeten, wissbegierigen und hochintelligenten betroffenen Person vor Augen, die stets rein rational agiert. Nach der dem Regelungsmodell der Art. 12 ff. DS-GVO offensichtlich zugrunde gelegten Theorie des Privacy Calculus[12] würde die Bereitstellung möglichst umfangreicher und detaillierter (entscheidungsrelevanter) Informationen auch dazu führen, dass Betroffene äußerst fundierte Entscheidungen treffen.[13] Paradoxerweise ist jedoch meist das Gegenteil der Fall: Studien belegen, dass die Aufnahmekapazität des Einzelnen sinkt, je mehr Informationen ihm zur Verfügung gestellt werden (sog. More-Is-Less-Paradoxon).[14] Es verwundert daher kaum, dass rund zwei Drittel der im Rahmen des Eurobarometers Befragten angeben, Datenschutzhinweise allein wegen ihrer enormen Länge nicht zu lesen.[15] Die Opulenz der Hinweise erschlägt ihre Adressaten bereits vor, spätestens aber während der Lektüre

---

10 Zu den Ausprägungen fehlender Effektivität siehe *Europäische Kommission*, Special Eurobarometer 487a "The General Data Protection Regulation", 2019, S. 47.

11 So war etwa 2015 die Bereitschaft, Datenschutzhinweise zu lesen noch deutlich höher, siehe *Europäische Kommission*, Special Eurobarometer 431 "Data Protection", 2015, S. 84.

12 Ausführlich zum Privacy Calculus siehe etwa *N. Bol/T. Dienlin/S. Kruikemeier/M. Sax/S. Boerman/J. Strycharz/N. Helberger/C. Vreese*, Understanding the Effects of Personalization as a Privacy Calculus: Analyzing Self-Disclosure Across Health, News, and Commerce Contexts, Journal of Computer-Mediated Communication 2018, 370.

13 *Ebner*, Weniger ist Mehr? (Fn. 6), S. 93 f.

14 *L. Moerel*, Big Data Protection: How to Make the Draft EU Regulation on Data Protection Future Proof, Tilburg 2014, S. 47.

15 *Europäische Kommission*, Special Eurobarometer 487a "The General Data Protection Regulation", 2019, S. 51.

(sog. Information Overload)[16].[17] Erschwerend tritt hinzu, dass dieses Phänomen zusätzlich durch ständig neue Informationspflichten (nicht ausschließlich, aber gerade auch) im Bereich des Daten(schutz)rechts potenziert wird.[18]

II. Komplexität der Datenschutzhinweise

Im Gleichlauf mit der Komplexität moderner Datenverarbeitungsmethoden nimmt auch der Komplexitätsgrad der erläuternden Datenschutzinformationen permanent zu.[19] Technische[20] wie juristische[21] Fachbegriffe erschweren das Verständnis des zu lesenden Textes erheblich. Dementsprechend stellt die schwere Verständlichkeit der Datenschutzhinweise im Rahmen der Eurobarometerumfrage mit 31 Prozent der Stimmen den zweithäufigsten Grund fehlender Lektüre dar.[22]

III. Rigide Art und Weise der Informationserteilung

Darüber hinaus ist auch die derzeit vorherrschende Art und Weise der Informationsbereitstellung weder einer Lektüre der Datenschutzhinweise noch ihrem Verständnis unmittelbar zuträglich.[23] Lange, ohne Unterbrechung durchgeschriebene und inhaltlich anspruchsvolle Texte auf weißem Grund sind schlicht wenig leserfreundlich. Beispielhaft sei an dieser

---

16 Ausführlich zum Information Overload siehe etwa bei *Ebner*, Weniger ist Mehr? (Fn. 6), S. 104 ff.; *I. van Ooijen/H. Vrabec*, Does the GDPR Enhance Consumers' Control over Personal Data? An Analysis from a Behavioural Perspective, Journal of Consumer Policy 2019, 91 (94 f.).

17 *T. Gerpott*, Datenschutzerklärungen – Materiell fundierte Einwilligungen nach der DSGVO, MMR 2020, 739 (740) m.w.N.

18 Siehe nur Art. 21 Abs. 1 DGA sowie insb. Art. 3 Abs. 2 DA-E, hierzu *Ebner*, Information Overload (Fn. 5), 364.

19 *B. Steinrötter* in: BeckOK IT-Recht, DS-GVO, 7. Ed. 2022, Art. 12 Rn. 4; *M. Pollmann/D. Kipker*, Informierte Einwilligung in der Online-Welt, DuD 2016, 378 (378).

20 *T. Gerpott*, Datenschutzerklärungen (Fn. 17), 740 m.w.N.

21 *R. Arnold/A. Hillebrand/M. Waldburger*, Personal Data and Privacy, 2015, S. 28.

22 *Europäische Kommission*, Special Eurobarometer 487a "The General Data Protection Regulation", 2019, S. 51.

23 *G. Ebner*, Information Overload (Fn. 5), 365.

Stelle auf die „Datenschutzerklärung"[24] von amazon.de verwiesen, die rund 4.400 Worte in meist vollständigen Sätzen und (bis auf die knapp 20 Links, die auf externe Seiten verweisen) ohne farbliche Hervorhebung umfasst.[25] Derartige Datenschutzhinweise bergen zudem die Gefahr, betroffene Personen von einer künftigen Lektüre anderer Datenschutzinformationen abzuhalten, da sie zu einer Aversion gegenüber Datenschutzhinweisen sowie entsprechenden Regelungen führen können.[26]

D. Lösungsansätze de lege ferenda

Nach hier vertretener Auffassung können die identifizierten Schwächen der Datenschutzhinweise – freilich im Bewusstsein der Grenzen des juristisch Regelbaren –[27] zumindest überwiegend[28] über eine Neuformulierung der Art. 12-14 DS-GVO nivelliert werden. Hierfür sollen zunächst die Leitmotive der Novellierung erörtert, Handlungsoptionen dargelegt und schließlich konkrete Modelvorschläge vorgestellt werden.

I. Leitmotive

Konsequenterweise müssen sich die Motive der Neugestaltung eng an den Ursachen für den Misserfolg der Informationspflichten *de lege lata* orientieren. Ziel der Novellierung soll insofern sein, die Informationspflichten dahingehend zu optimieren, dass ihr Produkt künftig tatsächlich möglichst kurz, inhaltlich leicht verständlich und optisch ansprechend ausgestaltet

---

24 Es handelt sich hierbei um den von amazon.de selbst verwendeten Begriff. Unabhängig davon ist diese Formulierung ebenso wie die der „Datenschutzrichtlinie" wegen des nur einseitig informierenden Charakters der Datenschutzinformationen irreführend und sollte besser vermieden werden, siehe dazu auch KG Berlin ZD 2019, 272 (274).

25 Stand der Datenschutzhinweise vom 04.12.2020, abrufbar unter https://www.amazon.de/gp/help/customer/display.html?nodeId=201909010&ref_=footer_privacy (zuletzt aufgerufen: 05.08.2022).

26 Ähnlich *Ebner*, Information Overload (Fn. 5), 364.

27 Vgl. *W. D'Avis/T. Giesen*, Datenschutz in der EU – rechtsstaatliches Monster und wissenschaftliche Hybris, CR 2019, 24 (32).

28 Schlichtes Desinteresse an Belangen des individuellen Datenschutzes, Naivität oder bereits etablierte Habituation können dagegen wohl auch durch die gelungensten neuen Informationspflichten nur in sehr begrenztem Umfang reduziert werden, vgl. *Ebner*, Weniger ist Mehr? (Fn. 6), S. 70.

wird.[29] Gleichzeitig können daneben auch konzeptionelle Schwächen der bisherigen Vorschriften behoben werden.

1. Kürzung

Das empirisch nachgewiesene Phänomen des Transparency Paradox[30] belegt eindeutig, dass die Kommunikation weniger Informationen in der Regel zu einem höheren Grad an Transparenz bei ihren Adressaten führt. Im Rahmen des Neuregulierungsprozesses ist deshalb jede einzelne bisherige Informationspflicht einer kritischen Abwägung zwischen gerade noch zu berücksichtigendem Informationsinteresse und drohender Informationsüberladung zu unterziehen. Dabei ist insbesondere unter Berücksichtigung der Existenz des Auskunftsanspruchs nach Art. 15 DS-GVO[31] zu prüfen, welcher der Verarbeitungshinweise zum Zeitpunkt der Datenerhebung wirklich unerlässlich ist, um das intendierte Handeln unter datenschutzrechtlichen Gesichtspunkten valide prüfen zu können.[32] Es liegt auf der Hand, dass unterschiedliche Akteure hierbei zu divergierenden Auffassungen gelangen werden. Entscheidend ist jedoch vielmehr, dass ein entsprechender Diskurs überhaupt erst einmal begonnen wird.

Nach hier vertretener Auffassung sollten die Informationspflichten inhaltlich gekürzt und das Auskunftsrecht gegebenenfalls ausgleichend angereichert werden. Auf diese Weise erhalten Betroffene über Art. 13 DS-GVO nur noch die für die anstehende Entscheidung absolut notwendigen Hinweise und können sich bei einem tiefer reichenden Interesse über Art. 15 DS-GVO informieren (lassen).[33] Deshalb sollten zusätzlich Anstrengungen unternommen werden, um die Ausübung des Auskunftsrechts zu erleichtern. Möglich wäre eine dahingehende Optimierung beispielsweise durch eine Bereitstellung weiterführender Hinweise zur praktischen Ausübung des Rechts über einen Medienbruch, etwa über einen QR-Code oder

---

29 Vgl. auch *Strassemeyer*, Tranzparenzvorgaben (Fn. 8), 178.
30 Grundlegend zum Transparency Paradox *H. Nissenbaum*, Daedalus, Journal of the American Academy of Arts & Sciences 2011, 32 (36 ff.).
31 Zum Stufenverhältnis zwischen Informationspflicht und Auskunftsersuchen siehe etwa *M. Eßer* in: Auernhammer, DS-GVO, 7. Aufl., Köln 2020, Art. 13 Rn. 3.
32 Ebenso bereits *Ebner*, Weniger ist Mehr? (Fn. 6), S. 319 f.
33 Eine ähnliche Regelungssystematik findet sich im California Consumer Privacy Rights Act in Sec. 1798.100 ff.

eine URL.[34] Unter Verweis auf Art. 15 DS-GVO könnten die Informationen über die Rechtsgrundlage der Verarbeitung, die berechtigten Interessen im Sinne des Art. 6 Abs. 1 lit. f DS-GVO, das Vorhandensein eines Angemessenheitsbeschlusses etc., die Speicherdauer, das Recht zum Widerruf der Einwilligung, das Beschwerderecht bei einer Behörde, über eine Bereitstellungspflicht, die Quelle der Daten (Art. 14 Abs. 2 lit. f DS-GVO) sowie insbesondere Erklärungen zur involvierten Logik sowie der Tragweite und den angestrebten Auswirkungen einer automatisierten Entscheidungsfindung zugrundeliegenden Verarbeitung unterbleiben. Als Kontaktdaten des Datenschutzbeauftragten reicht die Mitteilung entweder einer Telefonnummer oder einer E-Mail-Adresse. Dies sollte explizit so geregelt werden, um unnötigen Ballast zu vermeiden.[35]

2. Komplexitätsreduktion

Die Komplexität der Datenschutzhinweise könnte vor allem durch eindeutig formulierte Informationspflichten mit niedrigen Anforderungen an die „Auskunft" der Verantwortlichen reduziert werden. Besonders gut eignet sich hierfür die Formulierung von Informationspflichten, die der Verantwortliche zunächst für sich selbst mit „ja" oder „nein" bzw. in der Datenschutzinformation mit „findet statt" beantwortet werden kann.

In diesem Sinne könnte man (nach kalifornischem Vorbild)[36] nur eine Information darüber verlangen, ob seitens der Verantwortlichen beabsichtigt wird, die zu erhebenden Daten zu verkaufen. Damit kommt dem bisherigen Kanon zwar eine neue, nach hiesiger Auffassung für betroffene Personen allerdings höchst relevante und zudem einfach zu erteilende sowie leicht verständliche Information hinzu. Hegt der Verantwortliche keine dahingehende Intention, braucht er hierzu keinen Hinweis erteilen.

Dieselbe Vorgehensweise bietet sich für die bisherigen Art. 13 Abs. 2 lit. f bzw. Art. 14 Abs. 2 lit. g DS-GVO an. Diese Informationspflichten führen (schon wegen ihrer unverständlichen Formulierung seitens des EU-Gesetzgebers) zu langen, äußerst komplizierten Erklärungen, für deren Inhalt sich die betroffenen Personen zudem nur in Ausnahmesituationen

---

34 Derartige Vorschläge sehen etwa das brasilianische Datenschutzgesetz in Art. 9 VII oder das chinesische Personal Information Protection Law in Art. 17 Abs. 1 Nr. 2 vor.

35 Vgl. zum Ganzen bereits *Ebner*, Weniger ist Mehr? (Fn. 6), S. 318 ff.

36 Vgl. Section 1798.100 sub. (a) par. (1) CCPA.

interessieren dürften.[37] Um also die Anwendung für Verantwortliche und die Verständlichkeit für Betroffene gleichermaßen zu verbessern, sollte die Norm (inspiriert vom schweizerischem Vorbild)[38] so umformuliert werden, dass nur noch über das bloße Stattfinden entsprechender Praktiken unterrichtet werden muss.

Ebenso bietet sich eine Komplexitätsreduktion für die Hinweise hinsichtlich der Datenempfänger sowie des Drittstaatentransfers an. Um betroffenen Personen einen schnell überblickbaren und dennoch aussagekräftigen Überblick über die Weitergabe „ihrer" personenbezogenen Daten zu ermöglichen, sollten mögliche Empfänger stets in Kategorien eingeteilt und als solche mitgeteilt werden. Sofern relevant, muss zusätzlich darüber informiert werden, ob die Daten im Rahmen der Weitergabe an Drittstaaten übermittelt werden. Interessant und durchaus erwägenswert ist in diesem Zusammenhang Sec. 202 des American Data Privacy and Protection Act-Entwurfs, der Anfang Juni 2022 vorgestellt wurde. Die dort vorgesehene Informationspflicht verlangt lediglich eine detaillierte Information darüber, ob die Daten in die Volksrepublik China, nach Russland, den Iran oder nach Nordkorea übermittelt werden.[39]

3. Effektuierung der Informationserteilung

Im Idealfall sollte sich zudem auch die Art und Weise der Informationserteilung zum Besseren verändern. In der Literatur werden eine ganze Reihe an Effektuierungsmaßnahmen vorgeschlagen und diskutiert. Gleichwohl sollen an dieser Stelle lediglich die nach hiesigem Dafürhalten vielversprechendsten Maßnahmen, namentlich die Verwendung von Schlagworten bzw. Stichpunkten, Visualisierungsmaßnahmen und Privacy Bots diskutiert werden. Auf weitere Optionen wie Zertifizierungsverfahren,[40]

---

37 *Ebner*, Weniger ist Mehr? (Fn. 6), S. 324.
38 Vgl. Art. 21 Abs. 1 revDSG.
39 Ausführlich zum Entwurf des US-BDSG *Marin/Spirkl/Ebner*, US-Bundesdatenschutzgesetz (Fn. 7).
40 Zur Zertifizierung nach Art. 42 DS-GVO siehe etwa DSK, Kurzpapier Nr. 9 – Zertifizierung nach Art. 42 DS-GVO; *S. Kettner/C. Thorun/M. Vetter*, Wege zur besseren Informiertheit, 2018, S. 81 ff.

Etikettierung,[41] Gamification[42] oder Nudging[43] wird bewusst nicht eingegangen.[44]

a) Schlagworte, Stichpunkte etc.

Auf „konventionelle" Weise könnten Datenschutzhinweise vor allem durch eine vermehrte Verwendung von Schlagworten, Stichpunkten und einfacher Sprache gekürzt und damit Opportunitätskosten im Rahmen der Lektüre eingespart werden. Die eintretende Zeitersparnis könnte die Lesewahrscheinlichkeit deutlich erhöhen.[45] Entsprechende Aufforderungen an die Verantwortlichen sollten deshalb in Art. 12 Abs. 1 DS-GVO mitaufgenommen werden.[46] Auf dieses Prinzip der Vereinfachung setzen letztlich auch Formate wie One-Pager. Zwar vermitteln auch sie die Informationen ebenso grundsätzlich schriftlich. Allerdings werden die Hinweise durch grafische Darstellungen deutlich erkennbar voneinander abgegrenzt und auf lediglich einer (DIN-A4-)Seite zur Verfügung gestellt, wodurch die Übersichtlichkeit des Gesamttextes deutlich gesteigert wird.[47] Bedauerlicherweise wird die tatsächliche Effektivität von One-Pagern in Studien teilweise angezweifelt.[48] Dennoch spricht die bei entsprechender Straffung eintretende Reduzierung der Lesedauer für eine vermehrte Nutzung von Schlagworten, Stichpunkten und kurzen Sätzen.

Sehr interessant ist insofern auch der (soweit ersichtlich) erstmals im American Data Privacy and Protection Act-Entwurf enthaltene Vorschlag

---

41 Zum mittlerweile kaum mehr beachteten Etikettierungsverfahren *P. Kelley/L. Cesca/J. Bresee/L. Cranor*, Standardizing Privacy Notices: An Online Study of the Nutrition Label Approach, 2009, S. 3.

42 Zu den Möglichkeiten der Gamification siehe ausführlich *M. Scheurer*, Playing consent – Informationsvermittlung durch Gamification, PinG 2020, 13.

43 Zu Nudging in datenschutzrechtlichem Kontext siehe Art-29-Datenschutzgruppe WP 260 – Transparenz S. 24 Rn. 39; *R. Arnold/A. Hillebrand/M. Waldburger*, Informed Consent in Theorie und Praxis, DuD 2015, 730 (733).

44 Siehe hierzu aber ausführlich *Ebner*, Weniger ist Mehr? (Fn. 6), S. 121 ff.

45 Vgl. auch *BMWi*, Weissbuch digitale Plattformen, 2017, S. 75.

46 Dagegen könnte das quasi redundante Merkmal der Verständlichkeit gestrichen werden.

47 Vgl. *A. Auer-Reinsdorff*, Transparente Datenschutzhinweise – den inhärenten Widerspruch auflösen!, ZD 2017, 149 (150).

48 Insbesondere bei *O. Ben-Shahar/A. Chilton*, Simplification of Privacy Disclosures: An Experimental Test, The Journal of Legal Studies 2016, 41; siehe auch *Gerpott*, Datenschutzerklärungen (Fn. 17), 741.

zur Bereitstellung einer „Short-Form-Notice" für „Large Data Holder". In diesem aus oben genannten Gründen begrüßenswerten[49], kurzen (Vorab-)Hinweis sollen bereits vor der Kommunikation der „großen" bzw. „langen" Privacy Policy die relevantesten Informationen zur Verfügung gestellt werden.[50]

Zumindest diskutabel ist darüber hinaus auch eine „echte" Verpflichtung zur Erteilung der Datenschutzhinweise in „einfacher Sprache", wie dies beispielsweise auf Internetseiten deutscher Behörden praktiziert wird. Denn die Realität zeigt, dass die bisherigen Vorgaben des Art. 12 Abs. 1 DS-GVO („in einer klaren und einfachen Sprache") größtenteils nicht umgesetzt werden. Dies mag einerseits daran liegen, dass die formellen Anforderungen des Art. 12 Abs. 1 DS-GVO durch die Rechtsprechung bisher kaum durchgesetzt werden. Andererseits sind einige der derzeitigen Informationspflichten aufgrund der (technischen) Komplexität des zugrundeliegenden Sachverhalts kaum mittels einfacher Wortwahl erfüllbar.[51] Dieses Problem ließe sich jedoch über die oben angeregte Kürzung des Informationskataloges zumindest teilweise beheben. In diesem Fall könnte eine Verpflichtung zur Bereitstellung einer „Short-Form-Notice" in tatsächlich einfacher Sprache einen echten Mehrwert bergen.

b) Visualisierung

Eine bisher deutlich zu wenig genutzte Maßnahme zur Verbesserung der Informationspraxis sind die in Art. 12 Abs. 7 DS-GVO erwähnten standardisierten Bildsymbole. Mit ihrer Hilfe könnten einige Hinweise visuell dargestellt werden. Für einen Erfolg dieser Methode sprechen gleich mehrere Argumente: Zum einen zeigen Studien bereits seit längerem, dass die kognitiven Fähigkeiten des Menschen visuelle Informationen deutlich besser aufnehmen können, als dies für textbasierte Hinweise der Fall ist (sog. Bildüberlegenheitseffekt).[52] Zudem erfolgt das (Wieder-)Erkennen und Verarbeiten der Aussage eines Bildes in wesentlich kürzerer Zeit, als die Lektüre eines inhaltsgleichen Textes beansprucht.[53] Die dadurch bedingte

---

49 *Marin/Spirkl/Ebner*, US-Bundesdatenschutzgesetz (Fn. 7).
50 Siehe Sec. 202 sub. (e) American Data Privacy and Protection Act-Entwurf.
51 Vgl. *T. Wischmeyer*, Regulierung intelligenter Systeme, AöR 143 (2018), 1 (53).
52 *Strassemeyer*, Transparenzvorgaben (Fn. 8), 181 m.w.N.
53 *F. Richter*, Aus Sicht der Stiftung Datenschutz – „Der Einwilligungsassistent und die Chancen eines personal data ecosystem", PinG 2017, 65 (65); siehe genauer bei *L. Specht-Riemenschneider/L. Bienemann* in: L. Specht-Riemenschneider/S. Wer-

Zeit- und Kostenersparnis[54] könnte zu einer signifikanten Erhöhung der Lesewahrscheinlichkeit eines Datenschutzhinweises führen. Außerdem bergen Bildsymbole einen höheren Erinnerungswert als rein schriftliche Datenschutzhinweise,[55] wodurch insbesondere die Effekte der hyperbolischen Diskontierung[56] und der Habituation[57] abgeschwächt werden könnten. Schließlich belegt nicht zuletzt die Gewöhnung und Akzeptanz von Straßen- oder anderen Hinweisschildern, dass Menschen über ausreichende kognitive Fähigkeiten zur Aufnahme und Verarbeitung verbildlichter Informationen verfügen.[58] Die Implementierung von standardisierten Bildsymbolen birgt bei effektiver Umsetzung also einen echten Mehrwert für die Informationsvermittlung.

Um Verantwortliche wirksam an diese Möglichkeit zu erinnern und sie insbesondere zur Umsetzung anzuhalten, sollte man erwägen, Art. 12 Abs. 7 DS-GVO als „Soll-Vorschrift" auszugestalten und zudem eine § 161 Abs. 2 AktG ähnelnde Regelung als „Umsetzungsgarant" mitaufzunehmen. Danach müssen Verantwortliche, sofern sie sich gegen die Verwendung von Privacy Icons entscheiden, die hierfür relevanten Gründe dauerhaft einsehbar auf ihrer Homepage darlegen. Schließlich ist doch zumindest nicht grundsätzlich ausgeschlossen, dass sich Verantwortliche nach der Entwicklung des zur Umgehung der Vorschrift notwendigen (ersten) Bildsymbols Gedanken über die Kreation weiterer Zeichen machen. Dabei ist wichtig zu bedenken, dass es nicht darum geht, alle bisher schriftlichen Hinweise zu verbildlichen. Vielmehr bedeutet bereits jedes einzelne leicht interpretierbare Bildsymbol eine erhebliche Zeitersparnis für die betroffene Person.[59]

---

ry/N. Werry, Datenrecht in der Digitalisierung, Berlin 2020, S. 334 f. Rn. 18 m.w.N.: Zur Aufnahme eines Bildes in der Weise, dass es zu einem späteren Zeitpunkt leicht erinnert werden kann, benötigt das menschliche Gehirn ca. zwei Sekunden. Anstatt dessen können in der gleichen Zeit nur maximal zehn Worte eines wenig anspruchsvollen Textes aufgenommen werden.

54 *D. Heckmann/Paschke*, in: Ehmann/Selmayr, DS-GVO, 2. Aufl., München 2018, Art. 12 Rn. 53.

55 *Specht-Riemenschneider/Bienemann*, Datenrecht (Fn. 53), S. 335 Rn. 19 m.w.N.

56 Zum Effekt hyperbolischer Diskontierung siehe etwa *A. Acquisti/J. Grosslags*, Privacy ad Rationality in Individual Decision Making, IEEE Security & Privacy 2005, 26 (31).

57 Zur Wirkung von Gewöhnung siehe etwa bei *K. Quinn*, Why We Share: A Uses and Gratifications Approach to Privacy Regulation in Social Media Use, Journal of Broadcasting & Electronic Media 2016, 61 (82).

58 *Strassemeyer*, Transparenzvorgaben (Fn. 8), 181.

59 Zum Ganzen siehe bereits *G. Ebner*, Weniger ist Mehr? (Fn. 6), S. 118 ff.

c) Privacy Bots

Jedenfalls in digitalen Umgebungen erscheint eine Kombination der beiden zuvor dargelegten Effektuierungsoptionen mithilfe sog. Privacy Bots am vielversprechendsten. Dabei handelt es sich um Systeme, die die Datenschutzinformationen eines Verantwortlichen automatisiert analysieren und sie anschließend dergestalt aufbereiten, dass sie für betroffene Personen schnell überblickbar und leicht verständlich sind.[60] Im Ergebnis bedienen sich die Privacy Bots zur Darstellung der Hinweise den bereits geschilderten Methoden, namentlich einfacher Sprache, Stichpunkten, Schlagworten und Bildsymbolen bzw. sonstiger Visualisierung, wie Tabellen etc.[61] Die praktische Umsetzung erfolgt entweder über eine Website, in die die URL des Datenschutzhinweises des zu prüfenden Web-Dienstes eingefügt werden kann oder idealerweise mittels eines Browser-Plug-ins.[62] Für Einwilligungssituationen wäre es darüber hinaus (zumindest rein technisch)[63] möglich, eine Einwilligung im Einklang mit zuvor definierten, individuellen Datenschutzpräferenzen vollständig autonom, also ohne weitere Nachfrage bei der einwilligenden Person durch einen Privacy Bot erteilen oder verweigern zu lassen.[64] Hierbei handelt es sich gewiss um den „Königsweg"[65], für den es allerdings noch einige Schritte zu gehen gilt. Vor allen Dingen müssten effektive Privacy Bots überhaupt erstmal (weiter)entwickelt[66] und zudem in den Alltag der Menschen integriert werden.

---

60 Siehe etwa *C. Geminn/L. Francis/K. Herder*, Die Informationspräsentation im Datenschutzrecht – Auf der Suche nach Lösungen, ZD-Aktuell 2021, 05335.
61 *T. Gerpott*, Wirkungen von Formatvariationen bei Erklärungen zum Schutz personenbezogener Daten auf betroffene Personen, CR 2020, 650 (651).
62 *N. Nüske/C. Olenberger/D. Rau/F. Schmied*, Privacy Bots – Digitale Helfer für mehr Transparenz im Internet, DuD 2019, 28 (29).
63 Zum juristisch höchst umstrittenen Streitstand siehe etwa *L. Specht-Riemenschneider/A. Blankertz /P. Sierek/R. Schneider/J. Knapp/T. Henne*, Die Datentreuhand, MMR-Beil. 2021, 25 (38 ff.).
64 *Gerpott*, Formatvariationen (Fn. 61), 651; detailliert zu automatisierter und autonomer Einwilligung siehe bei *Hacker*, Datenprivatrecht, S. 606 ff.
65 *Specht-Riemenschneider/Bienemann*, Datenrecht (Fn. 53), S. 327 Rn. 3.
66 Vgl. *Gerpott*, Formatvariationen (Fn. 61), 651.

4. Konzeption

Neben den bereits erwähnten Verbesserungsoptionen sollte auch an der grundlegenden Konzeption der Art. 13 und 14 DS-GVO nachjustiert werden. Dabei kann die grundsätzliche Aufteilung der Informationspflichten auf zwei Normen wegen der unterschiedlichen Ausnahmen und des zwar weitestgehend ähnlichen, aber nicht vollständig identischen Informationsgehalts bestehen bleiben.

Aufgrund des im Einzelfall teilweise nicht leicht zu bestimmenden Anwendungsbereichs sollte jedoch der einleitende Wortlaut dahingehend geändert werden, dass (im Einklang mit der überzeugenden und in der Literatur wohl überwiegenden Auffassung)[67] zwischen einer Datenerhebung mit oder ohne Kenntnis der betroffenen Person bzw. einer Erhebung bei Dritten unterschieden wird. Deshalb sollte künftig auch auf den insofern irreführenden Begriff der „Dritterhebung" verzichtet werden. Überflüssig ist außerdem die stets doppelte Erwähnung der Hinweise in Art. 13 und 14 DS-GVO. Ausreichend wäre es vielmehr, die Informationspflichten einmal ausführlich in Art. 13 DS-GVO zu normieren und in Art. 14 DS-GVO sodann hierauf zu verweisen. Der für die Situation des Art. 14 DS-GVO zusätzlich relevante Hinweis über die Kategorien der erhobenen Daten kann dann unkompliziert in den ersten Absatz mitaufgenommen werden. Die durch diese Kürzung der Norm eintretende leichtere Handhabbarkeit erleichtert die Rechtsanwendungspraxis für Verantwortliche deutlich und führt somit im Ergebnis zu Rechtssicherheit.[68]

Für eine Effektivitätssteigerung der Informationspflichten im Falle der Direkterhebung ist der Informationszeitpunkt grundsätzlich auf den Moment unmittelbar vor der Datenerhebung vorzuziehen.[69] Hiervon können sich im Einzelfall Ausnahmen aus technischen oder tatsächlichen Gründen ergeben.[70]

---

67 Siehe nur *R. Schwartmann/J. Schneider* in: SJTK, DS-GVO, 2. Aufl., Heidelberg 2020, Art. 13 Rn. 15; *L. Franck* in: Gola, DS-GVO, 2. Aufl., München 2018, Art. 13 Rn. 4; zust. *Schmidt-Wudy*, BeckOK DSR, 40. Ed. 2022, Art. 13 Rn. 30; *B. Paal/M. Hennemann* in: Paal/Pauly, DS-GVO, 3. Aufl., München 2021, Art. 13 Rn. 11; *A. Ingold* in: Sydow/Marsch, DS-GVO, Baden-Baden 2022, Art. 13 Rn. 8; ausführlich zum Streitstand siehe bei *Ebner*, Weniger ist Mehr? (Fn. 6), S. 185 ff.

68 Ebenso *Ebner*, Weniger ist Mehr? (Fn. 6), S. 323.

69 So bereits *A. Roßnagel/C. Geminn*, Datenschutz-Grundverordnung verbessern, Baden-Baden, 2020, S. 65; Umgesetzt wurde die Anregung etwa im kenianischen Data Protection Act in Sec. 29 oder im chinesischen Personal Information Protection Law in Art. 17.

70 Vgl. *Ebner*, Weniger ist Mehr? (Fn. 6), S. 322 f.

Da sich der (*de lege lata* in Art. 13 und 14 DS-GVO enthaltene[71] und zur Vermeidung der Informationsüberladung an sich äußerst sinnvolle) risiko-basierte Informationserteilungsansatz *in praxi* bedauerlicherweise nicht durchzusetzen vermochte, ist in einer Neuregelung hiervon Abstand zu nehmen. Stattdessen sind die in einem Absatz kumulierten Hinweise stets mitteilungspflichtig.

Neu ist zudem die Verpflichtung zur Einhaltung einer bestimmten In-formationsreihenfolge. Dadurch soll gewährleistet werden, dass die nach hier vertretener Auffassung relevantesten Informationen in Datenschutz-hinweisen als erstes bereitgestellt und mit höherer Wahrscheinlichkeit wahrgenommen werden. Dementsprechend soll auf das Auskunftsrecht aus Art. 15 DS-GVO zwingend als erstes hingewiesen werden, um einer-seits die Kenntnis und den Zweck der Regelung bei den betroffenen Perso-nen zu gewährleisten. Das ist essentiell, da der Informationsgehalt der Art. 13 und 14 DS-GVO zur Wiederherstellung des Stufenverhältnisses zwischen den Informationspflichten und dem Auskunftsrecht deutlich re-duziert, das Recht auf informationelle Selbstbestimmung der Betroffenen aber gleichzeitig nicht (erheblich) eingeschränkt werden soll. Andererseits kann durch den direkten Hinweis auf das Auskunftsrecht womöglich vor-herrschendem Überoptimismus[72] entgegengewirkt werden, indem gleich zu Beginn der Datenschutzhinweise ein Bewusstsein für die Relevanz und die Ausübung der Betroffenenrechte geschaffen wird.

Konzeptionell besteht auch hinsichtlich der Ausnahmetatbestände so-wohl bei Art. 13 als auch bei Art. 14 DS-GVO Verbesserungspotenzial. Bis-her wird in Fällen der Direkterhebung für Situationen, in denen ein Zu-gang der Datenschutzhinweise bei den Betroffenen ohne Verschulden des Verantwortlichen bzw. mangels Kenntnis ihrer Person nicht möglich ist, eine analoge Anwendung des Art. 14 Abs. 5 lit. b HS. 1 Alt. 1 DS-GVO an-geregt.[73] Um dieses Problem zu vermeiden, ist Art. 13 DS-GVO *expressis verbis* zusätzlich dann einzuschränken, wenn und soweit es unmöglich ist, die Datenschutzinformationen zu erteilen.[74] Daneben sollte Art. 14 Abs. 5 lit. b DS-GVO strukturell geglättet und der Anwendungsbereich der Ausnahmen eindeutig formuliert werden. Da insbesondere die dort aufge-

---

71 Ausführlich hierzu *Ebner*, Weniger ist Mehr? (Fn. 6), S. 186 ff.; a.A. etwa *M. Bä-cker*, in: J. Kühling/B. Buchner, DS-GVO, 3. Aufl., München 2020, Art. 13 Rn. 20.

72 Zum Optimism-Bias siehe bspw. *A. van Aaken*, Harvard International Law Jour-nal 2014, 421 (431).

73 *Franck* (Fn. 65), Art. 13 Rn. 45.

74 Ausführlich auch zu denkbaren Anwendungsfällen in der Praxis *Ebner*, Weniger ist Mehr? (Fn. 6), S. 217, 275 f.

zählten Regelbeispiele lediglich zu Unsicherheit hinsichtlich der Reichweite der Ausnahmetatbestände führten, sind diese zu streichen.[75] Die sehr ähnliche Regelung in Art. 20 Abs. 2 des revidierten schweizerischen Datenschutzgesetzes[76] zeigt, dass es der Nennung von Regelbeispielen für ein Verständnis der Norm nicht bedarf.

II. Konkrete Novellierungsvorschläge

Berücksichtig man all die bisher dargelegten Erwägungen, könnten „neue" Informationspflichten beispielsweise folgendermaßen gestaltet werden:[77]

1. Art. 12 DS-GVO überarbeitete Fassung

(1) Der Verantwortliche trifft geeignete Maßnahmen, um der betroffenen Person alle Informationen gemäß den Artikeln 13 und 14 und alle Mitteilungen gemäß den Artikeln 15 bis 22 und Artikel 34, die sich auf die *aktuelle*[78] Verarbeitung beziehen, in präziser, transparenter, *übersichtlicher* und leicht zugänglicher Form in einer klaren und einfachen Sprache, *wenn möglich, stichpunktartig und mithilfe von Schlagworten* zu übermitteln; dies gilt insbesondere für Informationen, die sich speziell an Kinder richten. Die Übermittlung der Informationen erfolgt schriftlich oder in anderer Form, gegebenenfalls auch elektronisch. Falls von der betroffenen Person verlangt, kann die Information mündlich erteilt werden, sofern die Identität der betroffenen Person in anderer Form nachgewiesen wurde.

[...]

(7) Die Informationen, die den betroffenen Personen gemäß den Artikeln 13 und 14 bereitzustellen sind, *sollen* in Kombination mit standardisierten Bildsymbolen bereitgestellt werden, um in leicht wahrnehmbarer, verständlicher und klar nachvollziehbarer Form einen aussagekräftigen Überblick über die *konkret* beabsichtigte Verarbeitung zu vermitteln. Werden die Bildsymbole in elektronischer Form dargestellt,

---

75 Ebenso *Ebner*, Weniger ist Mehr? (Fn. 6), S. 328.

76 Siehe allgemein zum revDSG M. *Hennemann* in: FS Ebke, 378 ff.

77 Die Vorschläge orientieren sich maßgeblich an denen von *Ebner*, Weniger ist Mehr? (Fn. 6), S. 314. ff.

78 Ebenso *Roßnagel/Geminn*, DS-GVO verbessern (Fn. 69), S. 119 f.

müssen sie maschinenlesbar sein. *Entscheidet sich der Verantwortliche gänzlich gegen die Verwendung standardisierter Bildsymbole, hat er die hierfür relevanten Gründe in einer separaten Erklärung auf seiner Internetseite dauerhaft öffentlich zugänglich zu machen.*

2. Art. 13 DS-GVO neue Fassung

(1) Werden personenbezogene Daten mit Kenntnis der betroffenen Person von ihr erhoben, so teilt der Verantwortliche der betroffenen Person jeweils unmittelbar vor, spätestens aber zum Zeitpunkt der Erhebung in dieser Reihenfolge folgendes mit:

a) das Bestehen eines Rechts auf Auskunft gegenüber dem Verantwortlichen für über lit. a-h hinausgehende Details der Datenverarbeitung. Der Verantwortliche stellt eine URL oder einen QR-Code bereit, über den die betroffene Person Informationen zur praktischen Ausübung des Rechts auf Auskunft erhält;

b) den oder die Zwecke, zu denen die personenbezogenen Daten verarbeitet werden sollen;

c) gegebenenfalls die Absicht, die erhobenen Daten zu verkaufen;

d) gegebenenfalls das Stattfinden
   1. einer automatisierten Entscheidungsfindung, die für die betroffene Person mit einer Rechtsfolge verbunden ist oder sie erheblich in ihren Rechten beeinträchtigt;
   2. von Profiling;

e) gegebenenfalls eine möglichst genaue Bezeichnung der Kategorien von Empfängern und ob es sich um eine Übermittlung an einen Drittstaat handelt;

f) den Namen und die Kontaktdaten des Verantwortlichen;

g) gegebenenfalls die Telefonnummer oder E-Mail-Adresse des Datenschutzbeauftragten;

h) das Bestehen eines Rechts auf Berichtigung oder Löschung oder Einschränkung der Verarbeitung oder eines Widerspruchsrechts gegen die Verarbeitung sowie des Rechts auf Datenübertragbarkeit.

(2) Beabsichtigt der Verantwortliche, die personenbezogenen Daten für einen anderen Zweck weiterzuverarbeiten als den, für den die personenbezogenen Daten erhoben wurden, so teilt er der betroffenen Person diesen Umstand und den neuen Verarbeitungszweck vor der Weiterverarbeitung mit. Bedingt der neue Zweck eine Änderung der nach Absatz 1 mitzuteilenden Hinweise, so ist die betroffene Person

vor der Weiterverarbeitung auch über diese neuen Umstände zu unterrichten.

(3) Die Absätze 1 und 2 finden keine Anwendung, wenn und soweit
   a) die betroffene Person bereits über die Informationen verfügt oder
   b) die Erteilung der Informationen sich als objektiv unmöglich erweist.

Art. 13 Abs. 4 [a.F.] entfällt.

3. *Art. 14 DS-GVO neue Fassung*

(1) Werden personenbezogene Daten ohne Kenntnis der betroffenen Person bei ihr oder bei Dritten erhoben, so teilt der Verantwortliche der betroffenen Person zusätzlich zu den in Art. 13 Abs. 1 [n.F.] genannten Informationen die Kategorien der erhobenen Daten mit.

(2) Der Verantwortliche erteilt die Informationen gemäß Absatz 1
   a) unter Berücksichtigung der spezifischen Umstände der Verarbeitung der personenbezogenen Daten innerhalb einer angemessenen Frist nach Erlangung der personenbezogenen Daten, längstens jedoch innerhalb eines Monats,
   b) falls die personenbezogenen Daten zur Kommunikation mit der betroffenen Person verwendet werden sollen, spätestens zum Zeitpunkt der ersten Mitteilung an sie,
   c) falls die Offenlegung an einen anderen Empfänger beabsichtigt ist, vor, spätestens aber zum Zeitpunkt der ersten Offenlegung.

(3) Beabsichtigt der Verantwortliche, die personenbezogenen Daten für einen anderen Zweck weiterzuverarbeiten als den, für den die personenbezogenen Daten erlangt wurden, so teilt er der betroffenen Person diesen Umstand und den neuen Verarbeitungszweck vor der Weiterverarbeitung mit. Bedingt der neue Zweck eine Änderung der nach Absatz 1 mitzuteilenden Hinweise, so ist die betroffene Person vor der Weiterverarbeitung auch über diese neuen Umstände zu unterrichten.

(4) Die Absätze 1, 2 und 3 finden keine Anwendung, wenn und soweit
   a) die betroffene Person bereits über die Informationen verfügt,
   b) die Erteilung dieser Informationen sich als unmöglich erweist, einen unverhältnismäßigen Aufwand erfordern oder die Erteilung der Information voraussichtlich die Verwirklichung der Ziele der Verarbeitung unmöglich machen oder ernsthaft beeinträchtigen würde. In diesen Ausnahmefällen dokumentiert der Verantwortliche die Gründe der Verweigerung und die verwehrten Informationen in Textform. Er ergreift außerdem geeignete Maßnahmen

zum Schutz der Rechte und Freiheiten sowie der berechtigten Interessen der betroffenen Person, einschließlich der Bereitstellung dieser Informationen für die Öffentlichkeit,

c) die Erlangung oder Offenlegung durch Rechtsvorschriften der Union oder der Mitgliedstaaten, denen der Verantwortliche unterliegt und die geeignete Maßnahmen zum Schutz der berechtigten Interessen der betroffenen Person vorsehen, ausdrücklich geregelt ist oder

d) die personenbezogenen Daten gemäß dem Unionsrecht oder dem Recht der Mitgliedstaaten dem Berufsgeheimnis, einschließlich einer satzungsmäßigen Geheimhaltungspflicht, unterliegen und daher vertraulich behandelt werden müssen.

Art. 14 Abs. 5 [a.F.] entfällt.

4. Art. 15 DS-GVO neue Fassung

Soweit die aus Art. 13 und 14 DS-GVO gestrichenen Informationspflichten noch nicht Bestandteil des Auskunftskataloges des Art. 15 Abs. 1 DS-GVO sind, werden sie in ebendiesen Katalog mitaufgenommen. Hierdurch erlangen betroffene Personen bei entsprechendem Interesse jedenfalls auf der „zweiten Stufe" alle relevanten Informationen über die erfolgte Datenverarbeitung. Die neuen Hinweispflichten werden an den vorgeschlagenen Stellen eingefügt, die bisherigen *Literae* verschieben sich entsprechend:

(1) Die betroffene Person hat das Recht, von dem Verantwortlichen eine Bestätigung darüber zu verlangen, ob sie betreffende personenbezogene Daten verarbeitet werden; ist dies der Fall, so hat sie ein Recht auf Auskunft über diese personenbezogenen Daten und auf folgende Informationen:

a) *die Rechtsgrundlage oder Rechtsgrundlagen der Verarbeitung;*
   [...]

f) *wenn die Verarbeitung auf Artikel 6 Absatz 1 Buchstabe f beruht, die berechtigten Interessen, die von dem Verantwortlichen oder einem Dritten verfolgt werden;*
   [...]

h) *wenn die Verarbeitung auf Artikel 6 Absatz 1 Buchstabe a oder Artikel 9 Absatz 2 Buchstabe a beruht, das Bestehen eines Rechts, die Einwilligung jederzeit zu widerrufen, ohne dass die Rechtmäßigkeit der aufgrund der Einwilligung bis zum Widerruf erfolgten Verarbeitung berührt wird;*

[…]

E. Fazit/Ausblick

Jede betroffene Person hat das durch das Grundgesetz verbürgte Recht, selbstbestimmt über die Preisgabe „ihrer" personenbezogenen Daten zu entscheiden.[79] Um ebendiese Entscheidung auf einer ausreichend fundierten Wissensbasis treffen zu können, sind Informationspflichten unerlässlich.[80] Da die auf den bisherigen Informationspflichten beruhenden Datenschutzhinweise diesem Zweck aufgrund ihrer Länge, Komplexität und der Art ihrer Informationsvermittlung nicht gerecht werden, bedarf das Regelungssystem der Art. 12–15 DS-GVO einer Überarbeitung. In deren Rahmen ist insbesondere darauf zu achten, das Stufenverhältnis zwischen Informationspflichten und Auskunftsanspruch wiederherzustellen. Durch eine Kürzung der Informationspflichten und entsprechende Anreicherung des Auskunftsanspruchs wird die ursprüngliche Intention beider Rechtsinstitute wieder gewährleistet. Alle betroffenen Personen werden vor einer Datenerhebung knapp über die entscheidenden Modalitäten der bevorstehenden Verarbeitung unterrichtet und können sich bei einem über die erteilten Hinweise hinausgehenden Interesse anschließend über ein Auskunftsersuchen an den Verantwortlichen wenden. Dieser Mehraufwand ist den (erfahrungsgemäß zahlenmäßig deutlich unterlegenen[81]) Interessierten zum „Wohle" der restlichen, weniger interessierten Betroffenen zuzumuten. Es bleibt abzuwarten, wann entsprechende Diskussionen im juristischen Diskurs endlich die verdiente Aufmerksamkeit finden. Mit diesem Beitrag soll jedenfalls ein erster Anstoß zur Neuregulierung dieses für alle betroffenen Personen extrem relevanten Themas gegeben werden.

---

79 Siehe bereits BVerfGE 65, 1.
80 *Ebner*, Information Overload, (Fn. 5), 366.
81 Siehe nur BT-DruckS. 19/9168, S. 4.

II. Algorithms and Automation

Algorithm-friendly consumers – Consumer-friendly algorithms?

Elena Freisinger and Juliane Mendelsohn

A. Introduction and Overview

In the digital era algorithms are ever increasingly integrated into our daily lives and structure almost every consumption decision and consumer choice. This contribution combines two distinct fields of research: i) Human-AI-Interaction (HAI), an interdisciplinary research field spanning disciplines from technology and innovation management, behavioural economics and marketing, to information systems research (all of which analyse barriers and enablers of algorithm adoption); and ii) consumer protection law and theory (which protects consumers from encroachments of their autonomy). While the premises of these two fields of research seem at odds with one another – HAI predominantly strives to bring the consumer closer to the algorithm, while consumer protection law wishes to protect the consumer from the black box – we argue that the ubiquitous use of algorithms creates a common perspective. Both HAI and consumer protection law should strive to enhance the understandability and transparency of algorithms, making their use not only more commonly accepted, but also a true expression of autonomous choice. In addition, a combination of the two fields provides unique insights into how consumers interact with algorithms and how choices are made by algorithmically-enhanced consumers. We suggest that some of these insights can be used to design more concise and effective consumer protection tools in the future.

This article thus does two things. It, first, describes novel ways in which humans are interacting with algorithms and how this changes the rational choice paradigm and may even give rise to a new type of consumer. It then suggests that consumer protection tools should be designed around this form of interaction and knowledge and shows ways how trust and transparency can be increased.

In order to do so we first describe how consumers encounter algorithms. We also describe and elaborate on normative notions of algorithmically-enhanced consumers. Here we suggest that consumers are not only assisted or nudged by algorithms, but that a new type of consumer is emerging: the *hybrid consumer*, whose choices are the combined result of human and machine rationality, agency and subjective inclination. Since such developments can lead to large information asymmetries, the loss of autonomy and also a reluctance of consumers to employ such tools and mechanisms, we look at how consumer acceptance is driven by understandability, trust and transparency in current literature evolving around human-AI research. Last, we look at how these findings can perhaps support the development of new consumer protection tools. While mandated disclosures are classical tools to reduce information asymmetries, we show that more nuanced and novel ways to create more intuitive forms of understandability and transparency are emerging. Before suggesting that these findings may speak in favour of personalised or dynamic and integrated disclosures, we reflect on the function of consumer protection law and the development of the notions of agency and autonomy.

B. *Consumer interaction with algorithms*

In the digital world, consumers encounter algorithms (digital tools representing a fixed step-by-step decision-making process, making use of statistical calculations, mathematical tabulations, and/or computer programs) everywhere – regardless of whether they want to actively use them or not.[1]

This is primarily due to the fact that many current business models and products – e.g., streaming services, dating portals, or recommendation systems on online shopping platforms – are based on algorithms.[2] For example, in the case of a new product purchase, the digital purchasing process differs significantly from an offline purchase due to the algorithms used. In the latter case, the decision-making process and the decision-making criteria (e.g., product type, price) are known. When the buying process is shifted to the digital world, however, the process takes a different form. The input (product search) remains the same, but the output (suggestions of products) and the decision-making process differ, and while it is traceable and reproducible in the non-digital space, it resembles a 'black box' in the digital space. The algorithm decides which products appear in which place and thus implies a kind of popularity. This is often done by

---

1 B. J. *Dietvorst/D. M. Bartels*, Consumer Object to Algorithms Making Morally Relevant Tradeoffs Because of Algorithms' Consequentialist Decision Strategies, Journal of Consumer Psychology, 2021, 406.
2 Examples based on *Dietvorst/Bartels.*, Algorithms (n. 1).

so called 'neighbourhood-based collaborative algorithms', which suggest products that have the highest rating among a customer group which is similar to the user.[3] However, algorithms structure the decision-making process not only for product purchases, but also for other online services, such as algorithmic dating websites, online calculators for insurance and loans, or robo-advisors for investment decisions.[4] These examples show that the most typical form of interaction between humans and AI-based algorithms in a digital environment is the use of so-called search and recommendation systems. Yet, although similar, search and recommendations are different.[5] While search algorithms provide a system response toward an active search action (e.g., Google search or Amazon product search), recommendations will then rank the search results – implying a good fit for the search activity.[6] Pure recommender systems show recommendations without actively searching for information or products, e.g., landing pages of YouTube, Amazon or Google.[7]

In spite of this ubiquity and the feeling that one cannot avoid these systems, consumers generally show adverse behaviours with regard to the use of algorithms. This adversity may be troublesome for two reasons. Either consumers are not using and reaping the benefits of certain algorithms, or consumers are employing algorithms but do so begrudgingly and at the cost of their autonomy (and in many cases privacy). Safeguarding consumer autonomy and thus repairing this market failure is the classical function of consumer protection law. Before we turn to consumer protection law and questions of transparency, we look at new normative notions of the consumer that are emerging in the digital world.

---

3 *F. Ricci/L. Rokach/B. Shapira.*, Introduction to recommender systems handbook, in: Recommender Systems Handbook, Boston, Springer, 2011, 1.

4 Examples based on *Dietvorst/Bartels,* Algorithms (n. 1).

5 *O. Budzinski/B. A. Kuchinke,* Industrial organization of media markets and competition policy, in: M. B. Rimscha/S. Kienzler (eds.), Handbooks of communication science [HoCS]: Bd. 30. Management and Economics of Communication, Berlin/Boston, 2020, p. 21.

6 *B. Edelman,* Bias in Search Results?: Diagnosis and Response, Indian Journal of Law and Technology, 2011, 16.

7 For a detailed discussion see *O. Budzinski/S. Gaenssle/N. Lindstädt,* Data (r)evolution: The economics of algorithmic search and recommender services, in: S. Baumann (ed.), Handbook of Digital Business Ecosystems, Cheltenham: Elgar, 2022, p. 349.

C. Algorithmically enhanced consumers

Consumers' choice and actions interactions can be altered and enhanced by algorithms in a number of different ways. In the following section, we therefore describe and elaborate on normative notions of algorithmically-enhanced consumers and suggest that consumers are not only assisted or nudged by algorithms, but that a new type of consumer is emerging: the *hybrid consumer*.

I. Consumers as products

It is trite fact that consumers are mined and targeted for their data.[8] While the notion of the 'consumer as a product' is not a new category of consumer and does not specifically describe changes in consumer choice, it has brought some underlying and fundamental features of digital capitalism and digital market mechanisms and their effects on consumers to our attention. In 2016/2018 *Tim Wu* and *Shoshana Zuboff* coined the related terms 'surveillance capitalism' and the 'attention economy',[9] to describe mechanisms and strategies to capture consumer attention and human experience – information about us, our interactions, habits and interconnections – in the form of data, as though they were a natural resource,[10] and in turn making platforms and products ever more targeted and personalised, thereby aiding further attention and extraction.[11] *Zuboff* shows how, in the platform economy,[12] consumers become supply chain interfaces as their personal information, experiences and interactions are harvested as

---

8 S. *Zuboff*, The Age of Surveillance Capitalism, New York, PublicAffairs, 2018; for a review of how this has been incorporated into contract law: *T. Bauermeister*, Die "Bezahlung" mit personenbezogenen Daten bei Verträgen mit digitalen Produkten, AcP 222, 2022, 372.

9 The attention economics itself is not a new phrase or field of study, but has been an essential part of media economics for decades. See *T. Davenport/J. Beck*, The Attention Economy: Understanding the New Currency of Business, Harvard Business School Press, 200.

10 *Zuboff*, The Age of Surveillance Capitalism (n. 8).

11 *Zuboff*, The Age of Surveillance Capitalism (n. 8); *T. Wu*, The Attention Merchants, New York 2016.

12 For the economic foundations of the platform economy see *O. Budzinski/J. Mendelsohn*, § 1 Hintergründe, Ziele und wettbewerbspolitische Einordnung des Digital Markets Act, *J. P. Smidt/D. Hübener*, Das neue Recht der digitalen Märkte, forthcoming, Nomos, 2022.

data.[13] They are thus distanced from their traditional role in the market and, in part, become the commodity,[14] *Wu* first used the phrase 'consumers as products' by pointing out that *"when an online service is free, you're not the customer – you're the product"*.[15] While the addictive elements of several platform services, as well as the integration of consumers in the product test process have long been considered problematic, both *Zuboff's* and *Wu's* focus on the 'hidden' elements[16] and the pervasive expanse of these technologies (from online stores, to communication platforms, to games) offer insights into the more fundamental shifts taking place, which in turn inform consumer protection law.

The first shift is the effect on autonomy and the traditional idea that the act of autonomous choice is located with the individual. In fact, while the economy (its products and services) has become ever more targeted, 'customised' and 'personalised', *Wu* and *Zuboff* argue that the role of the autonomous individual – the person beyond their data – is fading.[17] Second, with the commodification of consumers, or rather their data, and „*unilaterally claims human experience as free raw material for translation into behavioural data*"[18], information (and power) asymmetries grow. In addition, information asymmetries become more pervasive as they now include not only market factors and transaction parameters, but information on the consu-

---

13 *A. Jenkins*, Shoshana Zuboff on the age of surveillance capitalism, interview 16.09.2019, contagious, available at https://www.contagious.com/news-and-vie ws/shoshana-zuboff-on-the-age-of-surveillance-capitalism (last access: 04.10.2022): „There is a complete misunderstanding of what all these things are. They are supply chain interfaces. The only thing that surveillance capitalists really have to worry about is supply chain. It's about expanding new flows of behavioural surplus. Every interface for the internet becomes a supply chain interface." also *Zuboff*, The Age of Surveillance Capitalism, (n. 8) p. 129 et seq.

14 *Zuboff*, The Age of Surveillance Capitalism (n. 8) p. 63 et seq.

15 *Wu*, The Attention Merchants (n. 8).

16 *Zuboff*, The Age of Surveillance Capitalism, (n. 8) p. 87 et seq.: Zuboff states that these business models, which are founded on predictive algorithms, mathematical calculations of human behaviour are designed to extract the maximum amount of information about any consumer or interaction and managed to shade or disguise such intention. See interview also *S. Naughton*, The goals is to automate us: welcome to the age of surveillance capitalism, The Gurdian online 20.01.2019, available at https://www.theguardian.com/technology/2019/jan/20/shoshana-zubo ff-age-of-surveillance-capitalism-google-facebook (last access: 04.10.2022).

17 „Surveillance capitalists no longer rely on people as consumers. Instead, supply and demand orients the surveillance capitalist firm to businesses intention anticipating the behaviour of populations, groups and individuals." See *Naughton*, The goals is to automate us (n. 16).

18 *Naughton*, The goals is to automate us (n. 16).

mers themselves. Last, while the participation (and the lending of data) in such services or markets is seen as voluntary, and it is often stipulated that consumers simply don't care enough to opt out of sharing their data with large platforms (this is the logic underlying so-called 'privacy paradox'). *Zuboff*, however, points out that consumers barely have a choice at all: „*we are trapped in an involuntary merger of personal necessity and economic extraction, as the same channels that we rely upon for daily logistics, social interaction, work, education, healthcare, access to products and services, and much more, now double as supply chain operations for surveillance capitalism's surplus flows*".[19] This may not always be true, but is certainly worth reflecting upon when reviewing designing remedies to reclaim consumer autonomy.

II. Assisted consumers

Several search and rank algorithms, as well as algorithms based on previously determined preferences, can help consumers make decisions.[20] If we could assume that consumers consciously and willingly use these algorithms, we could stipulate an enhancement, rather than an encroachment, of autonomy and consumer choice throughout.[21] Several factors, however, point to growing limitations on 'true' consumer choice. The more such algorithms are incorporated in large ecosystems, the more path dependencies and 'lock-in' effects become likely. In several platforms, consumers are already concerned with orchestrated choices, in much the same way as they are caught in 'filter bubbles' on media platforms.[22] In addition, even where algorithms make simple choices, the line between the human decision and that of the algorithm can easily become blurred. Studies find that consumers are likely to align their choice with that of the algorithm and, for instance, choose products or services marketed as the 'best deal'[23] (e.g., 'Amazon's Choice'[24]). In addition, rather than enabling the consu-

---

19 *Naughton*, The goals is to automate us (n. 16).
20 For examples see M. *Gal/N. Elkin-Koren*, Algorithmic Consumers, Harvard Journal of Law & Technology 2017, 309 (314).
21 *Gal/Elkin-Koren*, Algorithmic Consumers (n. 20) 309 (314).
22 E. *Pariser*, The Filter Bubble: How the Personlized Web is Changing What We Read and How We Think, New York 2011.
23 E.g., D. *DelVecchio*, Deal-prone consumers' response to promotion: The effects of relative and absolute promotion value, Psychology & Marketing 2005, 373
24 L. *Matsakis*, What Does It Mean When a Product is Amazon's Choice, Wired magazine 4.6.2019, available at https://www.wired.com/story/what-does-amazons

mer, the increased use of such algorithms may diminish the role of the (non-assisted) consumer in such choice processes and as a (fully) rational agent. It will increasingly be assumed that a choice made with the use of an algorithm is *per se* the better choice and that the choice suggested by the algorithms is already fully rational. The use of an investment app (e.g., 'eToro') is one blatant example. The amount of data fairly simple algorithms can process alone will increasingly make unassisted choices or those based on idiosyncrasies or a 'gut feeling' appear less rational and thus suboptimal.

III. Algorithmic consumers

A new generation of algorithms takes such assistance one step further, making and executing decisions for the consumer by directly communicating with other systems through the internet. As per the analysis of *Michal Gal* and *Niva Elkin-Koren*, 'algorithmic consumers' are no longer people or human agents, but algorithms and devices that have taken over the function of making independent and autonomous decisions and purchasing choices: a refrigerator that stocks up on milk, a car that drives itself to the gas station or an investment tool that purchases a certain stock at a certain price.[25] While a range of benefits are driving this development – speed, analytical sophistication, the reduction of transaction and information costs,[26] and even the overcoming of language and information

---

-choice-mean/ (last access: 04.10.2022); *J. Luguri/L. Strahilevitz*, Shining a light on dark patterns, Journal of Legal Analysis 2021, 43.

25 *Gal/Elkin-Koren*, Algorithmic Consumers, (n. 20) 310: "The next generation of e-commerce, researchers say, will be conducted by digital agents based on algorithms that can handle entire transactions: using data to predict consumers' preferences, choosing the products or services to purchase, negotiating and executing the transaction, and even automatically forming coalitions of buyers to secure optimal terms and conditions. Human decision-making could be completely bypassed. Such algorithms might be written by consumers for their own use or supplied by external firms. We call these digital assistants 'algorithmic consumers'.

26 *Gal/Elkin-Koren*, Algorithmic Consumers (n. 20) 318–320.

constraints[27] – it will have large implications for consumer autonomy,[28] since the consumer will now always be at least *"one step removed from the consumption decision"*.[29] Of course, the consumer chooses the tool, some of the primary factors, and may even be able to influence or deviate from the choices made, but, as stated by *Gal* and *Elkin-Koren*, these remaining instances of autonomous choice will largely be dependent on the design and transparency of the algorithm.[30] While the reduction of autonomy is a grave principle problem, as it detaches individuals ever more from the contractual conditions that form the legal architecture of their lives, there are potential welfare and equality harms as well. Individual welfare harms can result from an imperfect reflection of a consumer's preferences, i.e., personalized pricing according to luxury rather than standard preferences. In addition, welfare concerns go hand-in-hand with concerns about manipulation and coercion. As *Gal* and *Elkin-Koren* put it: *"when human judgment is replaced by non-transparent code, consumers are harder pressed to protect themselves against such manipulation due to their inability to understand, decipher, and challenge the algorithms."* Equality concerns, on the other hand, arise from a group of individuals being cut off from these technologies and thus from the cost benefits.

IV. Hypernudged consumers

Even where consumers have not intentionally outsourced their choice, algorithms increasingly influence consumer purchasing decisions, by pre-selecting offers and 'nudging' them in a certain direction.[31] In any digital consumer environment, be it a store website, a platform, a mobile applica-

---

27 Indeed, algorithms can potentially 'read' contractual terms, thereby avoiding at least some contractual limitations that human consumers might fall into due to time, language, or information constraints. See also *O. Bar-Gill*, Seduction by Contract: Law, Economics, And Psychology In Consumer Markets, Oxford 2012, 19; *O. Ben-Shaher/C. Schneider*, More than you wanted to now: the failure of the mandated disclosure, Princeton 2014, 7–9.

28 See also *Gal*, Technological Challenges to Choice 24 (Feb. 19, 2017) (unpublished manuscript) (on file with the Harvard Journal for Law & Technology).

29 *Gal/Elkin-Koren*, Algorithmic Consumers (n. 20) 322.

30 *Gal/Elkin-Koren*, Algorithmic Consumers (n. 20) 322, 323.

31 *J. Mendelsohn*, Die normative Macht der Plattformen, MMR 2021, 857 (859); *L. E. Willis*, When Nudges Fail: Slippery Defaults, University of Chicago Law Review 2013, 1155; *K. Yueng*, "Hypernudge": Big Data as a Mode of Regulation by Design, Information, Communication & Society 2016, 19; *N. Zingales*, Anti-

tion (app) or an IoT-interface, navigation takes place through algorithms and consumers are increasingly confronted with so-called 'dark patterns'.[32] In this context hypernudging – a term derived from *Sunstein* and *Thaler's* 2008 notion of nudging[33] – refers to *"algorithmic real-time personalization and reconfiguration of choice architectures based on large aggregates of personal data."*[34] A large amount of this nudging is both necessary to make large online platform manageable for the consumer and in the interest of the consumer, who would otherwise drown in an information and choice overload.[35] At the same time, the risk of manipulation and coercion is virulent and increases with lack of transparency and the inability of the consumer to comprehend the choice architecture. While choices in the real world have never been perfect (based on perfect information) and have always been (at times severely) limited, hypernudging can mean that autonomous consumers are removed from at least the first steps of the decision process, limiting their choice from the outset.

V. Hybrid consumers

In all of the constellations of interactions between algorithms and consumers listed above, it is striking that the consumer is still considered a separate and distinguishable entity. The consumer is described as being either assisted or guided by, nudged towards, or replaced with, algorithms. Little attention, however, is payed to the more fundamental shift taking place: the merger of human and machine (or algorithmic) choice and agency. We notice that these lines are blurred. Not only is it becoming increasingly difficult to locate instances of isolated consumer choices; but consumers will be making choices together with algorithms in the future,

---

trust Intent in an Age of Algorithmic Nudging, Journal of Antitrust Enforcement 2019, 3.

32 See *Luguri/Strahilevitz*, Shining a light on dark patterns (n. 24), 43.

33 R. *Thaler/S. Sunstein*, Nudge: *Improving decisions about health, wealth, and happiness*, New Haven 2008, p. 3: „any aspect of choice architecture that alters people's behaviour in a predictable way without forbidding any options or significantly changing their economic incentives. To count as a mere nudge, the intervention must be easy and cheap to avoid."

34 M. *Lanzing*, "Strongly Recommended" Revisiting Decisional Privacy to Judge Hypernudging in Self-Tracking Technonologies, Philosophy and Technology 2019, 549; K. *Yeung*, Information Communication and Society 2017, 118 (126); see also *Mendelsohn*, Normative Macht (n. 31), 859.

35 *Budzinski/Gaenssle/Lindstädt*, Data (r)evolution (n. 7).

and that the point where the one begins and the other ends will barely be determinable. Where a choice is nudged, assisted and then partly executed by an algorithm, any such choice will be made simultaneously by a machine and a human. We thus suggest that a new generation of consumer algorithms and a new notion of the consumer is emerging. We call this the **hybrid consumer**. The hybrid consumer is the choice agent that results from the combined and interacting rationality between an algorithm or machine and an autonomous human individual. A good example is the use of 'trial-and-error'-based algorithms that require a lot of interaction and 'learn' from an ongoing set of user choices, while, in turn, the user too adapts her choices, interaction, expectation, and in part even her rationality, as she gets used to the way the algorithm works.

For closer insights, imagine investment decisions in the digital space: Investment tool algorithms often employ machine learning techniques and thus learn from the users already on the platform to identify and allocate their wishes and needs. When a new customer registers with such a platform, the algorithm typically already knows her gender, age, education, marital status, income and race categorization. With the use of neighbor-based-algorithms, the algorithm first matches the new user with other similar user groups and offers her initial choices in line with preferences that are popular in this group. Afterwards, the new user can interact with the platform by scrolling through investment plans and – potentially -making first investment decisions. The algorithms are designed to learn about the customer and the customer learns about the algorithm while providing it with further data, filtering decision outcomes and describing preferences. The algorithm is thus designed to make ever better suggestions for investment plans. Vice versa, in an ideal setting, the customer learns ever more about the algorithm and its behavior. This interactive environment is said to provide the (hybrid) consumer with ever better and ever more tailored options. The emergence of the hybrid consumer, however, also raises a number of concerns and challenges. The stronger the lines between the machine and user are blurred, the more important it is to secure human autonomy. We assume that more transparency and understandability of algorithms can enhance trust, acceptance and thus autonomy. We thus look at algorithm acceptance and transparency in more detail.

D. Acceptance of algorithms: current state of research

Research on factors that facilitate or impede technology adoption has a long tradition in marketing, technology, and innovation research. Well-known models such as the TAM (Technology-Acceptance-Model)[36] or the UTAUT (Unified Theory of Acceptance and Use of Technology)[37] model have long formed the starting point for research into acceptance factors of new technology. However, with the advent of algorithms, this type of research has taken on a new angle, as current models do not yet fully represent the far-reaching consequences that arise from the application of algorithms and artificial intelligences, e.g., in employee scenarios,[38] but also in consumer research.

The adoption of AI and algorithms is thus unique in the following four ways:[39] (1) AI tools are considered 'black boxes', i.e., the input and output is usually transparent, but not the process to produce the output; (2) underlying models and computations are never 100% error-free – although often superior to human capabilities – and often have an error rate that even increases in very dynamic environments or with little data access; (3) models need time to learn, and thus are more error-prone in early than in later applications; (4) algorithms are subject to biases that can vary in severity, at times with far-reaching consequences. These points create resistance among users who have to interact with algorithms. Negative reactions often occur even when users know that the algorithm provides better insights than human decision makers.[40] While this finding has been confirmed in numerous studies, some studies indicate that algorithms are, in some cases, preferred over human decision-makers.[41] Overall, four thematic areas can be listed that influence algorithm adoption: (1) higher-level factors (e.g., cultural, societal, or environmental factors); (2) individual factors (e.g., personality, demographics, psychological attributes); (3) task-related factors (e.g., complexity and moral classification of the task); and

---

36 *F. D. Davis*, Perceived Usefulness, Perceived Ease of Use, and User Acceptance of Information Technology, MIS Quarterly 1989, 319.

37 *V. Venkatesh/M. G. Morris/G. B. Davis/F. D. Davis*, User acceptance of information technology: Toward a unified view, MIS Quarterly 2003, 425.

38 *V. Venkatesh*, Adoption and use of AI tools: a research agenda grounded in UTAUT, Annals of Operations Research, 2021, 641.

39 *Venkatesh*, Adoption and use of AI tools (n. 38).

40 *B. J. Dietvorst/J. P. Simmons/C. Massey*, Algorithm aversion: people erroneously avoid algorithms after seeing them err, Journal of experimental psychology, 2015, 114.

41 *Dietvorst/Bartels*, Algorithms (n. 10).

(4) algorithm-related factors (e.g., design, decision, delivery mode of the outcome)[42]. We argue, that algorithm-related factors in particular play a critical role in the acceptance of algorithms in the consumer sector and thus also in consumer protection, since they can be influenced by companies and also by consumer protection law.

Current research from the field of dedicated consumer research shows that consumers are not willing to employ algorithms in every purchase decision[43] and overwhelmingly reject them for very subjective tasks.[44] We know from HR research that human decision makers are more likely to be seen as having the ability to consider individual and moral circumstances, while algorithms are perceived as reductionist and limited to consider qualitative information as well as contexts.[45] Consumers are particularly prone to such conclusions, if the algorithms are not transparent. Current studies show that even experts are often unable to understand how an algorithm works in detail.[46] It is thus necessary to look at transparency in more detail.

I. Transparency

The transparency of an algorithm is generally understood to be the degree to which the underlying rules of operation and internal logic of a technology are apparent to users, and is considered critical to the development of trust in new technologies.[47] Researchers therefore suggest creating more

---

42 *H. Mahmud*, What influences algorithmic decision-making? A systematic literature review on algorithm aversion, Technological Forecasting and Social Change, 2021.

43 *B. J. Dietvorst/D. M. Bartels*, Consumers Object to Algorithms Making Morally Relevant Tradeoffs Because of Algorithms' Consequentialist Decision Strategies, Journal of Consumer Psychology 2021, 406.

44 *N. Castelo/M. W. Bos/D. R. Lehmann*, Task-Dependent Algorithm Aversion, Journal of Marketing Research 2019, 809.

45 *D. T. Newman/N. J. Fast/D. J. Harmon*, When eliminating bias isn't fair: Algorithmic reductionism and procedural justice in human resource decisions, Organizational Behavior and Human Decision Processes 2020, 149.

46 *J. Burrell*, How the machine 'thinks': Understanding opacity in machine learning algorithms, Big Data & Society 2016; *J. Kroll/J. Huey/S. Barocs/E. W. Felten/J. R. Reidenberg/D. G. Robinson/H. Yu*, Accountable algorithms, University of Pennsylvania Law Review, 2016, 633.

47 *K. A. Hoff*, Trust in Automation: Integrating Empirical Evidence on Factors That Influence Trust, Human factors 2015, 407.

transparency on both sides of the human-algorithm interaction to form more trust and trust calibration.[48] A great driving force of acceptance is to open the 'black box' and disclose the decision-making process of an algorithm.[49] People arguably have an intrinsic interest in knowing the underlying principles of algorithmic decision making, that is, in understanding the algorithm and its rationale.[50] This means that transparency must be increased to gain acceptance. Increasing transparency can be influenced by five factors in particular: access to decision patterns; explanation of decision rationale; understanding of what is explained; interaction with the algorithm; and integration of personal opinions.[51]

1. **Accessibility** Current research shows that human decision makers are preferred to algorithmic decision makers because it is felt that there is more and better access to them and they can be asked for their rationale.[52] On the other side, algorithms cannot be consulted about their decision making[53] and thus the reasons for the decision-making cannot be understood, which ultimately leads to a loss of trust in algorithms.[54]

2. **Explainability** This can be countered by making algorithmic decisions more explainable.[55] For example, studies show that linking a decision

---

48 *J. W. Burton/M. Stein/T. B. Jensen*, A systematic review of algorithm aversion in augmented decision making, Journal of Behavioral Decision Making 2020, 220.

49 *R. Litterscheidt*, Financial education and digital asset management: What's in the black box?, Journal of Behavioral and Experimental Economics, 2020; *N. N. Sharan/D. M. Romano*, The effects of personality and locus of control on trust in humans versus artificial intelligence, Heliyon 2020.

50 *H. Mahmud/A. K. M. Najmul Islam/S. I. Ahmed/K.* Smolander, What influences algorithmic decision-making? A systematic literature review on algorithm aversion, Technological Forecasting and Social Change 2022, 1.

51 For an overview and a detailed review see *Mahmud/Najmul Islam/Ahmed/Smolander*, Decision-making (n. 50); Criteria by *A. Chander*, Working with Beliefs: AI Transparency in the Enterprise, IUI Workshops 2018.

52 *D. Önkal/P. Godwin/M. Thomson/M. S. Gönül/A. Pollock*, The relative influence of advice from human experts and statistical methods on forecast adjustments, Journal of Behavioral Decision Making 2009, 390.

53 *U. Kayande*, How Incorporating Feedback Mechanisms in a DSS Affects DSS Evaluations, Information Systems Research 2009, 527; *Önkal/Godwin/Thomson/Gönül/Pollock*, Influence (n. 52).

54 *P. Goodwin/M. S. Gönül/D. Önkal*, Antecedents and effects of trust in forecasting advice, International Journal of Forecasting 2013, 354; *Önkal/Godwin/Thomson/Gönül/Pollock*, Influence (n. 52).

55 *M. S. Gönül et al.* The effects of structural characteristics of explanations on use of a DSS. Decision Support Systems, 2006, 1481.

to a provided explanation of how the algorithm works increases the acceptance of algorithms.[56]

3. **Understandability** However, an explanation alone is not sufficient to fully increase acceptance. Another important factor is to understand the algorithm itself.[57] An increase in comprehensibility can be achieved by personalized language,[58] a friendly tone of voice,[59] descriptive illustrations[60] and a convincing style of speech.[61]

4. **Interactability** Furthermore, an interaction of consumers with the algorithm to find out which factors lead to which result, by a so-called trial-and-error procedure,[62] can have a positive effect on transparency. This calibration process increases confidence in the algorithmic decision maker,[63] feedback on the algorithm's performance alone, on the other hand, is not sufficient; there must be some kind of iterative learning process by the user.[64]

5. **Integratability** Finally, it is also crucial that algorithms are integrative, i.e., considers the input of users ('human-in-the-loop')[65]. Although this does not necessarily lead to better results, consideration in the sense of including points important to the individual is helpful in accepting the algorithm output.[66]

---

56 *Goodwin/Gönül/Önkal,* Forecasting, (n. 54); *L. Zhang,* Who do you choose? Comparing perceptions of human vs robo-advisor in the context of financial services, Journal of Services Marketing 2021, 634.

57 *M. Yeomans,* Making sense of recommendations, Journal of Behavioral Decision Making 2019, 403.

58 *J. H. Yun/E. Lee/ D. H. Kim,* Behavioral and neural evidence on consumer responses to human doctors and medical artificial intelligence, Psychology & Marketing 2021, 610.

59 *Yun/Lee/Kim,* Artificial Intelligence (n. 58).

60 *L. Zhang,* Who do you choose? Comparing perceptions of human vs robo-advisor in the context of financial services, Journal of Services Marketing 2021, 634.

61 *Önkal/Godwin/Thomson/Gönül/Pollock,* Influence (n. 52).

62 *K. van Dongen,* A framework for explaining reliance on decision aids, International Journal of Human-Computer Studies 2013, 410.

63 *Van Dongen,* Framework (n. 62).

64 *Van Dongen,* Framework (n. 62).

65 *N. Köbis/L. D. Mossink,* Artificial intelligence versus Maya Angelou: Experimental evidence that people cannot differentiate AI-generated from human-written poetry, Computers in human behavior 2021, 1.

66 *B. J. Dietvorst/J. P. Simmons/C. Massey,* Overcoming algorithm aversion: People will use imperfect algorithms if they can (even slightly) modify them., Management Science 2018, 1155.; *K. Kawaguchi,* When will workers follow an algorithm? A field experiment with a retail business., Management Science 2021, 1670.

II. Creating transparency

While we often think about increasing transparency in very straight-forward terms, the sub-factors identified above as well as experimental studies with 'trial-and-error'-based learning and 'human-in-the-loop' mechanisms, show that both transparency and acceptance are more fluid notions and can be achieved in a number of ways. While opening the so-called black box is primarily determined by transparency, especially the subfactor familiarity with algorithms and algorithmic tasks has a major impact on the willingness to accept an algorithm. Studies have shown that a perceived general unfamiliarity with the algorithm leads to higher aversion.[67] Yet, familiarity can be a double-edged sword, as becoming familiar with an algorithm can also mean becoming familiar with algorithmic errors.[68] People lose trust in buggy algorithms faster, especially for supposedly simple tasks.[69] Similarly, *Andrew Prahl* and *Lyn Van Snow*l show in their experimental work that humans loose trust in bad algorithmic advice more quickly than in the bad human advice.[70] However, the experimental work of *Berkeley Dietvorst* and his co-authors shows that people might distrust algorithms, but that this aversion can be overcome by giving them the opportunity to slightly influence the outcome.[71] When users can personally experience that algorithms are capable of learning, acceptance increases.[72] In addition, studies have shown that users will accept algorithms more frequently if they feel that the results of the algorithms will be favourable to them.[73] Hence, not only the typical transparency aspects help to over-

---

67 *J. S. Lim/M. O'Connor*, Judgemental adjustment of initial forecasts: Its effectiveness and biases, Journal of Behavioral Decision Making 1996, 149; *S. M. Whitecotton*, The effects of experience and a decision aid on the slope, scatter, and bias of earnings forecasts, Organizational Behavior and Human Decision Processes 1996, 111.

68 *Mahmud/Najmul Islam/Ahmed/Smolander*, Decision-making (n. 50).

69 *P. Madhavan/D. A. Wiegmann/F. C. Lacson*, Automation Failures on Tasks Easily Performed by Operators Undermine Trust in Automated Aids, Human Factors 2006, 241.

70 *A. Prahl/L. Van Snowl*, Understanding algorithm aversion: When is advice from automation discounted? Journal of Forecasting, 2017, 691.

71 *Dietvorst/Simmons/Massey*, Overcoming aversion (n. 66).

72 *B. Berger/M. Adam/A. Rühr/A. Benlian*, Watch Me Improve—Algorithm Aversion and Demonstrating the Ability to Learn, Business & Information Systems Engineering 2021, 55.

73 *I. Toma/D. Delen/G. Moscato*, Impact of Loss and Gain Forecasting on the Behavior of Pricing Decision-making, International Journal of Data Science and Analysis 2020, 12.

come negative prejudices, but the interaction with the algorithm itself contributes immensely to a profound understanding of how the algorithm works, which errors it is prone to and if it is positive for one to use the algorithm.

We therefore argue that key to an informed and comfortable usage with algorithms is the interplay between an informed understanding of the algorithm's functionality and the ability to experiment with or to learn about the algorithm in a mock-up environment. We argue that trial-and-error-experience in a learning environment is just as important as being intellectually educated about how the algorithm works and was made. Through interaction, human-in-the-loop and trial-and-error, the black box can open up even further, and the user can begin to find its mechanisms and functionality transparent in ways that are more intuitive and also closer to the user's experience. Ultimately, consumers are able to make more informed decisions when interacting with algorithms in a digital environment.

In summary, we have suggested that a comfortable user interaction with algorithms depends on transparency and familiarity. Explanations for the algorithms would have to be available, describing how the algorithm works. In particular, clear, understandable language and illustrations should be used. It should also be possible to interact with the algorithm. One method would be to learn about the algorithm in a test environment and through trial-and-error. Ultimately, it is also crucial for an increase in acceptance that users feel that their voices are heard and their preferences are incorporated. One possible approach here would be to allow factors to be weighted or criteria to be included or excluded.

E. *Consumer protection in the age of algorithms*

In light of current developments in digital spaces, large information asymmetries, the loss of autonomy and also a reluctance of consumers to employ such tools and mechanisms are likely to occur. We thus explore how to design new consumer protection tools to overcome these barriers by incorporating the findings and results of the research on consumer acceptance of algorithms into the design of these remedies.

I. The aims and rationale of consumer protection law

According to classical law and economics dogma, the function of consumer protection is to remedy market failure resulting from information asymmetries that exist between consumers and businesses.[74] In contract theory and economics, information asymmetry deals with transactions where one party has more or better information than the other. This causes market failure and at times even moral hazards and a 'monopoly of knowledge'.[75] These imbalances affect the formal preconditions of private and contract law, that stipulate that contracting parties are 'equal' and also autonomous. Standard consumer protection tools such as mandated disclosures, 'notice and consent' (privacy), but also withdrawal rights, aim to boost autonomy and counteract asymmetry by lending ever more information to the consumer. The mandated disclosure (*Informationspflichten*) is a regulatory instrument and contract law tool that requires the discloser to give the disclosee information which she may use to make a more informed and hence better decision and to prevent the discloser from abusing his information power.[76] Notice and consent is a form of mandated disclosure most commonly used to protect privacy and requires that consumers/users are notified and give permission before any information may be stored or used about them.[77] Withdrawal rights grant consumers a period during which they can cancel and revoke their contract or purchase.

Both the normative assumptions and the effectiveness of these consumer protection tools have been debated for a long time.[78] Significantly, behavioural economics has shed light on several irrationalities and idiosyn-

---

74 R. *Cooter*, Law and Economics, 6th ed., Boston 2016, 276; O. *Bar-Gill*, Seduction by Contract, Oxford 2012; O. *Williamson*, Legal Implications of Imperfect Information in Consumer Markets, The New Institutional Economics Market Organization and Market Behavior 1995, 49.

75 See G. A. *Akerlof*, The Market for „Lemons": Quality Uncertainty and the Market Mechanism, The Quarterly Journal of Economics 1970, 488.

76 See O. *Ben-Shahar/C. E. Schneider*, The Failure of Mandated Disclosure, University of Pennsylvania Law Review 2010, 647.

77 See D. *Susser*, Notice after Notice and Consent: Why Privacy Disclosures Are Valuable Even If Consent Frameworks Aren't, Journal of Information Policy 2019, 37.

78 *Ibid;* A. Ferrell, Measuring the Effects of Mandated Disclosure, Berkeley Business Law Journal 2004; *Ben-Shahar/Schneider*, The Failure of Mandated Disclosure (n. 76).

crasies driving consumer choice.[79] While this has not changed consumer protection law, it has meant that its assumptions and foundational stipulations are increasingly 'formal' in function and say little about actual or material consumer choice.[80] We are thus forced to admit that simply giving consumers extensive additional information, may serve to empower them legally, but does little to change the rationality of their choices or to remedy related market failure.[81] Instead, tools such as mandated disclosures have found more nuanced and theoretical justifications.[82] The interactions with algorithms further blur the conditions for rational choice. On the one hand consumers use algorithms to guide and steer their choices, thereby in part assisting or outsourcing them. Here the algorithm may be considered the *agent* of the consumer and the consumers are assumed to be making autonomous and rational choice by choosing to integrate algorithms into the process.[83]

---

79 *Cooter*, Law and Economics, (n. 74), 50; In 2013 Richard Posner described it as follows: "What is called 'behavioral economics' […] has undermined the economic model of man as a rational maximizer of his self-interest and helped to expose the rampant exploitation by business of consumer psychology. Businesses know, and economists are learning, that consumers are easily manipulated by sellers into making bad choices—choices they would never make if they knew better." *R. Posner*, Why is there no Milton Friedman today?, Econ Journal Watch 2013, 210.

80 For the destinction between formal and material statements in contract law see: *W. Canaris*, Wandlungen des Schuldvertragsrechts – Tendenzen zu seiner "Materialisierung", 200 AcP 2000, 273.

81 *A. N. Scholes*, Behavioural Economics and the Autonomous Consumer, 14. Cambridge Yearbook of European Legal Studies 2012, 297 (306–318); *S. Issacharoff*, Disclosure, Agents, and Consumer Protection, Journal of Institutional and Theoretical Economics 2011, 56: *E. M. Tscherner*, Can Behavioral Research Advance Mandatory Law, Information Duties, Standard Terms and Withdrawal Rights?, Austrian Law Journal, 2014, 144; *H.-W. Micklitz/L. A. Reisch/K. Hagen*, An Introduction to the Special Issue on "Behavioural Economics, Consumer Policy, and Consumer Law", Journal of Consumer Policy 2011, 271.

82 *P. McColgan*, Abschied vom Informationsmodell im Recht der Allgemeinen Geschäftsbedingungen, Tübingen 2020; *Susser*, Notice after Notice and Consent (n. 77).

83 *Gal/Elkin-Koren*, Algorithmic Consumers (n. 20), 309 (314).

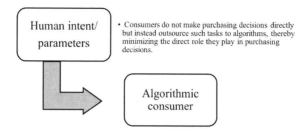

Human intent/ parameters

• Consumers do not make purchasing decisions directly but instead outsource such tasks to algorithms, thereby minimizing the direct role they play in purchasing decisions.

Algorithmic consumer

On the other hand, only a limited number of algorithmically-enhanced consumer decisions are this straightforward. If we assume that choices are increasingly made not just with the help of algorithms, but *with* algorithms and in algorithmic environments, where choices themselves are technically predefined and determined, the interaction between algorithms and humans seems far less linear. In addition, algorithms inform different stages of a consumer decision.[84] Increasingly consumer decisions will thus become choices that are made cooperatively by algorithms and consumers: they will be (hybrid) choices made by a culmination of machine and human intelligence and agency, both of which will be difficult to differentiate or untangle.

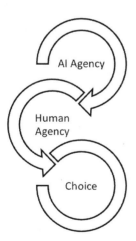

AI Agency

Human Agency

Choice

---

84 *Gal/Elkin-Koren* describe the different steps and stages typically involved, when algorithms become the agent of the consumer and make certain choices for them, see *Gal/Elkin-Koren*, Algorithmic Consumers (n. 20), 309 (317).

Since the choice ultimately made by the consumer can no longer be isolated from that made in combination with the algorithm, the question arises of how best to integrate disclosures and counteract asymmetries. Consumers must be made aware of their rights and the workings of the algorithms, but, increasingly, no longer stand apart from them as a separate, rational entity. This means that mandated disclosures could become even less effective and foreign to the process.

II. A brief reflection on autonomy and agency

Consumer protection tools have been a contentious issue for a long time.[85] While the practical ineffectiveness of disclosures and consent tools is overwhelmingly accepted and has been widely discussed,[86] these tools are still said to serve critical normative functions. Thus, before weighing in on any possible amendments to classical consumer protection tools and remedies, it seems prudent to reflect on some of the principles at stake. In economics, asymmetric information leads to consumer welfare losses. While this is certainly true for a range of different products and services, the legal mind may argue that something even larger is at stake: the principle of the equal autonomy of all contracting agents. This principle is the foundational assumption of both private law and economics in (modern) civil society.[87] For this reason, it helps to reflect on both the notion of 'agency' and 'autonomy' as the two principles that underlie several legal challenges with algorithmic transformation.

Agency is most fundamentally defined as legal capacity. It implies a capacity to act and to (normatively) shape reality.[88] We are currently accustomed to distinguish between the concept of an *agent*, as a static and

---

85 *O. Bar-Gill*, Seduction by Contract: Law, Economics, and Psychology in Consumer Markets, Oxford 2012; *O. Ben-Shahar/C. E. Schneider*, More Than You Wanted to Know: The Failure of Mandated Disclosure, Princeton 2014; *Y. Bakos/F. Marotta-Wurgler/D. R. Trossen*, Does Anyone Read the Fine Print? Consumer Attention to Standard-Form Contracts, Journal of Legal Studies 2014, 1.

86 *W. Kerber/K. Zolna*, Konsumentensouveränität und Datensouveränität aus ökonomischer Sicht, S. Augsberg, Steffen/P. Gehring (eds.), Datensouveränität. Positionen zur Debatte, Frankfurt a. M./New York 2022, 45.

87 See *M. Auer*, Der privatrechtliche Diskurs der Moderne, Tübingen 2014.

88 *I. Kant*, AA V: Kritik der praktischen Vernunft. Kritik der Urteilskraft, 1788, available at: https://korpora.zim.uni-duisburg-essen.de/kant/aa05/ (last access: 03.10.2022); *H. Kelsen*, Théorie pure du droit, Paris 1962; *B. Smith*, Legal Personality, Yale Law Journal 1928, 283; *A. Bertolini/F. Episcopo*, Robots and Ai as Legal

statutory notion and that of *agency*, a dynamic notion.[89] While algorithmic or AI systems are not considered agents or granted personhood, it is possible to describe their rationality, and capacity to act, i.e., the choices they make, as expressions of agency. In this case, consumer protection laws don't safeguard agency, but rather the agent. The agent must thus have features beyond the simple capacity to act or formulate a 'choice' – features beyond *agency*. Such distinguishing features may be described as the ability to act freely and to act morally – *"the ability to decide freely and coordinate one's action towards a chosen end"*.[90] This can be described as *autonomy*. It may thus be possible to distinguish agency (the capacity to act) from autonomy, as the 'free' and moral instance that makes us human and makes our choices our own.[91] Thus, while we suggest that algorithms increasingly have the capacity to act and thus possess the agency required to accept the hybrid consumer as a combination of human and machine agency, consumer protection law must still seek to guarantee the full autonomy of human agents. The ability to make both 'free' and moral choices only exists where the consumer has sufficient information to do so.

III. Towards personalised disclosures and dynamic disclosures?

Much of the private law community has long been unhappy with disclosure tools.[92] While mandated disclosures serve the abstract function of delivering the consumers plentiful information on the products or services

---

Subjects? Disentangling the Ontological and Functional Perspective, Frontiers in Robotics and AI 2022, 9.

89 This is the author's own thought, mainly grounded in the Kantian connection between agency, autonomy and morality, whereby an autonomous action is necessarily an expression of moral capacity. See also: *Bertolinin/Episcopo*, Robots and Ai as Legal Subjects (n. 88), 9: Ultimately, RAI applications do not share human's autonomy and moral awareness necessary according to an absolute—i.e., non-instrumental or sector-specific—definition of moral agency, as the latter "cannot abstract from the very determination of ultimate ends and values, that is, of what strikes our conscience as worthy of respect and concretization"- *F. Fossa*, Artificial Moral Agents: Moral Mentors or Sensible Tools?, Ethics and Information Technology 2018, 115.

90 *Bertolini/Episcopo*, Robots and Ai as Legal Subjects? (n. 88), 9.

91 *V. Dignum*, Responsibility and Artificial Intelligence, Berlin 2019; *M. D. Dubber/F. Pasquale/S. Das*, The Oxford Handbook of Ethics of AI, Oxford 2020, p. 215; *A. Bertolini*, Robots as Products: The Case for a Realistic Analysis of Robotic Applications and Liability Rules, Law, Innovation and Technology 2013, 214.

92 See all authors n. 85.

in question and their corresponding rights and obligations, it is broadly accepted that only a marginal number of consumers (or rather legal advisers)[93] read or take note of such disclosures at all.[94]

Many authors have suggested that as goods and services become more personalised and targeted, and so should disclosures.[95] Hereby *"personal information duties and standardised notices (w)ould be replaced by granular legal norms that provide personalized disclosures based on the personal preferences and informational needs of an individual."*[96] In addition to disclosures being tailored to the individual, we suggest that they could also be more tailored and integrated into the hybrid decision making process. The findings of algorithm aversion research indicate that users accept algorithms more when the functions of an algorithm are communicated in a clear, understandable language with accompanying illustrations, but that this also has to be accompanied by 'getting to know' the algorithm. Hence, interaction with the algorithm is crucial. These conclusions could be used to design such interactive and *dynamic disclosures*. Disclosures would thus not be static: the necessary information would not be provided all at once, but would be disclosed at every step and be precisely related to it – to each mechanism and the rights-sensitive relation in question. In this way, information asymmetries could be counteracted in a continued and interactive manner. Technically this could feature 'pop-up' functions and granular consent forms. Another method would be to learn about the algorithm in a test environment through trial-and-error, to understand how it works and reacts to different factors. Such a test environment should be similar to the real environment in which the customer will encounter algorithms, but broken down to the essential features that explain how an algorithm makes its decision. In addition, algorithms could be designed to incorporate mechanisms that explain the algorithm and its risks during the process of learning and adoption. Such methods could add another layer of interaction and of learning. We suggested above that learning (trail-and-error) and testing environments, as well as the continued development and

---

93 *C. Armbrüster*, McColgan, Peter: Abschied vom Informationsmodell im Recht allgemeiner Geschäftsbedingungen, Zeitschrift für die gesamte Versicherungswissenschaft 2020, 129.

94 *Bakos/Marotta-Wurgler/Trossen*. Does Anyone Read the Fine Print? (n. 85); *Bar-Gill*, Seduction by Contract (n. 85).

95 See in particular, *C. Busch*, Implementing Personalized Law: Personalized Disclosures in Consumer Law and Privacy Law, University of Chicago Law Review 2019, 309.

96 *Busch*, Implementing Personalized Law (n. 95).

incorporation of preferences and 'back-steps' are important ways in which consumers come to trust and understand algorithms.

IV. *Withdrawal rights*

Many of these suggestions and developments rely on market-driven mechanisms and market actors, that intrinsically may not always have the consumer's best interest at heart. Far-reaching withdrawal rights are thus essential to safeguard autonomy and to give consumers a way out of choices that may very well have overwhelmed them or do not serve them.[97]

F. *Conclusion*

We began this research endeavour with the assertion that algorithms and their integration into consumer decisions are treated differently in the (interdisciplinary) research field of HAI and the field of consumer protection law. However, this is only partially true. While the former focuses on bringing humans and algorithms together in an enlightened way, the latter focuses on the reduction of information asymmetries. Both areas of investigation attempt to find a way for a consumer to act in an informed and comfortable manner when faced with a decision in a consumer context. We first described how consumers act in a digital environment and how they encounter algorithms, before we elaborated on normative notions of algorithmically-enhanced consumers. We concluded that a new type of consumer is emerging: the *hybrid consumer*, whose choices are the combined result of human and machine rationality, agency and subjective inclination. This development surely leads to large information asymmetries, followed by a loss of autonomy and – potentially – a hesitation to make use of the algorithms. Before proposing measures, we elaborated on the current state of research on consumer acceptance and its driving forces. While mandated disclosures are classical tools to reduce information asymmetries, we showed that more nuanced and novel ways to create more intuitive forms of understandability and transparency are emerging.

---

97 See in particular G. *Wagner/H. Eidenmüller*, Down by Algorithms? Siphoning Rents, Exploiting Biases and Shaping Preferences – The Dark Side of Personalized Transactions, University of Chicago Law Review 2019, 582 (569 et seq.); *H. Eidenmüller*, Why Withdrawal Rights?, European Review of Contract Law 2011, 1.

Personalised and dynamic disclosures could allow users to get to know the algorithm in testing environment and through the learning ('trail-and-error') process. If done correctly and accepted by the consumers, this could reduce information asymmetries and enhance consumer autonomy in their interaction with algorithms.

Building Trust in Smart Legal Contracts

Alessandro Parenti and Marco Billi

A. Introduction

Since its birth, the interest around blockchain technologies has experienced a continuous growth. Especially in the last 2–3 years, this sector received high fundings by many venture capital firms and other investors (23 billion in 2021 for the whole sector).[1] We can mention two domains above all that gained the most success worldwide: the NFTs market, where the new interest for digitalized ownership drew investments in the millions for many projects,[2] and Decentralized Finance (DeFi).

Both technologies, like many others within the blockchain sector, are built upon software running a distributed ledger, a distributed, immutable database, on which information can be registered, such as *smart contracts*.

The term "smart contract" was originally coined by computer scientist and cryptographer *Nick Szabo* in 1994 as "a computerized transaction protocol that executes the terms of a contract".[3] He explains his idea by bringing forward the example of a vending machine: the vending machine is programmed to automatically perform (dispense the product) when certain conditions are met (a coin is inserted). This mechanism has the advantages of removing the need for intermediaries thus reducing transaction costs and making breaches of contract expensive or non-convenient (the cost of breaching the machine would likely be higher than the amount in the till). As we can notice also from the wording, *Szabo*'s idea of smart contract was closely related to the legal domain.

After the 90s, the term smart contract remained unused for more than 15 years, also because of the lack of technologies capable of fully realizing this theoretical idea in all its features. In 2014, however, *Vitalik Buterin*

---

1 *Team Blockdata*, The 10 biggest funding rounds in blockchain / crypto ever, 2021, available at https://www.blockdata.tech/blog/general/top-10-funding-rounds-in-blockchain-crypto

2 Although lately is has seen a decline in interest (last access: 05.09.2022).

3 *N. Szabo*, Smart Contracts, 1994, available at https://www.fon.hum.uva.nl/rob/Courses/InformationInSpeech/CDROM/Literature/LOTwinterschool2006/szabo.best.vwh.net/smart.contracts.html (last access: 05.09.2022).

used *Szabo*'s idea when he published Ethereum's whitepaper. One of the main innovative features of *Buterin*'s blockchain enabled the implementation of smart contracts on it.

The concept that originated from Ethereum smart contracts, however, diverges from *Szabo*'s original idea in that it loses the link with the legal field. *Buterin* refers to smart contracts as "cryptographic 'boxes' that contain value and only unlock it if certain conditions are met".[4] Therefore, for today's understanding, we need to bear in mind *Stark*'s[5] distinction between a *smart contract* (code), which simply refers to a piece of software running on a blockchain that self-executes its code once certain conditions (pre-defined inside it) get satisfied; and a *smart legal contract*, i.e., a smart contract used to represent and automatically execute an agreement enforceable by law.

As we will explain throughout the present paper, a smart legal contract, given its intrinsic features, raises an explainability issue, especially because of the potential impact that such a tool could directly have on people's personal legal sphere.

Traditionally, as far as the field of xAI (explainable AI (Artificial Intelligence)) is concerned, the focus is on providing the user with a rationale behind the outcome of AI system, often seen in decision support systems and other user-oriented applications. There are two main ideas in this research field. The first focuses on building additional systems that mimic the original, showing to which extent the model and/or its predictions are human understandable.[6] The two most common methods to achieve this are (1) by either creating a second model that provides a global explanation to the opaque system, achieving transparency and interpretability, (2) explaining only the reason for the prediction on a specific instance, basically providing a justification for the outcome of the black box considering a pair of input and decision.[7] The second research current, instead of

---

4 V. *Buterin*, Ethereum: A Next-Generation Smart Contract and Decentralized Application Platform, 2014, available at https://ethereum.org/en/whitepaper/ (last access: 05.09.2022).

5 J. *Stark*, Making Sense of Blockchain Smart Contracts, Coindesk.Com, 2016, available at https://www.coindesk.com/making-sense-smart-contracts (last access: 05.09.2022).

6 R. *Guidotti/A. Monreale/ S. Ruggieri/ F. Turini/ F. Giannotti/ D. Pedreschi*, A Survey of Methods for Explaining Black Box Models, in ACM Computing Surveys 2019, 1 (1 et seqq.).

7 H. *Prakken/R. Ratsma*, Case-based argumentation for explanation: formalisation and experiments, Argument and Computation 2021.

an ex-post explanation, tries to embed in the original system a symbolic representation of the knowledge-base.

With regard to smart contracts, we depart from this distinction, as explainability may be replaced with intelligibility. The parties of a contract may not require, strictly speaking, an "explanation" behind what the contract does, instead the focus shifts to describing, in computable and human terms, what the contract states. The step of contract creation can be quite unclear for non-software developers as it occurs in a programming language, aiming at guaranteeing the automated execution of the contract.[8] This paper aims at providing a solution to help these contracting parties communicate in a common language, understandable to both users and programmers alike.

In Smart Legal Contract research, there are two main currents that try to solve these issues from different points of view. The most classical *hybrid* approach is Ricardian Contract,[9] which places all information from the legal document in a format that can be executed by software. The code and the legal prose are then connected through the use of parameters, keeping the two separate and connected at the same time.

Our contribution aims to move beyond this approach, through the so-called *standalone* approach, using a sole source to represent both the contract and the code. Particularly, we shall focus on (1) what legal concepts can be successfully represented using a domain-specific language and (2) whether it is possible to isomorphically translate a legal contract into code using a general-purpose language.

B. Smart Legal Contracts

As we mentioned above, when we use smart contract technology for the purposes of representing legal agreements between two or more parties enforceable by law, we refer to Smart Legal Contracts. For purposes of completeness, we shall also say that, just like any other contract, they must satisfy a certain number of conditions that are usually laid down by the relevant legal provisions, in order to be considered valid by the legal system and thus to be enforceable before a court of law.

---

8 *P. Qin/W. Tan/J. Guo/B. Shen*, Intelligible Description Language Contract (IDLC) – A Novel Smart Contract Model, Information Systems Frontiers 2021, available at https://link.springer.com/article/10.1007/s10796-021-10138-4 (last access: 13.10.2022).

9 *I. Grigg*, 2004; *I. Grigg*, 2017.

In literature we can find different approaches to the use of this technology. First, we shall highlight the distinction defined by the ISDA-Linklaters Whitepaper[10] between external and internal model of smart contract. In the former, code is not part of the legal contract and is employed simply as a means for the execution of some parts of it. The latter refers to a *"legal contract rewritten in a more formal representation than the current natural human language form. A computer would then take that more formal representation and execute the conditional logic automatically."* In this model the code is a necessary part of the contract, as agreed and signed by the parties.

Furthermore, we can distinguish three ways to implement internal models of smart contracts, taking into account the approaches identified by *Clack*.[11] First, it is possible to link the written contract with its associated code through the use of markup languages, which have the task of annotating certain parts of the code and the text, providing a direct link between the two. This approach is represented by the concept of Ricardian Contracts[12] introduced by *Grigg* in 1996 and by all the evolutions that stemmed from it. These include Smart Contract Templates,[13] Intelligible Contracts[14] and the Accord Project.[15] We will not go into further detail, as this approach falls outside the scope of this contribution.

The other two approaches are (1) domain specific programming languages and (2) controlled natural language. The former helps towards the creation of a single artefact expressing both the contractual obligations and the computer code (in the light of the concept of *Computable* Contracts).[16] Moreover, thanks to its specificity, it is better suited for expressing and identifying aspects (e.g., payments, assets, and logic) that are proper to the legal domain of smart legal contracts, thus facilitating the activity of contract drafting. This approach was particularly explored for the financial

---

10 *ISDA/Linklaters,* Whitepaper: Smart Contracts and Distributed Ledger-A Legal Perspective, 2017, available at https://www.isda.org/2017/08/03/smart-contracts-and-distributed-ledger-a-legal-perspective/ (last access: 05.09.2022).

11 *C. D. Clack*, Languages for Smart and Computable Contracts, 2021.

12 *I. Grigg*, The Ricardian Contract, 2021, available at https://iang.org/papers/ricardian_contract.html (last access: 05.09.2022).

13 *H. Haapio/J. Hazard,* Wise contracts: smart contracts that work for people and machines, in: Trends and communities of legal informatics. Proceedings of the 20th international legal informatics symposium IRIS, 2017, 425 (425 et seqq.).

14 *L. Cervone/M. Palmirani/F. Vitali,* Intelligible Contracts, 53rd Hawaii International Conference on System Sciences, 2020, 1780 (1780 et seqq).

15 Available at https://www.accordproject.org/ (last access: 05.09.2022).

16 *H. Surden*, Computable Contracts, UC Davis Law Review 2012, 629 (626 et seqq.).

sector: we can mention the *Marlowe*[17] language for the Cardano block-chain and *Goodenough et. al.*[18] with a state-transition system to represent a financial contract.

The controlled natural language approach aims at making lawyers, and non-technical people in general, comfortable in the use of the programming language, thus contributing to the creation of the smart contract code directly, or at least in their ability to understand the written contract. Furthermore, this would help remove the error-prone step of manual conversion from natural language to a specification or programming language. An example of this approach is the Lexon language.[19]

C. Intelligibility

The concept of Smart Legal Contracts necessarily raises questions on whether it could fit in the current contract law framework. The main issue is represented by the language in which these are written, i.e., code, unintelligible for non-experts, aka those without a background in computing or logic.

On the one hand, we must say that current contract law (from a European point of view) is firmly based on the principle of freedom of form. This means that a contract, as a general rule, is not subject to any formal requirement.[20] National laws can then require a specific form for particular types of contracts, both *ad substantiam* and *ad probationem*. Moreover, the EU Blockchain Observatory & Forum has affirmed that blockchains fall under the scope of the e-IDAS regulation as an electronic document and that, consequently, "the data, including smart contracts, contained

---

17 *P. Lamela Seija/S. Thompson.* Marlowe: Financial contracts on blockchain. In International Symposium on Leveraging Applications of Formal Methods, Cham 2018, p. 356 (356 et seqq.).

18 *M. D. Flood/O. R. Goodenough.* Contract as Automaton: The Computational Representation of Financial Agreements (Office of Financial Research Working Paper), 2021. Although recently Goodenough has tried the logic programming approach.

19 *F. Idelberger,* Merging Traditional Contracts (or Law) and (Smart) e-Contracts – a Novel Approach, in: Proceedings the 1st Workshop on Models of Legal Reasoning, 2020, available at https://lawgorithm.com.br/wp-content/uploads/2020/09/MLR2020-Florian-Idelberger.pdf (last access: 05.09.2022).

20 PECL 2:101 (2); DCFR II – 1:106; UNIDROIT 1.2.

therein cannot be denied legal force solely because of their electronic nature".[21]

On the other hand, the fact that a contract is expressed in a language that is inaccessible to the average person may affect the correct formation of contractual intent that, together with a sufficient agreement, represents the only necessary requirements.[22] In fact, the difficulty in ascertaining the mutual expression of the intention to be legally bound is highlighted when the parties cannot read or understand their obligations.[23] A solution was found by assimilating smart contracts to adhesion contracts, for which the expression of the intention to be bound was undoubtably recognized, and by applying the relative discipline to it. This means requiring the drafting party to take reasonable steps to bring terms not individually negotiated or imposed by one party to the other party's attention, before or when the contract is concluded.[24] The EU Directive of Unfair Contract Terms states that the consumer should have a 'real opportunity of becoming acquainted' with the terms in order for those not to be considered unfair.[25] This provision has been considered satisfied for wrap contracts (Click-wrap or browse-wrap),[26] where the expression of consent has been recognized just by using a website where the terms and conditions are accessible through hyperlinks. The EU directive on consumer rights takes one more step by also providing that, in order for the consumer to be bound by a contract falling under the scope of the directive (B2C relationships), the trader shall provide certain information to the consumer "in a clear and comprehensible manner".[27]

---

21 *EU blockchain Observatory & Forum*, REPORT – Blockchain and digital Identity, 2018.
22 G. *Christandl*, Art 2:101 (1): Conditions for the Conclusion of a Contract, in: N. Jansen/R.Zimmermann (eds.), Commentaries on European Contract Laws, Oxford 2018, p. 236 (236 et seqq.).
23 B. *Carron/ V. Botteron*. "How smart can a contract be?" Blockchains, Smart Contracts, Decentralized Autonomous Organizations and the Law, Cheltenham 2019, p. 128.
24 N. *Jansen*, Art 2:104: Terms not Individually Negotiated, in: N. Jansen/R. Zimmermann (eds.), Commentaries (n. 23), p. 272 (272 et seqq.).
25 Directive 1993/13/EC, annex 1(i).
26 "Wrap contracts" are adhesion contracts concluded online. The most common are "click-wrap" and "browse-wrap" agreements. In the former the user accepts the terms by clicking on an "I agree button", while in the latter, he does so by simply continuing using the website. C. *Bomprezzi/G. Finocchiaro*, A legal Analysis of the use of blockchain technology for the formation of smart legal contracts, mediaLAWS 2020, 122.
27 Directive 2011/83/EU, Art. 5–6.

Under such legal framework, the most commonly proposed solution, at least in B2C relationships, entails accompanying the smart contract code with a natural language translation of the contract.[28] In B2B relationships such need does not arise since the parties are deemed to have equal contracting power. The legislator assumes that they had enough resources to understand the contents of the agreement, without having to directly intervene in order to protect the weak party.

The present contribution follows instead the abovementioned *standalone* approach, where the whole agreement is expressed directly in the smart contract code. By using programming languages whose understandability level is far higher than usual smart contract languages the goal is to build trust in the source code for both the end user and for the legal professional.

It is argued that with a hybrid smart contract there is no way to determine whether the code behaves according to what is written in the natural language section of the document (i.e.t, the original contract).[29] Such a situation can occur both because of intentional deceit by the drafting party, who taking advantage of the other, or just because of a translation mistake made by the programmer. In fact, where two parties decided to conclude an agreement in the form of a smart contract, they would need, other than a lawyer to lay out the contract terms, also a programmer to write the agreement into computer code. This new level of intermediation increases both the transaction costs and the risk of errors. Not having a legal background, a programmer could be unaware of the different meanings a term can have and thus implement code that is slightly different in its legal effect.

For all the above-mentioned reasons, we believe that approaching trust in the system by using human readable code could empower both the user to be more aware of the behavior of the program, and the legal professionals to build or understand the content of contracts on their own. In case of B2C relationships intelligibility of the source code is necessary for a standalone smart contract to be compliant with EU provisions on consumer rights, according to which "Before the consumer is bound by [...], or any corresponding offer, the trader shall provide the consumer with the following information in a **clear and comprehensible manner...**". This principle can and should be applied also outside the B2C field, rather in

---

28 C. *Bomprezzi*, Implications of Blockchain-Based Smart Contracts on Contract Law, Baden-Baden 2021, p. 140.

29 F. *Idelberger*, Merging Traditional Contracts (n. 22).

all cases in which intelligibility of the code could foster trust between the parties, as well as in the contract itself.

In order to properly reach our goal, it would be important to transpose in the smart contract code the whole agreement, at least to the extent permitted by the programming language. This means having a smart contract representation in an intelligible form both legal and non-legal elements, i.e., the parts exclusively necessary for the execution of the code and that would not be mentioned in a traditional contract; as well as elements that do not affect the execution of the transactions, but that are nonetheless part of the contract, such as the header or the competent forum. By doing so, one can acknowledge all the distinct aspects of the agreement in relation to the execution of the obligations.

In the following sections we employ two newly developed programming languages for the purpose of testing our approach to smart legal contract drafting. We will start with a simple contract example and evaluate its transpositions in both languages explaining their functioning.

D. Example

For the purpose of displaying the effect of the two methods we will analyse throughout this paper, we must first present the running example, taken from *Governatori et al.*[30] and readapted to better show what we are proposing. The contract concerns a license agreement between two parties. The licensor is willing to grant the licensee a temporary license to test the product, only under the conditions that the licensee pays the full fee in advance. From the moment he receives the temporary license, the licensee has a limited amount of time (called evaluation period) to test the product and either send confirmation of his intention to buy the full version or let the evaluation period expire and get reimbursed.

Below, the contract in full:

1. Licensor is willing to grant to the Licensee a License to use the Product for the term and specific purpose set forth in this Agreement, subject to the terms and conditions set out in this Agreement.

---

30 G. *Governatori/F. Idelberger/Z. Milosevic/R. Riveret/G. Sartor/X. Xu.*, On legal contracts, imperative and declarative smart contracts and blockchain system, Artificial Intelligence and Law 2018, 377 (377 et seqq.).

2. Licensor grants Licensee a temporary license to evaluate the Product and fixes (i) the evaluation period – in 10 days – and (ii) the cost of the Product – in 1000 Euros -, in case the Licensee will buy the Product.
3. In consideration of the License Product described in Clause 1 of this License Agreement, Licensee shall pay in advance the License fee as stated in Clause 2 of the Agreement.
4. The licensee can decide to purchase the permanent version of the license by sending an explicit communication to this end to the licensor, within the end date of the evaluation period.
5. This Agreement and the License granted herein commences upon the moment the payment has been received by the Licensor.
6. This Agreement shall terminate upon (a) the moment of purchase or, in any case, (b) once the evaluation period has expired.
7. Once the evaluation period has expired, the Licensee will be reimbursed if the Product has not been bought.

I. TECHNOLOGIES – *Stipula*

The first approach we present is represented by a domain-specific programming language, *Stipula*. It was recently developed by professors *Cosimo Laneve*[31] and *Silvia Crafa*[32] in collaboration with *Giovanni Sartor*[33], designed for the creation of Smart Legal Contracts. Stipula's distinctive characteristic is that it was built starting from a small set of abstractions aimed at capturing the main concepts of contract law. These include elements such as *permission, prohibition, obligation, agreement* or *alea*: basic patterns that can be found in any legal contract. Each of these are represented in code with a specific primitive. The idea is that such a structure would make the code more understandable and, especially, easier to handle for legal professionals when drafting smart legal contracts. Moreover, Stipula is based on a relatively straightforward syntax, consisting of terms that recall their commonly understood meaning.

In the next sections we put forward the implementation of our example using Stipula. We will explain the meaning of the different elements constituting the language while describing the various steps of the contract execution.

---

31 cosimo.laneve@unibo.it
32 silvia.crafa@unipd.it
33 giovanni.sartor@unibo.it

1. Agreement

Every Stipula contract begins with the execution of the *Agreement* constructor. This represents the moment in which the parties have reached a consensus on the contents of the arrangement they want to create, such as the end of negotiation.

At this stage, each party is asked to either set and/or accept certain values of the contract terms. In Stipula, these values are called *fields,* and in our example, these are the cost, the deadline for the activation of the contract and the deadline of the evaluation period.

```
stipula License {

asset balance, token

field t_start, t_limit, cost, code

init Inactive


agreement (Licensor, Licensee)(t_start, t_limit, cost){

Licensor , Licensee : t_start, t_limit, cost

} ==> @Inactive
```

Fig. 1. Contract header and agreement constructor in Stipula's code. Asset values and agreement constructor are highlighted.

```
# Please, Licensor insert your id:
ga3xl
# Please, Licensor insert the values for the fields:
t_start:
2022/07/23:00:00
t_limit:
2022/07/26:00:00
cost:
10
```

Fig. 2: Stipula's interface during the execution of the agreement constructor.

As you can see from the contract header, field values must be distinguished from *asset* values, which refer to the actual goods managed by the smart contract like a currency or a token representing a good or a right. Such resources have to preserve a total supply in the context of the program: "the sender of the asset must always relinquish the control of the transferred asset".[34] This feature implements, by design, a safety against the risks of double-spending, accidental loss, or lock-in assets, since there is a finite predetermined amount that can be exchanged.

In the license agreement, the assets are the *Balance* (money sent to the contract) and a *token* representing the permanent license. Note how only fields, and not assets, are part of the agreement constructor.

2. *Offer*

An offer is an expression to another party or to the community at large, to be bound by the stated terms. The deployment of smart contract code on a distributed ledger is generally deemed to correspond to an offer, at least for those individuals who are allowed to interact with the smart contract.[35] When any participant in the network can interact with it and conclude the agreement, then the uploading represents an offer to the public. In order to be valid, an offer must contain all the terms of the agreement (*essentialia negotii*).

After the agreement, the contract's state is set to "Inactive". The first action can be taken by the licensor by calling the "offerLicense" function, through which he or she is asked to send the token representing the license to the smart contract. By doing so, where the licensee accepted, the contract could automate the licensor's performance of granting the license.

---

34 *S. Crafa/C. Laneve/G. Sartor,* Pacta sunt servanda: smart legal contracts in Stipula, 2021 available at https://arxiv.org/abs/2110.11069 (last access: 13.10.2022).

35 *M. Durovic/A. Janssen,* The Formation of Blockchain-based Smart Contracts in the Light of Contract Law. European Review of Private Law 2019, 753 (753 et seqq.).

```
@Inactive Licensor : offerLicense (x)[n]{

n --o token

x --> code;

now + t_start >> @Proposal{

token --o Licensor

} ==> @End

} ==> @Proposal
```

Fig. 3: offer function in the Stipula's syntax. The 'state' is highlighted

```
# Please, choose which function should run:    ############
      Licensor.offerLicense(Type4 x)[Asset n]  Next state Proposal
ga3xl.offerLicense(useCode)[100]               ############
```

Fig. 4. Stipula's interface during the execution: Offer.

After the offer the contract's state switches to "Proposal". *States* are another basic feature of Stipula. They can be seen as the various stages of a contract's lifecycle and the transition between one another is triggered by the occurrence of an event (external or produced by one party). Events are indicated in the source code with an "@".

From the legal standpoint, *States* are used to implement the concepts of *prohibition* or *permission*. In every state, certain actions (i.e., functions call) are allowed, while others are precluded. As an example, in the license agreement, the Licensee is allowed to buy the license only in the "@Trial" state and not before.

3. Acceptance

An acceptance is a form of statement or conduct that indicates assent to the offer. In a smart contract, parties express acceptance by signing a transaction with their cryptographic keys and by sending it to the contract address. As it was noted, the majority of today's smart contracts represent unilateral contracts, stating, for example, that if X happens, I will give you Y.[36] With these types of contracts, acceptance always comes through the act of performance. The transaction expressing consent will likely represent the transfer of control over a digital asset to the smart contracts as, for example, money, cryptocurrency, or digital token representing a material good.

In our example, after the licensor's proposal, the licensee can accept it by calling the function "activateLicense". He or she receives a usecode which grants a temporary access to the software. At the same time, the licensee is required to send to the contract the price necessary to buy the permanent license. This money will be credited automatically to the licensor if the licensee buys the permanent license by calling the relative function (in another version of the same contract, the upfront escrow can be used to issue a penalty where the licensee infringed some contract terms). Should the licensee not buy the permanent license within the evaluation period, the money will automatically be sent back to him and the token back to the licensor.

```
@Proposal Licensee: activateLicense()[b] (b == cost) {

b --o balance

code --> Licensee;

now + t_limit >> @Trial {

balance --o Licensee

token --o Licensor

} ==> @End

} ==> @Trial
```

Fig. 5: the acceptance function in Stipula's syntax. The 'event' is highlighted.

Such a procedure is implemented through an *event*, another Stipula's primitive. Events are employed to schedule the execution of future operations if specific preconditions are met. Usually, preconditions are represented by the different states defined in the contract. From the legal perspective, events are used to enforce contractual *obligations*. They consist of a timeout (timer), which is initiated when the function is called, a precon-

---

36 *M. Durovic, A. Janssen*, 2019 (n. 33).

dition (state) and the consequential operation that may be triggered (a statement). According to an event, if the timer expires and the contract state is still "@X", then the contract executes a certain operation such as terminating the contract, issue an automatic penalty etc. In our example, the event is used to invalidate the temporary usecode for the software at the expiration of the evaluation period and, as already mentioned, to send the resources managed by the contract to the respective owner.

4. Purchase

The licensee can decide to purchase the permanent license by calling the "Buy" function. The money previously escrowed by the contract is sent to the licensor address and the licensee receives the token representing the permanent license. By receiving the token, the licensee acquires a full right on the license which cannot be limited by other actors.

```
@Trial Licensee : buy ()[]{

balance --o Licensor

token --o Licensee;
```

Fig. 6. The buy function in Stipula's Syntax. The lollypop operator is highlighted.

This particular kind of transfer is indicated by a special operator, the lollypop (-o). This operator is used for the movement of *assets*. This means that the location previously holding the asset is emptied and it loses control over it. On the legal side, this represents the translative effect of a previously existing right.

II. TECHNOLOGIES – *Logical English*

Logical English is a controlled natural-language interface that provides syntactic sugar for logic programming languages (namely Prolog and sCASP). It enables the user to write logic rules in quasi-natural language form, which is then translated internally in Prolog, evaluated, and the solution presented to the user in natural language form. This language, developed by *Robert Kowalski* in 2020,[37] is aimed at providing the ability to understand the code and what it represents even to non-programmers, thus virtually giving everyone access to the underlying logic of a program. This language differs from Stipula, as while the latter excels at inferring legal meaning and concepts from the syntax, this approach is focused on representing the source code as faithfully as possible to the contract as written in natural language.

We will now present a brief overview of the technical aspects of this language.

A LE (Logical English) document consists of a knowledge base of facts and rules, scenarios, queries, and templates. The templates are declarations of the predicates contained in the knowledge base and scenarios, such as

> *"according to clause1 *a licensee* and *a licensor* conclude *a contract* for *a product*"*

A template identifies a sentence and the variables contained in it. The arguments are identified by a being surrounded by asterisks and starting with an indefinite article "a" or "an". The predicate itself is represented by the rest of the template. The templates are used to identify instances of the predicates in the knowledge base and elsewhere. For example, the template above can be used to identify a sentence such as

> *"according to clause1 Ale and Marco conclude Contract1 for licenseNFT"*

as an instance of a predicate, which is translated into Prolog or s(CASP) resulting in the symbolic representation:

> *"according_to_clause1_and_conclude_for('Ale', 'Marco', 'Contract1', 'licenseNFT')"*.

The translation can be then processed by any standard Prolog interpreter.

This next section will focus on the conversion process, e.g., how to translate the natural language text into Logical English. In legal logic programming one of the key conditions for the representation of legal rules in code is isomorphism, defined as one-to-one correspondence between norms in the formal model and natural language. Each concept or condition must be accurately translated, not only the automated process that is the foundation of a smart legal contract, but also the surrounding

---

37 R. *Kowalski*, Logical English A position paper prepared for Logic and Practice of Programming 2020.

information that the parties decide is useful to better interpret the contract itself.

For example, let us take a look at clause 1 of this hypothetical contract (Figure 6).

```
according to clause1 a licensee and a licensor conclude a contract for a product
    if the licensee is of type licensee
    and the licensor is of type licensor
    and the parties agree to the contract
    and the product is the object of the contract.
```

Fig. 7: the logical transposition of clause 1.

The representation of this clause exemplifies the process behind it. First, we must recall Article 1321 of the Italian Civil Code, which states that a contract is an agreement between two or more people, to establish, regulate or terminate a patrimonial legal relationship.

After having established the minimum requirements behind the definition of a contract, it becomes easier to visualize the purpose of the clause. The LE representation, as seen in Figure 6, clearly identifies the conditions behind the applicability of the clause and therefore of the contract. The parties have been identified as 1) the licensor and 2) the licensee. Furthermore, the parties have agreed to the contract. Finally, the object of the contract is the license to use the product, here referred to as simply "product", which has monetary value and establishes a legal relationship between the two parties.

The same process applies to all other contract clauses. We shall take a slightly deeper look at clause 6, which states that the Agreement shall terminate upon (a) the moment of purchase or, in any case, (b) once the evaluation period has expired.

```
63  according to clause6 the agreement shall terminate by purchase on a date D
64      if according to clause4 a licensee purchases a permanent license on the date D.
65
66  according to clause6 the agreement shall terminate by expiration on a date D
67      if according to clause2 a licensor grants a product to a licensee for a number days for an amount on a date D0
68      and according to clause5 an evaluation period starts on a date D1
69      and D is the number days after D1
70      and it is not the case that
71          according to clause6 the agreement shall terminate by purchase on a date D2.
```

Fig. 8: the logical transposition of clause 6.

Since clause 6 introduces two moments in time related to the termination of the contract, we have decided to divide this rule into two. The first is related to the moment of purchase, while the second relates to the expiration date. It is interesting to introduce at this point one of the logical features of LE, which is negation as failure, and is written as "it is not the case that", followed by the negated literal. Through negation as failure, just like traditional Prolog programs, it is possible to write exceptions to norms as defeasible rules.

For this clause, we have stated that in all cases where the contract has not terminated with the purchase of the product by the licensee, it shall terminate by expiration of the trial period.

1. Execution

Now that the contract has been represented into computational language, the next step concerns telling the systems which steps must be taken to execute the contract itself. Basically, how to go from "what the contract states" to "what the contract does"?

```
86  a contract sends NFTuseCode to a licensee on a date D
87      if according to clause1 the licensee and a licensor conclude the contract for a product
88      and according to clause2 the licensor grants the product to the licensee for a number days for an amount on D.
89
90  a contract sends a product to a licensee on a date D
91      if according to clause1 the licensee and a licensor conclude the contract for the product
92      and according to clause4 the licensee purchases a permanent license on D.
93
94  a contract sends an amount to a licensee on a date D
95      if according to clause1 the licensee and a licensor conclude the contract for a product
96      and according to clause7 the licensee gets refunded the amount on the date D.
97
98  a contract sends a product to a licensor on a date D
99      if according to clause1 a licensee and the licensor conclude the contract for the product
100     and according to clause7 the licensee gets refunded an amount on the date D.
```

Fig. 9: the transposition of the execution rules.

Each goal originates from the same template – "*a contract* sends *a thing* to *an agent* on *a date*" – which is being recalled, providing a trace of all token movements. Furthermore, it can be observed that each action is linked to the computable representation of the legal prose. Particularly, each transaction can be directly connected to an article being applied in the current case.

For example, the first rule in Figure 8, lines 86–88, states that a contract sends a temporary use code to the licensee if clauses 1 and 2 of the contract are positively instantiated. Each executable step is triggered by the satisfactory outcome of a clause in the contract.

2. *Explaining the contract*

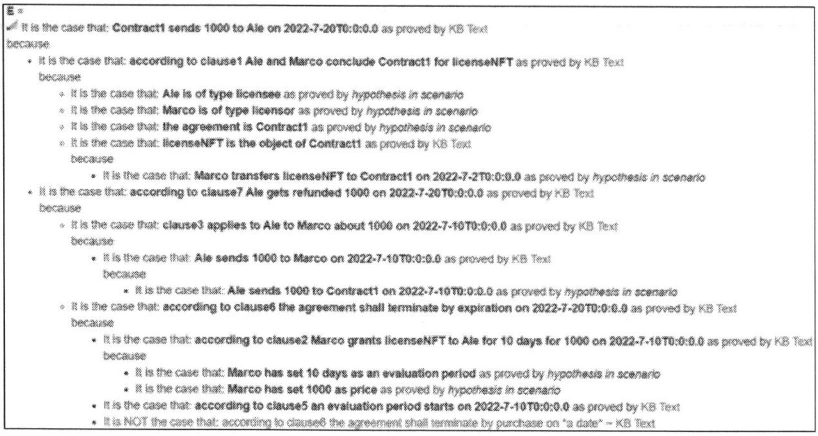

Fig. 10: the results of the execution.

In figure 9 we can visualize one of the advantages provided by mixing declarative programming with quasi-natural language translation. It is possible to query the system regarding the actions taken by the contract, as well as whether any clause applies in the present case. The system looks through all known facts, inserted by the user, as well as any inferences that can be made based on the applicable rules.

Based on the information which has been given as input, the system runs through the available options, checking which articles can be applied in the current situation, and by tracing the executable steps, gives a complete overview of the relevant clauses and the actions that can be taken. For example, by looking at Figure 9, we can visualize that the contract has sent the price of the contract back to the licensee (*Ale*) on a date since 1) a contract was successfully concluded (clause 1 was correctly applied) and 2) the licensee is supposed to be refunded the price on this date (clause 7 was correctly applied). Each of these clauses has sub-conditions for their applicability, and it is possible to verify each step of the reasoning process.

Each indentation reflects a goal that shall be satisfied by the conditions in the next indentation level. The system also returns negative conditions, highlighted in red, which tell the user which requirements were not met.

Therefore, by approaching smart legal contracts from a declarative-isomorphic point of view, it is possible to both provide the user with a trace of the movement of tokens from and to the contract, as well as enable the parties to interact with the contract directly, asking questions regarding the applicability of certain clauses, their effect on the overall validity of the contract, and the conditions that must be satisfied or not satisfied.

E. *Conclusion & discussion*

In this paper we have presented Stipula, a domain specific language aimed at supporting lawyers in the drafting of smart legal contracts, by capturing the essential concepts of contract law and transposing them into an easy-to-use programming language. We highlighted certain concepts, such as what constitutes an agreement, an offer or the acceptance of the contract, and the way Stipula conveys such information to the user.

Furthermore, we experimented with Logical English, a logic programming language. Transposing a contract by maintaining the same structure and syntax sacrifices certain semantic and contextual definitions in order to provide non-IT experts with the ability to read the code and understand the logical steps required in order to fulfill the obligations of the contract.

We believe that these solutions could greatly contribute to the transparency of this innovative technology, thus fostering people's trust in it. Moreover, these can become useful for legal practitioners, them to either draft smart legal contracts directly, or to validate the program written by a programmer.

An observation that stemmed out from our work, particularly from the implementation of Logical English, is that the translation of a contract in logic form is facilitated when the original contract has been written computable logic in mind. With regard to execution steps, certain logical structures must be present in the text in order to facilitate the transposition. Generally, having a clear distinction between goals (the actions that must be automatically executed) and requirements (which conditions must apply) is essential to write a precise isomorphic representation of the contract clauses.

These two solutions can help contracting parties communicate in a common language, available to both users and programmers alike, and the use case shown supports, at least preliminarily, this conclusion.

From Bilateral to Ecosystemic Transparency: Aligning GDPR's Transparency Obligations with the European Digital Ecosystem of Trust

Kostina Prifti, Joris Krijger, Tamara Thuis and Evert Stamhuis

A. Introduction

Trustworthiness plays a crucial role in the ambition of Europe's digital leadership plans. With its vision for innovation and data technologies such as Artificial Intelligence (AI), the EU seeks to make ethics 'a core pillar' for developing a unique approach to digital innovation. Guidelines and regulatory frameworks of recent years, such as the Ethical Guidelines for Trustworthy AI and the Draft AI Act, are shaped by the ambition to ensure excellence and trust. By enacting the General Data Protection Regulation (GDPR), Europe already introduced the most human centred data protection law in the world, but questions remain about its efficacy[1] and its ability to address all normative data protection concerns in the age of AI.[2] In this chapter we highlight a specific concern related to transparency, one of the core components of human centred AI. More specifically we focus on the relation between the ambition of fostering trustworthiness and the approach to transparency obligations in the GDPR and potentially ensuing AI regulation. As a general characteristic these regulatory frameworks view transparency as a one-dimensional obligation between organizations and data subjects. As such, the functioning and conceptualization of transparency in the GDPR is determined by the overall rationale to "strengthen individuals' fundamental rights in the digital age". This rationale situates transparency obligations in the bilateral relation between individuals and organizations, imposing an implicit duty of care on individuals to safeguard their legal rights and consequently ensure legal compliance of data controllers. Taking recent developments in the fields

---

1 S. *Mercer*, The Limitations of European Data Protection As A Model for Global Privacy Regulation, AJIL Unbound 2020, 20.
2 M. *Finck*, The Limits of the GDPR in the Personalisation Context. Forthcoming in: U. Kohl, J. Eisler (eds.), Data-Driven Personalisation in Markets, Politics and Law, Cambridge 2021.

of legal, psychological, and organisational science into account, we contest that transparency in its current functioning, with primacy on informing data subjects, placing responsibility on the side of the individual to enforce their rights, results in a realistic and thus fair allocation of responsibilities. As trust correlates with a clear and fair allocation of responsibilities the trustworthiness ambitions of Europe's digital leadership will suffer when the arrangement of obligations remains as incongruent as we will show it is, vis-à-vis the reality in which data driven systems operate.[3]

This chapter provides an exploration, critique, and expansion of the transparency concept in the GDPR by juxtaposing its functioning with the European ambition of becoming a digital ecosystem of trust. We begin with describing the current transparency obligations that are applicable in the case of data science applications, automated individual decision-makings (ADMs) more in particular exposing and abstracting the transparency rationale underlying the GDPR. We chose ADMs as our focal point because these are explicitly specified as data driven practice in the GDPR. ADMs will, despite limitations in Art. 22 of the GDPR, become increasingly more common with the introduction of AI and will, in their current and future appearance, for a considerable proportion fall under the future regulation for AI. In that way our analysis of incumbent regulation also speaks for future regulation. Briefly put, we challenge the positioning of transparency obligations in the bilateral relation between individuals and organizations and the subsequent distribution of responsibilities that is structured around individuals proactively enforcing their rights. We discuss some key issues of the current functioning of transparency obligations in the GDPR and examine the limitations to the underlying rationale in relation to the notion of a trustworthy digital ecosystem. As a result, the chapter advances the claim that the incongruence between the legal notion of transparency and the rationale of fostering trust ought to be reduced by expanding the concept of transparency to a multilateral concept with more actors in an applied manner, thus diversifying and rebalancing the allocation of responsibilities. Transparency as currently conceptualized in the GDPR is insufficient to meet the trustworthiness objectives behind transparency obligations.

Existing literature on transparency in the case of ADMs and other AI powered applications focuses mainly on developing various mechanisms

---

3 *J. van den Hoven/G. Comandé/S. Ruggieri/J. Domingo-Ferrer/F. Musiani/F. Giannotti/F. Pratesi/M. Stauch/I. Lishchuk* Towards a Digital Ecosystem of Trust: Ethical, Legal and Societal Implications, Opinio Juris In Comparatione 2021, 131.

that contribute to increasing transparency for the individual, facilitating as such the creation of the "informed individual" who then uses the information enabled by transparency to act rationally in defence of their rights.[4] The novelty of the analysis and proposed solution in this chapter is a shift from the direction of improving transparency towards a direction that simultaneously expands and applies the concept of transparency. We suggest that an approach rooted in the digital ecosystem renders an implementation of transparency that better serves the aim to promote trust. Our approach seeks to improve the congruency between the normative allocations of responsibilities and the empirical reality of the actor-relation networks that we call the ecosystem. We first criticize the lack of realism in the currently dominant perception of how it works in the relation between organization and individual. A second line of critique aims at the narrow recognition of relevant relations in current policy developments. In a way, we endorse the plea of Felzmann et al. who worked on transparency in the relation between technology providers and users and we extend their contextualisation effort in the direction of the ecosystem of trust.[5]

B. *Current transparency obligations*

This section is structured as follows. Owing to the limited technological scope of ADMs when reviewing transparency, the meaning of ADMs is firstly clarified. Secondly, an overview and analysis of legal transparency obligations pertaining to ADMs is provided. Lastly, the section abstracts the legal regulation of transparency for ADMs by exposing the overarching rationale and its main implications. The main takeaway from the transparency rationale in reference to ADMs is that it is positioned in a two-party relation between an organization and an individual, a relation in which or-

---

4 See for example: *H. Felzmann/E. Fosch-Villaronga/C. Lutz/A. Tamò-Larrieux*, Towards transparency by design for artificial intelligence, Science and Engineering Ethics 2020, 3333; *E. Bayamlıoğlu*, The right to contest automated decisions under the General Data Protection Regulation: Beyond the so-called "right to explanation", Regulation & Governance 2021, available at https://onlinelibrary.wiley.com/doi/full/10.1111/rego.12391 (last access: 05.09.2022); *S. Wachter/B. Mittelstadt/L. Floridi*, Transparent, explainable, and accountable AI for robotics, Science robotics 2017, available at https://www.science.org/doi/10.1126/scirobotics.aan6080 (last access: 05.09.2022).

5 *Ibid.*

ganizations are obliged to provide information intelligibly and individuals are expected to utilise the information to protect their legal interests.

I. ADMs and profiling: AI powered or not

ADMs were firstly regulated by law in a direct manner in Art. 22 GDPR. This article being positioned between Arts. 12–23 GDPR, the ruling on ADMs seems to be categorised by the legislator as part of rights of data subjects, specifically phrased as a right not to be subjected to a decision based solely on automated processing. Briefly explained, there are a few elements that qualify a decision as an ADM and consequently trigger Art. 22 GDPR. Firstly, the decision must have been made *solely* by automated (what may be termed "autonomous") processing. In other words, the human intervention is missing in the decision-making process. Importantly, this must not be understood as there being no human intervention, as humans are the ones that develop and operate the system. Instead, it means that once the system is designed and composed with the necessary data and logic of processing the data, the system works autonomously, and its results are not reviewed by a human in the loop.[6] Secondly, Art. 22 GDPR takes under its regulative effect only those kinds of autonomous decisions that either produce a legal effect on the individual, or significantly affect them. A legal effect may be losing a job, or being denied healthcare, whereas a significant effect on individuals relates to cases like discrimination. Therefore, a decision falls under the applicability of Art. 22 GDPR if it is autonomous and produces legal effects or similarly affects individuals. As profiling can be done with or without ADM applications, Art. 22 GDPR covers ADM applications with or without profiling. ADMs processing personal data are, in principle, banned – individuals have a right not to be subjected to these kinds of decisions. The techno-empirical reality however is that ADMs are widely used, often based on consent, but also in places where its usage is authorized in the implementing legislation in the member state. Indeed, paragraph 2 of Art. 22 GDPR provides a gateway by outlining three exceptions: when it is necessary for a contract (e.g. in the case of a job opening for which there are 3000 applicants and only 4 HR mem-

---

6 Article 29 Data Protection Working Party, Guidelines on transparency under Regulation 2016/679, 17/EN WP260.

bers), when it is authorised by member state law, or when it is based on explicit consent.[7]

II. Legal obligations for transparency

To these ADM applications several transparency obligations apply. Transparency is one of the overarching principles in the GDPR, and it is further deduced to several types of obligations, which may be grouped in three categories. The first group of obligations relates to *the right of individuals to get access to information*. Present mainly in Arts. 13–15 GDPR, access to information obligations aim to ensure that individuals are informed about the details of the processing activities, like the identity of controller and processor, the purposes of data processing, its length, data transfers etc. These details are expected to provide the individual with a clear view of the processing activities.

The second group of obligations is concerned with *information about the rights* that individuals have in relation to the processing of their personal data. Individuals' rights about their personal data are outlined in Arts. 15–22 GDPR, and they include the right to erasure, right to accuracy, portability, access, etc. Particularly applicable in cases of ADMs, data controllers must safeguard the individual's rights by enabling the possibility for human intervention, providing the chance for the individual to express their views, as well as to contest the decision when they believe it is inaccurate and/or unfair. In general, data controllers and processors are obliged to inform individuals, pursuant these two groups of obligations, on details of the processing and what rights individuals have in relation to these details.

The first two groups of obligations relate to the "what" dimension of information, namely what information ought to be given to individuals. The third group of obligations relates to the "how" dimension of information, comprising obligations that aim to ensure concise, intelligible, transparent, and easily accessible information. This third group of obligations is also referred to as "intelligibility". Intelligibility is one of the prevailing challenges of ADMs, exacerbated by the non-transparent nature of the decision-making process in machine learning, and particularly deep learning, algorithms.[8] When an ADM is already opaque to experts who developed

---

7 *Ibid.*
8 *N. Burkart/M. F. Hubner*, A survey on the explainability of supervised machine learning, Journal of Artificial Intelligence Research 2021, 245.

an ADM system, intelligibility to individuals as laypersons is, even more, a considerable challenge.

On a related note, scholars discuss the nature and exact content of a right to an explanation in the GDPR. This Regulation assumes an ex-ante approach to explainability, aiming to ensure that individuals receive an explanation before the processing starts. As a result, individuals, it seems, do not have the right to receive an ex-post explanation, through which the data controller explains the autonomous decision in their particular case.[9] An ex-ante approach to explainability disengages the explanation from contextuality, as the individual may be explained the algorithmic logic in general terms, but would still not know (before, during, and after the ADM) how these general rules of logic apply in their context. For instance, an individual may be explained that the logic of the ADM entails correlating expenditures with the ability to pay back a loan. However, the individual may not be aware, for example, that the loan was rejected because of a gambling addiction in the past, detected by an autonomous data collection and interpretation process. This kind of explanation would only be feasible ex-post. However, data controllers do not have an explicit obligation for ex-post explainability, which means that individuals must challenge and contest the decision before they become aware of what they are contesting specifically.

In summation, there are three kinds of transparency obligations in the GDPR. One kind aims to ensure that individuals are informed on the details of the processing. The second kind aims to ensure that individuals are informed on what their rights are in relation to the details of the processing. The third kind relates to the manner through which the first and second kind of transparency is delivered, usually referred to as explainability.

III. *Abstracting the transparency rationale*

The objective of the transparency obligations in the GDPR is to provide the necessary information to individuals in an intelligible way, thus empowering individuals to manage their legal rights and legal protection. In

---

9 S. *Wachter/B. Mittelstadt/L. Floridi*, Why a right to explanation of automated decision-making does not exist in the general data protection regulation, International Data Privacy Law 2017, 76.

this regard, transparency is often viewed as instrumental to due process.[10] The rationale for why individuals must receive information about the processing of their personal information and their rights in an intelligible manner is so that they can exercise their rights, which connects directly with due process. Relating this understanding to the traditional dichotomy found in the law between obligations of conduct and obligations of result, transparency obligations can be perceived as obligations of conduct. As a result, the assessment of whether data controllers have fulfilled their transparency obligations is based on their conduct, not on whether individuals are able to exercise their rights based on the information provided.

Secondly, the transparency obligations as outlined in the previous subsection are positioned mostly in the bilateral relation between organizations and individuals. Data controllers face transparency obligations to the individuals whose data they process, while the involvement of enforcement agencies like national Data Protection Authorities (DPAs) takes a secondary role. Specifically, since DPAs have the duty to monitor and enforce the GDPR, data controllers and processors must be transparent to DPAs about their work. The monitoring notwithstanding, the locus of transparency obligations is clearly the bilateral relation between organizations and individuals. Similar to consumer protection laws, the GDPR puts the weight on individuals to enforce their legal rights, with some support from enforcement agencies.[11]

Lastly, it is worth noting the exoteric conception of transparency that the GDPR advances.[12] The explainability obligations discussed above are guided by the aim of information being intelligible to laypersons. Scholars have evidenced that the GDPR lacks, and may benefit from, an esoteric conception of transparency, where the intricacies of ADMs are made transparent to experts, which would allow scrutiny on a deeper level.[13] The implementation of this idea would require transparency obligations that are different both in shape and form from the obligations that exist to support individuals whose data are being processed.

In conclusion, the positioning of transparency obligations in the bilateral relations between individuals and organizations means the individual,

---

10 *E. Bayamlıoğlu*, The right to contest automated decisions (n. 4).

11 *O. Butler*, Obligations imposed on private parties by the GDPR and UK Data Protection Law: Blurring the public-private divide, European Public Law 2018.

12 *M. Grochowski/A. Jabłonowska/F. Lagioia/G. Sartor*, Algorithmic transparency and explainability for EU consumer protection: unwrapping the regulatory premises, Critical Analysis of Law 2021, 43.

13 *Ibid.*

being privileged with information rights, is implicitly attributed with the main responsibility of ensuring that data controllers and data processors comply with their legal obligations – at least as regards the processing of personal data of that individual. In other words, to individuals *a duty of care* is allocated, expecting them to be informed and act on that information in defence of their legal rights. In this regard, transparency is an enabler of due process, facilitating consent, contestation, and other rights for individuals. However, the practical limitations which disable or hinder the transparency obligations from fulfilling their aim and role as it extends to trust need our attention, now that we have shown how transparency is defined by its rationale. We will display the critique on the transparency regulation for ADMs in the next section.

C. *Empirical, legal and organisational critique*

Transparency obligations for ADMs in the GDPR aim to provide individuals with information that enables them to safeguard their rights in cases when their personal data is processed. This regulatory aim is coherent, insofar as it assumes that rational individuals would take action to safeguard their rights. However, the theoretical rationale for transparency in ADMs must be understood in relation to the empirical context in which it operates. As a result, this section will put forward practical and contextual considerations that challenge the transparency rationale for ADMs in the GDPR. Exposing practical limitations serves as a basis for critique and further development of the concept of transparency and its obligations in the case of ADMs. The section presents and reviews six practical problems that show lack of congruence between the conceptual intentions and the techno-empirical context of operation: information, knowledge, resources, manipulation, enforcement, and public interest problems.

Information problems

Transparency may be understood as an infrastructure for information, enabling access and intelligibility of the latter; information is a central tenet of transparency. However, besides the obligations that the GDPR provides in relation to transparency discussed in the previous section, there are two kinds of information problems that hinder the effectiveness of transparency obligations in the GDPR. These problems relate to cases when individuals are not aware that a decision about them is made autonomously, which can occur for illegitimate or legitimate reasons.

Data controllers may illegitimately withhold information from individuals when a decision about them is made autonomously.[14] In such cases, the information asymmetry between organizations and individuals is strong considering that the information is entirely in the hands of data controllers who run the ADM. Individuals depend for the information on the organization itself, which may not always have an incentive to comply with the legal obligation to inform individuals.[15]

The legitimate reasons why organizations do not provide the necessary information to individuals as required by law may spring from effective use and competition considerations.[16] Consequently, as scholars point out, the picture in practice is more nuanced than what the GDPR suggests, often involving a balancing exercise.[17] One reason for effective use relates to the integrity of the algorithms behind the ADM. Operating organizations, in the context of their activities, must avoid risks of adversarial learning, referring to cases when users manipulate or circumvent the logic of the ADM.[18] Moreover, data controllers as businesses are weary of competition-related problems that may arise from giving information about the logic of the system. In some cases, that information may be protected under Intellectual Property (IP) rights, in other cases be perceived as a valuable trade secret.[19]

As a result, a closer look at the practical implementation of transparency obligations reveals that the right to access information, while seemingly clear and straightforward in legal doctrine, encounters practical challenges

---

14 M. *Hildebrandt*, Smart technologies and the end (s) of law: novel entanglements of law and technology, Cheltenham 2015.

15 R. *Mancha/D. Nersessian*, From Automation to Autonomy: Legal and Ethical Responsibility Gaps in Artificial Intelligence Innovation, Michigan Technology Law Review 2021, 55.

16 Burell 2016 classifies opaqueness because of manipulation and IP as intentionally opaque: *J. Burrell*, How the machine 'thinks': Understanding opacity in machine learning algorithms, Big Data & Society 2016, available at https://journals.sagepu b.com/doi/full/10.1177/2053951715622512 (last access: 14.10.2022)

17 T. *Wischmeyer*, Artificial intelligence and transparency: opening the black box, in: T. Wischmeier/T. Rademacher (eds.), Regulating artificial intelligence, Cham 2020, p. 75.

18 C. *Meek/D. Lowd*, Adversarial learning, in: Proceedings of the eleventh ACM SIGKDD international conference on Knowledge discovery in data mining 2005, p. 641.

19 E. *Bayamlıoğlu*, Tright to contest automated decisions (n. 4).

that may disable the objective and instrumental role of transparency in relation to due process and empowering individuals.

Knowledge problems

The EU regulator adopts an implicit assumption, when regulating ADMs in the GDPR, that an informed individual is always able to safeguard their rights in relation to organizations that control and process their data. As behavioural economics clarifies, the expectation that more information leads to more rational choices is often fallacious and may frequently have the opposite effect.[20] The fallacy arises out of an approach towards information and knowledge as being the same. In other words, the EU regulator assumes that once an individual is informed, they *know how* to utilise the information for their benefit in safeguarding legal rights. Knowledge relates to being able to process information in a way that makes it actionable in a variety of ways, and we could question whether individuals, even after having acquired the information about the processing and their rights, do possess the knowledge to utilise the acquired information to their benefits. The fulfilment of the aim behind transparency obligations requires not informed, but knowledgeable individuals. However, transparency obligations focus only on producing informed individuals, which results in a misalignment between the aim of transparency and its actual obligations.

The literature on consumer attitudes and information points to a combination of this knowledge problem and the previous information problem. Koolen summarizes these as "apathy, attrition and disinterest".[21] Individuals do not give attention to information, are worn out by the frequency and inaccessibility of the information and effectively do not internalize that it is in their personal interest that information is provided. 'Why bother, I have nothing to hide', is the attitude that puts pressure on the whole chain from providing information to acquiring knowledge and dedicating energy to action, which is the next problem.

---

20 G. *Gigerenzer*, Moral satisficing: Rethinking moral behavior as bounded rationality, Topics in cognitive science 2010, 528.
21 C. *Koolen*, Transparency and Consent in Data-Driven Smart Environments, European Data Protection Law Review 2021, 174 with further references.

Resources problems

It is challenging to ensure that individuals are informed, and even more challenging to ensure that they are knowledgeable in how to safeguard their legal rights in the context of ADMs. Another practical challenge concerns the resources required for an individual to utilise the information provided because of transparency obligations to safeguard their legal rights. Limitations of resources may be financial, particularly worrying in cases of poorer and vulnerable groups. Contesting an ADM may require the hiring of professional legal services, which is affordable by only a few. Furthermore, limitations of resources may also be time related. To be informed, individuals are expected to spend time reading lengthy texts written in legalese language, sometimes even simply to accept or reject cookies, let alone in cases of complex ADM. When it comes to contesting, too, time constraints are significant as it may take years for a case to be finalised.

The problem of resources is challenging even in contexts where individuals are exposed to an ADM rarely, perhaps once or twice in their lifetime such as having applied for a loan or for a high-end job position. The advent of autonomous technologies like personal intelligent assistants, care robots, autonomous vehicles, and more, expand these challenges even further. With autonomous technologies, which operate without constant human supervision, an individual may be exposed to tens or hundreds of automated decisions in a single day.[22] The regulatory expectation that individuals would have resources to contest ADMs in such quantities would be simply unrealistic.

The resources problem challenges consent, too, considering that paragraph 2 of Art. 22 requires individuals to give explicit consent (as one of the bases) before an autonomous decision is taken about them. While this obligation may work in cases when individuals are rarely exposed to ADMs, although even then with many limitations,[23] it is severely challenged in cases where individuals are exposed to a large quantity of automated decisions. Individuals would not have the time, assuming they would have the desire and the ability, to engage in giving consent multiple times du-

22 *B. Liu*, Recent advancements in autonomous robots and their technical analysis, Mathematical Problems in Engineering 2021, available at https://www.hindawi.co m/journals/mpe/2021/6634773/ (last access: 05.09.2022).

23 *E. Kosta*, Peeking into the cookie jar: the European approach towards the regulation of cookies. *International journal of law and information technology* 2021, 380; *Koolen*, Transparency and Consent (n. 21).

ring the days. It is also not an acceptable solution for consent to be given in an overarching "blanket" manner, as that does not fit the notion of consent that the GDPR advances.

The quantitative increase of ADMs, particularly in autonomous technologies, poses challenges also in the work of national DPAs. As the institution responsible for the enforcement of the GDPR and the competent authority to handle complaints against data controllers, DPAs are notoriously struggling to handle all complaints and requests within due and reasonable time.[24] These challenges arise as a combination of a lack of resources, funding, and staff members, and a quantitative increase in data processing activities, particularly ADMs. The rational model of due process that transparency supports, namely that informed individuals would complain to relevant authorities when their rights are infringed, is challenged not only from the individual perspective, who may not be informed, knowledgeable, or have the resources, but also from the institutional perspective.

Manipulation problems

Besides information, knowledge, and resource related problems, individuals may be manipulated in making choices in the context of ADMs, which might not necessarily align with their data processing preferences. Consent for data processing is to a great extent self-management by individuals. However, privacy protection based on privacy self-management frameworks (consent and contest) fails to protect individual privacy and misses the collective dimension of privacy.[25] The implication of privacy self-management is that individuals make their own decisions whether to accept or reject the conditions presented to them by a data processor. Important to consider is that in making choices, outcomes are, besides rational deliberation, influenced by the design of the choice environment.[26] Consequently, the way the choice is presented by the data processor may

---

24 *B. Daigle/M. Khan*, The EU general data protection regulation: an analysis of enforcement trends by EU data protection authorities, Journal of International Commerce and Economics 2020, available at https://www.usitc.gov/staff_publicat ions/jice/eu_general_data_protection_regulation_analysis (last access: 05.09.2022).

25 *L. Baruh/M. Popescu*, Big data analytics and the limits of privacy self-management, New Media & Society 2017, 579.

26 *M. Weinmann/C. Schneider/J. vom Brocke*, Digital Nudging, Business & Information Systems Engineering 2016, 433.

influence to a great extent how an individual chooses to reject or accept terms and conditions.[27]

One way to influence decisions through choice architecture is through making use of nudging techniques. According to Thaler and Sunstein,[28] a nudge is "any aspect of the choice architecture that alters people's behaviour in a predictable way without forbidding any options or significantly changing their economic incentives". Nudging in the context of consent for data processing can include altering the provision of information, correcting misapprehensions about social norms, altering profiles of different choices, or implementing default options.[29] In a digital environment, such as websites or mobile applications, nudging implies the use of design-elements in the user interface to alter the behaviour and thus choices of data subjects.[30] Examples of digital nudges in the realm of cookie consent is for instance the use of different colours or the two-step cookie design, presenting the accept option as more attractive choice.

Transparency objectives are, therefore, hindered by manipulation problems such as the case of nudging, where organizations may abide by the legal obligations of transparency while still nudging individuals to make certain choices that suits the organizations' cost-benefit considerations.

Enforcement problems

Mercer notes that, despite the advanced and established status of the GDPR, its efficacy can be questioned as, so far, there have been only few notable enforcement actions.[31] We see at least three causes that can be discerned for this lack of enforcement, that come on top of the resources problem we mentioned above. The first relates to the discrepancy between attitudes towards privacy and actual behaviour. This discrepancy is known as the 'privacy paradox': although users value privacy they take very little

---

27 *E. J. Johnson/S. B. Shu/B. G. C. Dellaert/C. Fox/D. G. Goldstein/G. Häubl/R. P. Larrick/J. W. Payne/E. Peters/D. Schkade/B. Wansink/E. U. Weber*, Beyond nudges: Tools of a choice architecture, Marketing Letters 2021, 487.

28 *C. R. Sunstein/R. H. Thaler*, Nudge: Improving decisions about health, wealth, and happiness, New Haven 2008.

29 *Y. Lin/M. Osman/R. Ashcroft.*, Nudge: Concept, Effectiveness, and Ethics, Basic and Applied Social Psychology 2017, 293.

30 *Weinmann/Schneider/vom Brocke*, Digital Nudging (n. 26).

31 *S. Mercer*, The Limitations of European Data Protection (n. 1).

action to protect their personal data or enforce their privacy rights.[32] A second reason for the relatively small number of enforcement actions concerns the nature of risks and harms that, from a traditional regulatory perspective, are not significant enough to warrant enforcement action. Compared with other chapters and articles in the Charter of Fundamental Rights of the European Union, such as freedom of expression or right to integrity of the person, the harms resulting from a violation of privacy regulation seem relatively small, especially when they are addressed on an individual level. The third concerns the 'enforceability' of these privacy regulations. As Finck remarks,[33] advanced algorithms are trained on training data, which is often personal data, before being deployed. This way of training raises the question of how data subjects' rights that involve the modification or deletion of data can be reconciled with the nature of these technologies. She stresses that this might make it difficult, if not impossible, to implement their rightful request to have their data removed. Given the time and costs of retraining models, enforcing GDPR rights comes close to removing the entire model that has been fed with their data.

Public interest problems

The GDPR relies on consent as a notion of individual self-determination. As discussed above there is good reason to question the understanding individuals have to the digital ecosystem they operate in, rendering the basis of their consent problematic. However, there is another problem with this focus on individual rights and consent, as this "fails to capture communal repercussions and the impact of individual consent on the public interest".[34] Fairfield and Engel therefore proposed to view privacy not as a private good, but as a public good since 'an individual who is careless with data exposes not only extensive information about herself, but about others as well'.[35] By focusing on grounds for making data available on an individual level, such as consent for data collection or processing, the GDPR misses the repercussions this consent can have on a public level. An individual decision about data sharing can, through storing, aggregating, or combining data sets, affect others in ways they never consented to. In

---

32 A. Acquisti/J. Grossklags, Privacy and rationality in individual decision making, Security & Privacy 2005, 26.

33 Finck, The Limits of the GDPR in the Personalisation Context (n. 2).

34 Ibid., p.1.

35 C. Engel/J. A.T. Fairfield, Privacy as a Public Good, Duke Law Journal 2015, 385.

a transparency framework tailored to informed proactive individuals this public aspect is overlooked.

D. Trust and Transparency

The shortcomings and limitations discussed above raise the question as to what extent transparency obligations in the GDPR serve the ecosystem of trust the European Union seeks to establish. To align the functioning of transparency with the notion of a European trustworthy digital ecosystem we propose a focus on redefining the notion of transparency from bilateral to ecosystemic, recognizing the empirical reality of the individual and the context of deployment of advanced technologies that warrant approaching the relevant relations more broadly. Before further fleshing out this complementary conceptualization of transparency we will first analyse in more detail how the current functioning of transparency, and subsequent distribution of responsibilities centred on proactive individual enforcement of rights, relates to an ecosystem of trust.

In its Data Governance Act the European Union describes a 'trustworthy environment' as something that "requires instruments able to ensure that data from the public sector, industry and citizens is available for use in the most effective and responsible manner, while citizens retain a reasonable degree of control over the processing of data they generate, and businesses can rely on adequate protection of their investments in data economy".[36]

Trust, however, is a complex concept that needs to be outlined somewhat more to pinpoint how GDPR's shortcomings might impact this ecosystem of trust. Trust, as a psychological state, is a subjective attitude where one accepts a vulnerability based on positive expectations of the intentions or behaviour of another.[37] It has often been remarked that trust functions as an important prerequisite of technology acceptance and adoption.[38] Trust, in the context of AI, is often related to trust in machines and transparency, then, is regarded as a method to enhance trust in

---

36 Data Gouvernance Act, Explanatory Memorandum.
37 *D. M. Rousseau/ S. B. Sitkin/R. S. Burt/C. Camerer*, Introduction to Special Topic Forum: Not so Different after All: A Cross-Discipline View of Trust, The Academy of Management Review 1998, 393.
38 E.g. *V. Venkatesh/J. Y. L. Thong/X. Xu*, Unified Theory of Acceptance and Use of Technology: A Synthesis and the Road Ahead, Journal of the Association for Information Systems 2016, 328; *K. Siau/W. Wang*, Trust is hard to come by.

technological artefacts. For example, the positive effect on trust when AI assistants provide a transparent reasoning for choosing one solution over a set of alternatives.[39] However, trust in the digital economy requires something else than trust in AI as a technology. When it comes to the digital economy and the role of AI in it, it is much more relevant to assess data infrastructures, institutions and mechanisms. To relate this notion of trust to a digital ecosystem of trust we will use van den Hoven et al. definition of a digital ecosystem of trust.[40] They define a digital ecosystem of trust as "a system of interacting organisms and their environment, in which appropriate norms are clear to parties, and responsibilities are well defined and adequately and fairly allocated to actors and agents. Trust needs to be horizontal between citizens and parties and vertical between citizens and governments".[41]

Our main criticism of transparency as it functions in the GDPR is its strong but problematic emphasis on the proactive individual who shoulders the majority of the responsibility in making sure her rights are upheld and if necessary enforced. As the adequate and fair allocation of responsibilities is an important part of a digital ecosystem of trust, there emerges an incongruence between the current functioning of transparency and the role it could, or should, play in the broader digital ecosystem of trust.

We argue that the current conceptualization of transparency could or maybe even should be complemented with a functioning of transparency that addresses two aspects: a congruent representation of individuals' behaviour and of the relation-network in which the data driven technology operates. It is generally held that transparency, and transparency assessments, matter because access to relevant information is vital for maintaining accountability. Indeed, "transparency is thus a highly valued instrumental good, since it is an input into a process of monitoring that increases the odds that voters or consumers get what they want from institutional actors".[42] This is an important starting point for a different perspective on the role and function of transparency in the governance of

---

Building Trust in Artificial Intelligence, Machine Learning, and Robotics, Cutter Business Technology Journal 2018, 47.

39 *F. Biessmann et al.*, Transparency and trust in artificial intelligence systems, Journal of Decision Systems 2020. DOI: 10.1080/12460125.2020.1819094.

40 *van den Hoven/Comandé/Ruggieri/Domingo-Ferrer/Musiani/Giannotti/Pratesi/Stauch/Lishchuk*, Towards a Digital Ecosystem of Trust (n. 3).

41 *Ibid*, p. 134.

42 *N. Bowles/J. T. Hamilton/D. A. L. Levy* (Eds.), Transparency in Politics and the Media: Accountability and Open Government, Bloomsbury Publishing 2013, p. 15.

data driven systems. As we have shown, such a perspective goes beyond the bilateral individual and rights-oriented approach and requires a reconceptualization of transparency that is centred around its techno-empirical dimension. This approach complements the focus on possibilities for redress with an interpretation of transparency based on promoting trust in the data ecosystem and its accompanying accountability mechanisms. Where in the GDPR transparency may function as a normative limit to the power of organizations vis-à-vis individuals, we should focus on how the tool of transparency can also function to tailor power and responsibility to the more complex concrete context.[43]

Developing a transparency framework that redistributes responsibilities among multiple parties involved in the processing of data bears certain implications on the nature of transparency obligations in various spheres. To provide an impetus for the expansion of transparency from bilateral to ecosystemic, affecting multiple agents and actors rather than just an individual and an organisation, we will discuss three of these considerations such a framework should account for.

E. Expanding transparency obligations to foster trust; an exploration

As shown above, there is a clear need to broaden the conceptual domain of transparency obligations towards ecosystemic relationships. This requires redefining the bilateral individual-organization relationship and expand to, what *Brodie et al.*[44] describe as "network relationships among versatile actors in [...] ecosystems". To facilitate the development of this revised transparency notion, this section exploratively analyses the second leg of that revision: the expansion of transparency obligations in ADMs to a broader relation network. Expanding transparency obligations to foster trust in a digital ecosystem requires the consideration of multilateral relations between all actors in the ecosystem. Following *Li et al.*[45] we take digital ecosystems to be "complex and interdependent systems and their underlying infrastructures by which all constituents interact and exhibit

---

43 *S. Gutwirth/P. Hert*, Privacy, Data Protection and Law Enforcement. Opacity of the Individual and Transparency of Power, Privacy and Criminal Law 2006, 18.

44 *R. J. Brodie/J. A. Fehrer/E. Jaakkola/J. Conduit*, Actor Engagement in Networks: Defining the Conceptual Domain, Journal of Service Research 2019, 173.

45 *W. Li/Y. Badr/F.Biennier*, Digital ecosystems: challenges and prospects in: Proceedings of the International Conference on Management of Emergent Digital EcoSystems (MEDES '12), New York 2012, p. 117.

as a whole self-organizing, scalable and sustainable behaviors." Digital and business ecosystems are metaphorical to the biological ecosystem in which the interdependencies of all actors, coevolving in their capabilities in the environment, are highlighted.[46] Relating this field to technology and innovation one could say that a social innovation environment is about a set of actors from different societal sectors and their environment with legal and cultural norms, supportive infrastructures and many other elements that enable or inhibit the development of social innovations.[47]

Rather than situating transparency obligations solely in the information exchange between the individual and the organisation operating the technology, we seek to tailor transparency obligations to the specifics of the various relations that are part of a digital ecosystem. In the context of ADM applications, we distinguish, beyond the transparency interaction between individuals and organizations, transparency as related to the interactions within organizations, between organizations, between the organization and institutional bodies, between institutional bodies and individuals, either impacted by the technology or intermediary user/operator, between society/general public and organizations and society/general public and institutions. We will address a selection of these in the following section where we exploratively analyse some of the aspects of transparency obligations that require further alignment with the extent and complexity of interactions in the ecosystem in which advanced algorithms operate.

I. Experts, Oversight Institutions and Organizations

The positioning of transparency obligations beyond the bilateral relations between individuals and organizations bears certain implications on the nature of transparency obligations for other actors in the ecosystem. Specifically, since information must be made transparent to laypersons who are assumed to have little information and knowledge on the workings of AI, the "how" of transparency is guided towards simplicity. By being simple and concise, the information made transparent is intelligible to non-experts. As a result, an opportunity so far neglected is the relevance

---

46 *J.F. Moore*, The Death of Competition: Leadership and Strategy in the Age of Business Ecosystems, New York 1996.
47 *F. Sgaragli*, Enabling Social Innovation Ecosystems for Community-led Territorial Development, Rome 2014.

and utility of making information about ADMs transparent to experts.[48] Experts are involved in numerous capacities in the digital ecosystem, as representative of a professional user category or of a supervising mechanism, to name but a few. The duty to explain to experts bears some implications. Firstly, an inclusion of experts as beneficiaries of transparency obligations necessitates a change in the nature of transparency obligations, specifically because the information made transparent may be not only more technical and complicated but also more complete and thus more transparent. An expert-based level of scrutiny is higher than non-expert scrutiny. Therefore, the first change relates to the nature of the information that must be made transparent.

A second implication relates to the fact that an inclusion of experts creates the possibility for institutional oversight over the use of ADMs as regulated by the GDPR, a kind of oversight so far neglected by the regulatory framework. In this regard, expert-based institutional oversight may be categorised as: input, output, and throughput oversight.[49] Input oversight bears an ex-ante nature, relating to the involvement of institutional expertise before the ADM system is placed in the market. The proposed AI legislation by the European Commission may be understood closely to this type of oversight, insofar as AI powered ADM systems must pass a certification process before being placed in the market. However, the proposed legislation relies on market-based solutions since the ex-ante certification process is performed by licensed private actors,[50] so there is a possibility to expand the involvement of institutional expertise in an ex-ante manner. In principle, such expert-based oversight would ensure that only ADM systems that comply with legal requirements are made available to consumers.

Output-based oversight becomes necessary considering that, due to the unpredictable nature of AI powered ADMs, complying with ex-ante requirements does not guarantee that ADMs will not infringe individual's rights. In this regard, institutional expertise of the output-based type would benefit from transparent information to assess the impact of ADMs

---

48 *Grochowski/Jabłonowska/Lagioia/Sartor*, Algorithmic transparency and explainability for EU consumer protection (n. 12).

49 *B. Haggart/C. I. Keller*, Democratic legitimacy in global platform governance, Telecommunications Policy 2021, 1.

50 Article 19, Proposal for a Regulation of the European Parliament and of the Council laying down harmonised rules on Artificial Intelligence (Artificial Intelligence Act) and amending certain Union Legislative Acts {SEC(2021) 167 final} – {SWD(2021) 84 final} – {SWD(2021) 85 final}.

on individuals. National DPAs have some minor output-based oversight competences according to the GDPR; for instance, they have the right to conduct ex officio investigations.[51] However, the resources problems identified in the previous section hinder them from effectively exercising these competences on a large scale. Lastly, throughput type of oversight relates to overseeing the process of using ADMs between their ex-ante approval and their ex-post assessment. Throughput oversight allows institutions to be informed and have some form of control over the process of using ADMs, which is relevant considering that process-related problems may not be evident before or after the use of ADMs, but only in the course of their use.

II. Choice Architecture, Developers and Stakeholders

The conceptualization of transparency mainly or solely in the bilateral relations between individuals and organizations also bears some challenges and implications from a more organizational perspective. Transparency obligations to provide information in a concise, intelligible, transparent, and easily accessible way are – as previously mentioned – limitedly enforced and allow for manipulation of the individual's choice. That results in an undesirable level of uncertainty. Organizations currently have no directions on the way in which cookie consent notices should be designed and presented to individuals. As shown in a study by *Bauer et al.*,[52] the way the choice architecture is designed in terms of salience, effort, and framing impacts the decision-making process of the individual. Transparency obligations in the design of the choice environment would not only enable individuals to make an unmanipulated choice but potentially increase awareness about these choices in society at large. These obligations could imply for instance the same level of salience and effort in the choice options presented to individuals to decrease the level of manipulation by data processors. Considering the concept of nudging previously mentioned, organizations can self-nudge to behave in a way that is more socially

---

51 Article 57, GDPR.
52 *J. M. Bauer/R. Bergström/R. Foss-Madsen*, Are you sure, you want a cookie? – The effects of choice architecture on users' decisions about sharing private online data, Computers in Human Behavior 2021, 120.

preferable,[53] and enhances trust in the digital ecosystem in which they operate.

Besides the environment in which organizations and individuals interact, the current transparency obligation limitedly addressed the complex organizational structures in which ADMs are operating and interacting with individuals and their data. Instead of perceiving algorithms as constrained and procedural formulas, Seaver stresses the importance of understanding algorithms as "heterogenous and diffuse sociotechnical systems".[54] This understanding of algorithms includes the embedding of the algorithm in the specific organizational context in which it is developed and/or used. ADMs are designed, developed and deployed by different types of actors over time, and hence a holistic overview and understanding of all processes including interdependencies by these actors are often impossible.[55] Within organizations, users and developers may know how the technology works on a certain level of abstraction, but rarely know everything about the technology and the chain of actions and processes connected to it.[56] There are different knowledge levels to what they know about the technique they use, as for instance managers responsible for an AI system do not understand the details of what data scientists develop. Consequently, the traceability as to who decided on what at which point in time about how the data is collected and processed could be compromised.[57] This limited traceability of the decision-making process may not only affect the type of information the organizations can provide but also how responsibilities are attributed in cases of disparate impact or negati-

---

53 L. *Floridi/J. Cowls/M. Beltrametti/R. Chatila/P. Chazerand/V. Dignum/C. Luetge/R. Madelin/U. Pagallo/F. Rossi/B. Schafer/P. Valcke/E. Vayena*, AI4People — An Ethical Framework for a Good AI Society: Opportunities, Risks, Principles, and Recommendations, Minds and Machines 2018, 689.

54 N. *Seaver*, Algorithms as culture: Some tactics for the ethnography of algorithmic systems, Big Data & Society 2017, available at https://journals.sagepub.com/doi/full/10.1177/2053951717738104 (last access: 06.09.2022).

55 L. *Floridi/J. Cowls/M. Beltrametti/R. Chatila/P. Chazerand/V. Dignum/C. Luetge/R. Madelin/U. Pagallo/F. Rossi/B. Schafer/P. Valcke/E. Vayena*, Auditing algorithms: Research methods for detecting discrimination on internet platforms, Data and Discrimination: Converting Critical Concerns into Productive Inquiry 2014, available at https://link.springer.com/article/10.1007/s11023-018-9482-5 (last access: 14.10.2022).

56 M. *Coeckelbergh*, Artificial Intelligence, Responsibility Attribution, and a Relational Justification of Explainability, Science and Engineering Ethics 2020, 2051.

57 B. D. *Mittelstadt/P. Allo/M. Taddeo/S. Wachter/L. Floridi*, The ethics of algorithms: Mapping the debate, Big Data & Society 2016 available at https://journals.sagepub.com/doi/full/10.1177/2053951716679679 (last access: 14.10.2022).

ve outcomes of ADM. With advanced algorithms becoming opaque for experts in the organizations, they influence how roles and responsibilities are delegated in the ADM processes.[58]

So, in the operations of the organization, users and even experts are often unaware of the unintended consequences or moral significance of the ADM system that they are using.[59] Moreover, professionals on a more managerial level seem to be increasingly aware and concerned about using algorithms responsibly, yet do not perceive it as their personal responsibility to act upon this concern.[60] While this gap in organizational responsibility can be partly explained by the uncertain nature and unpredictability of the long-term societal impact of innovation processes,[61] regulatory transparency obligations that account for the organizational structures surrounding ADMs could result in a fairer and clearer allocation of responsibilities, both inside and outside the organizations. Multilateral transparency obligations from an organizational perspective imply a reflection on the different tasks and roles of actors in the ADM process. If systems are designed in a non-transparent way, transparency should challenge the people involved in the process to take responsibility for its outcomes. Therefore, both regulations, as well as institutions such as a DPA and the organization itself, should consider who is to be held accountable for the ADM's implications, and thus define what level of transparency is required. As it is important to address unanticipated issues with the ADM, the system's design should allow for the possibility to reverse actions and make its behaviour visible so it can be grasped by the stakeholders involved.[62]

One development that receives much attention in the past years, is the use of Explainable AI (XAI) methods and techniques to provide a post-hoc explanation of the system's output. But we do not assess these as the panacea for the incongruency we deal with in this chapter. While these methods provide experts with additional insights and information about the algorithms that are developing and deploying, there is little understan-

---

58 *K. Martin*, Ethical Implications and Accountability of Algorithms, Journal of Business Ethics 2019, 835.
59 *M. Coeckelbergh*, Artificial Intelligence (n. 56); *A. Matthias*, The responsibility gap: Ascribing responsibility for the actions of learning automata, Ethics and Information Technology 2004, 175.
60 *Mancha/Nersessian*, From Automation to Autonomy (n. 15).
61 *M. Sand/I. van de Poel*, Varieties of responsibility: Two problems of responsible innovation, Synthese 2018, 4769.
62 *Mancha/Nersessian*, From Automation to Autonomy (n. 15), p. 136.

ding of how organizations use XAI methods in practice.[63] Additionally, most of these methods are deployed for the purposes of developers and machine learning engineers to debug models, and they limitedly address the needs of users or individuals as specified in the GDPR. Mittelstadt et al.[64] question for instance to what extent the methods, making use of local approximations, could be considered reliable and useful for non-experts. Another concern is that the use of explainable AI in the ADM context could even lead to unfair allocations of responsibility as individuals are given the perception that they have control over their data and how it is processed by providing them a post-hoc explanation.[65] In this way, designers of the system processing the data may distance themselves from the responsibility for the ADM's behaviour.

Lastly, conceptualizing transparency multilaterally fostering trust in the ADM's digital ecosystem, requires transparency obligations that effectuate a shift in focus from the relation between the data processor and the individual to a format in which organization also relate to groups of individuals, institutional bodies, other organizations, e.g.in a value chain. For instance, business organizations hire data processors, third-party vendors, to implement an algorithmic application within their business processes. With the involvement of third-party vendors, an organization is not a single actor, but part of a chain of actors that have a potential obligation to share information with individuals.

III. Public

While current transparency obligations are focused on protecting individual rights, this focus might conflict with a fair allocation of responsibility

---

63 *U. Bhatt/A. Xiang/S. Sharma/A. Weller/A. Taly/Y. Jia/J. Ghosh/R. Puri/J. M. F. Moura/P. Eckersley*, Explainable machine learning in deployment, Proceedings of the 2020 Conference on Fairness, Accountability, and Transparency – FAT* '20, p. 648, available at https://dl.acm.org/doi/abs/10.1145/3351095.3375624 (last access: 06.09.2022).

64 *B. Mittelstadt/C. Russell/S. Wachter*, Explaining Explanations in AI, Proceedings of the Conference on Fairness, Accountability, and Transparency – FAT* '19, p. 279 available at https://dl.acm.org/doi/10.1145/3287560.3287574 (last access: 06.09.2022).

65 *G. Lima/N. Grgić-Hlača/J. Keun Jeong/M. Cha*, The Conflict Between Explainable and Accountable Decision-Making Algorithms, 2022 ACM Conference on Fairness, Accountability, and Transparency, p. 2103, available at https://arxiv.org/abs/2205.05306 (last access: 06.09.2022).

and the transparency objectives from the general public, society at large. From a more societal perspective, individuals could benefit from other data subjects sharing their data with data processing organizations to improve the accuracy and trustworthiness of the ADM process and outcomes. However, from an individual perspective, it might be worthwhile protecting one's own privacy and restrict organizations from collecting and processing personal data. One of the ways of balancing both interests is the involvement of stakeholders from multiple perspectives and invite them to co-design and co-own solutions,[66] hence cooperate with citizens and customers to create cohesion and collaboration in the ways transparency obligations are executed. An important element here is to make use of participatory mechanisms that help to assess to which extent tasks and decision-making should be delegated to ADMs in a way that is aligned with values and understanding of society.[67] A transparency obligation towards society at large could be compared to the current ESG related disclosure obligations of organizations to report on non-financial performance. Not only is this information useful to investors, it also fosters trust in an organization from a broader societal perspective when an organization is transparent about its policies and results.

In this way, transparency as a multilateral concept allows for dialogue between stakeholders in society varying from businesses, governmental institutions, and citizens, eventually collaborating to promote trust in the digital ecosystem as a whole.

F. Conclusion and further research

In this chapter we have developed the following point: Transparency obligations in the GDPR, in their current form – and to some extent the Draft AI Act – might have adverse effects on the 'envisioned digital ecosystem of trust' ambitions of the European Union, due to the unrealistic allocation of responsibility vis-à-vis individuals, as citizens, consumers or otherwise impacted persons. Our objections against the current conceptualisation can be summarized as: (a) it does not effectively help the data subject, (b) it does not provide guidance to the organization who operates the technology on what satisfactory transparency is, (c) it does not match the

---

66 *Floridi/Cowls/Beltrametti/Chatila/Chazerand/Dignum/Luetge/Madelin/Pagallo/Rossi/Schafer/Valcke/Vayena*, AI4People (n. 53).
67 *Ibid.*

complex ecosystem these technologies are part of, (d) it does not include the public interest as an accountable consideration.

A more just distribution of responsibilities, and therefore a more trustworthy ecosystem, might arise when transparency obligations are revised by (i) incorporating a realistic perception of what individuals can and will do and (ii) by extending transparency towards various other relations in the ecosystem, beyond the bilateral relation between individual and operating organization. We have highlighted several of these relations and provided suggestions for how transparency can have a role in them. How that plays out needs further attention in follow-up work.

A next step would be to define the actor-relation network around a concrete ADM use case, be it AI powered or not, and flesh out how in that network the transparency expectations exist, first in the normative perspective of law and ethics. It would certainly help the contextualisation of the outcome when the co-existence or interaction with incumbent transparency obligations is analysed more in-depth. With those we mean: transparency obligations that exist in a concrete use case but have nothing to do with GDPR or AI Act. It may be that incumbent obligations easily absorb the new ones, but more research is warranted. Examples of such situations are the disclosure between health care provider and patient, or the openness that is required for public administration bodies vis-à-vis citizens, the elected representatives, and the public at large.

Another line of research could follow-up on this and try to assess empirically what individual recipients appreciate as satisfactory information sharing in case of an ADM, both in process and in content, and under which conditions information sharing results in actionable knowledge. This would certainly move beyond the current research into algorithm appreciation,[68] as it takes algorithmic decision-making as a given and focuses more on contextual aspects. In that empirical project we would include

---

68 G. *Yalcin/E. Themeli/E. Stamhuis/S. Philipsen/S. Puntoni*, Perception of Justice by Algorithms, Artificial Intelligence and Law 2022, available at https://doi.org/10 .1007/s10506-022-09312-z (last access: 06.09.2022); N. *Helbergera/T. Araujob/C. H. de Vreeseb*, Who is the fairest of them all? Public attitudes and expectations regarding automated decision-making, Computer Law & Security Review 2020, available at https://www.sciencedirect.com/science/article/abs/pii/S02673649 20300613 (last access: 06.09.2022); *J. Gonçalves/I. Weber/G. M. Masullo/M. Torres da Silva/J. Hofhuis*, Common sense or censorship: How algorithmic moderators and message type influence perceptions of online content deletion, New Media & Society 2021, available at https://journals.sagepub.com/doi/10.1177/146144482110 32310 (last access: 06.09.2022).

the perceptions and practices of professionals that try to live up to the standards of transparency they are confronted with.

The impact that our revision of transparency might have on costs of compliance in organizations is another line of research that we have not pursued at all.[69] We may hypothesize that a better fit to the ecosystem increases satisfaction and therefore has a beneficial effect on cost-benefit ratios in the long run but whether this is the case is open for debate.

We can conclude by stating that, to live up to the promises of excellence and trust, the EU should start to conceptualize transparency broader than it currently does. It should move from bilateral to ecosystemic transparency if it wants trust in digital technologies to prevail as this will allow it to arrive at a fairer distribution of risks and responsibilities that will befit its value driven approach.

---

69 C. *Tikkinen-Piri/A. Rohunen/J. Markkula*, EU General Data Protection Regulation: Changes and implications for personal data collecting companies, Computer Law & Security Review 2018, 134.

Ent- und Redifferenzierung von Entscheidungsherstellung und -darstellung im Digitalen – Zum Wesensunterschied menschlicher und maschineller Entscheidungsbegründung aus rechtssoziologischer Perspektive

Tobias Mast

> *„Galileis Widerruf hatte auf die Bewegung der Gestirne keinerlei Einfluß. Im Bereich der Jurisprudenz wirkt jedoch die Leugnung der Wirklichkeit, anders als in der Naturwissenschaft, auf die Wirklichkeit zurück. "*[1]

Inwiefern die Herstellung einer Entscheidung in ihrer Darstellung abgebildet wird, darüber streitet die Rechtswissenschaft seit etwa 100 Jahren. Dabei spenden rechtssoziologische Einsichten seit inzwischen 50 Jahren der realistisch-pessimistischen Fraktion empirischen Aufwind. Wenn nun in den Köpfen der Justiz und Verwaltung aber doch vieles anders abläuft, als man annahm, als man die Lobgesänge auf die Funktionalitäten ihrer Begründungen und deren verfassungsrechtliche Rückbindungen verfasste, könnte dies legitimatorische Neubewertungen nahelegen.

Der vorliegende Beitrag setzt sich das nicht als Hauptziel, sondern möchte die Einwände gegen ein idealistisches, rein rechtlich geleitetes Begründungsverständnis als Vehikel dafür nutzen, Vor- und Nachteile automatisierter Entscheidungsbegründungen aufzuzeigen. Dafür sollen zunächst die Funktionen, die staatlichen Begründungen zugedacht sind und das hinter ihnen stehende verfassungsrechtliche Desiderat erörtert werden (A.). Anschließend befasst er sich mit der Differenzierung zwischen der Herstellung und Darstellung von Entscheidungen bei Menschen (B.), um sich sodann automatisierten, v.a. unter Einsatz von KI erstellten Entscheidungen zuzuwenden (C.) und schließlich deren Funktionalität auf einer hohen Generalisierungsebene zu vergleichen (D.).

Zwei klarstellende Eingrenzungen vorweg: Zum einen geht es mir nicht um die Qualität der *Entscheidungen selbst*. Zum anderen hinterfrage ich nicht die tatsächliche Umsetzbarkeit der in der KI-Forschung entwickelten

---

1 M. *Kriele*, Theorie der Rechtsgewinnung, Berlin 1976, S. 333 (Nachwort zur 2. Aufl.).

Erklärungsansätze,[2] sondern führe zu ihren Legitimitätspotenzialen für den Fall aus, dass sie ihren Versprechungen gerecht werden. Als Laie bin ich weitgehend gehalten, diese für bare Münze zu nehmen, ganz ähnlich den Empfängerinnen und Empfängern staatlicher Entscheidungsbegründungen.

A. Die Begründung und ihre Funktionen im Wandel der Zeit

I. Begründungsfunktionen

Mit ihrer Begründung erläutert die entscheidende Person, weswegen sie „so und nicht anders entscheidet, unabhängig davon ob [sie] dabei auf den klassischen Auslegungskanon, Präjudizieren oder allgemeine Gerechtigkeitsvorstellungen zurückgreift, eine verfassungskonforme Auslegung vornimmt oder die topischen [sic!] Methode anwendet."[3] Dass staatliche Stellen ihre Entscheidungen begründen, dient unterschiedlichen Funktionen. Im besten Falle werden Betroffene von ihrer Richtigkeit überzeugt und daher befriedet. Durch sie wird klar, was zukünftig geändert werden müsste, um ein anderes Ergebnis zu erzielen. Jedenfalls ermöglicht erst die Begründung den Betroffenen, eine Entscheidung zu kontrollieren und substantiierte Rechtsbehelfe gegen diese einzulegen. Innerhalb des Rechtsschutzsystems bildet die Begründung sodann die effizient abzuarbeitende Folie für höherrangige Instanzen. Die jeweils individuellen Chancen, auf Akzeptanz für einzelne Entscheidungen zu stoßen und damit justizielle Ressourcen zu schonen, kumulieren sodann der Idee nach auf systemischer Ebene zur Vertrauenswürdigkeit der Exekutive und Judikative.[4] Die-

---

2 Vgl. etwa die kritischen Beiträge von *C. Rudin*, Stop explaining black box machine learning models for high stakes decisions and use interpretable models instead, Nature Machine Intelligence 2019, 206 ff.; *K. de Vries*, in: L. Colonna/S. Greenstein (Hrsg.), Nordic Yearbook of Law and Informatics 2020–2021: Law in the Era of Artificial Intelligence, Stockholm 2022, S. 133 (151 ff.).

3 *U. Kischel*, Die Begründung, Tübingen 2003, S. 6; hieran anknüpfend *T. Wischmeyer*, Regulierung intelligenter Systeme, AöR 2018, 1 (56).

4 Vgl. die Funktionsbeschreibungen mit jeweils unterschiedlichen Schwerpunktsetzungen bei *F. Müller/R. Christensen*, Juristische Methodik I, Berlin 2013, Rn. 160; *Kischel*, Die Begründung (Fn. 3), S. 39 ff.; *K. Towfigh*, Die Pflicht zur Begründung von Verwaltungsentscheidungen nach dem deutschen und englischen Recht und ihre Europäisierung, Bern 2007, S. 11 ff.; *J. Saurer*, Die Begründung im deutschen, europäischen und US-amerikanischen Verwaltungsverfahrensrecht, VerwArch 2009, 364 (382 f.); *P. Stelkens*, in: ders./Bonk/Sachs (Hrsg.), VwVfG, 9. Aufl., Mün-

se Funktionen lassen sich zu unterschiedlichen Graden dem Demokratie- und Rechtstaatsprinzip zuordnen, in bestimmten Konstellationen auch weiteren Verfassungsnormen.[5]

II. Normative Kraft unter dem Vorbehalt des Möglichen

Die Art und Weise einer Begründung beeinflusst, in welchem Maße sie sich dazu eignet, die genannten Funktionen zu erfüllen und damit den verfassungsrechtlich gewünschten Zustand herzustellen. Die staatliche Begründungspflicht ist deswegen keine Regelvorgabe, die Begründungen zeitlos dieselbe Mindestqualität abverlangt, sondern ein *Prinzip*, das danach strebt, ihren Funktionen unter den jeweiligen tatsächlichen und rechtlichen Bedingungen gerecht zu werden.[6]

Dabei steht die Begründungspflicht wie jede Verfassungsvorgabe unter dem *Vorbehalt des tatsächlich Möglichen* und relativiert sich im Spannungsfeld zwischen Sein und Sollen in eine Vorgabe der möglichst weitgehenden Annäherung an den erwünschten Zustand.[7] Die normative Kraft der Verfassung kann schwanken. Mit *Konrad Hesse* lässt sich zu jedem Zeitpunkt gesellschaftlicher und technologischer Entwicklung fragen, ob „die verfassungsmäßige Ordnung den Gegebenheiten der geschichtlichen Situation entspricht".[8] Das verfassungsrechtliche Gewicht, das einer Begründung zukommt, variiert dabei in dem Maße, in dem sie nach ihrer

---

chen 2018, § 39 Rn. 1; *S. Wachter/B. Mittelstadt/C. Russell*, Counterfactual Explanations without Opening the Black Box: Automated Decisions and the GDPR, Harvard Journal of Law & Technology 2018, 841 (843 f., 863 ff.); *M. Martini*, Blackbox Algorithmus, Berlin 2019, S. 189 f.; *D. Roth-Isigkeit*, Die Begründung des vollständig automatisierten Verwaltungsakts, DÖV 2020, 1018 (1019); *F. Campos Zamora*, Das Problem der Begründung richterlicher Entscheidungen, Bern 2021, S. 194.

5 Ausführlich *Kischel*, Die Begründung, (Fn. 3), S. 63–142 m.w.N.

6 *Kischel*, Die Begründung (Fn. 3), S. 171 ff.; vgl. zur Prinzipienqualität materieller Gesetzespublizität und deren Verwirklichungsbedingungen im Digitalen *T. Mast*, Gesetzespublizität im Zeitalter der Vernetzung, ZG 2022, 35 (55 ff.).

7 *O. Depenheuer*, in: J. Isensee/P. Kirchhof (Hrsg.), Handbuch des Staatsrechts Band 12, 3. Aufl., Heidelberg 2014, § 269 Rn. 5 ff., 28; vgl. *S. Müller-Franken*, in: Staat im Wort: Festschrift für Josef Isensee, Heidelberg 2007, S. 229 (234 f.); *H. Kelsen*, in: M. Jestaedt (Hrsg.) Reine Rechtslehre, Studienauflage der 2. Aufl. 1960, Tübingen 2017, S. 37.; jüngst monographisch *L. Munaretto*, Der Vorbehalt des Möglichen, Tübingen 2022.

8 *K. Hesse*, Grundzüge des Verfassungsrechts der Bundesrepublik Deutschland, 20. Aufl., Heidelberg 1995, Rn. 692; vgl. *ders.*, Die normative Kraft der Verfassung, in: P. Häberle (Hrsg.), Ausgewählte Schriften, Heidelberg 1984, S. 10 ff.

konkreten Gestalt dazu geeignet ist, die ihr zugedachten Funktion zu erfüllen. Umgekehrt kann eine Begründung als so defizitär in Bezug auf eine ihr zugedachte Funktion ausfallen, dass sie der Norm, die die Begründungspflicht aufstellt, nicht mehr genügt.[9]

B. *Herstellung und Darstellung menschlicher Entscheidungen*

Nachdem die Multifunktionalität der Begründungen und das verfassungsrechtliche Streben nach ihrer Realisierung herausgestellt wurden, soll nun ein Blick auf die tatsächlichen Tücken dieses Unterfangens geworfen werden.

I. *Differenzierung*

Der Begründungsprozess einer rechtlichen Entscheidung lässt sich kategorial von ihrem Herstellungsprozess unterscheiden. Ob sie auch mündlich verkündet oder schriftlich verfasst ist, die Begründung teilt nicht einfach den Entscheidungsfindungsprozess mit. Die zunächst präferierten Alternativbegründungen, alsbald wieder verworfenen Gedanken und erst zögerlich verlassenen Sackgassen bleiben allesamt verborgen. Empirisch fraglich ist gar, ob sich überhaupt das nach dem letztlich gewählten Lösungspfad als entscheidungserheblich Ausgewiesene mit den Herstellungserwägungen deckt. Mit *Hermann Isay*, *Josef Esser* und *Martin Kriele* hatten bereits einige Klassiker der Rechtstheorie hieran Zweifel. Sie gingen stattdessen davon aus, dass die Suche und Darstellung eines juristischen Begründungsweges der eigentlichen Entscheidung nachlaufe, diese sekundär rechtfertige statt primär anleite.[10] Die Unterscheidung erlebte sodann ein Revival,

---

9 Vgl. *H. Christensen/R. Kudlich*, Theorie richterlichen Begründens, Berlin 2001, S. 327; *Kischel*, Die Begründung (Fn. 3), S. 336 f., 338.

10 *H. Isay*, Rechtsnorm und Entscheidung, Nachdruck Aalen 1970 [Erstveröffentlichung Berlin 1929], S. 153, 162 ff., 177; Darstellung bei *R. Nierwetberg*, Die Lehre Hermann Isays von Entscheidung und Rechtsnorm: Versuch einer Verbindung von Recht und Ethik, ARSP 1983, 529–549; *J. Esser*, Grundsatz und Norm in der richterlichen Fortbildung des Privatrechts: Rechtsvergleichende Beitr. zur Rechtsquellen- u. Interpretationslehre, Tübingen 1956, S. 256 f.; *Kriele*, Theorie der Rechtsgewinnung (Fn. 1) [Erstveröfflichung 1967], S. 21 ff., 169, 195; zu alldem *P. Schwerdtner*, Rechtswissenschaft und kritischer Rationalismus I, Rechtstheorie 1971, 67 (69 ff.); Kritik bei *K. Larenz*, Methodenlehre der Rechtswissen-

zuvörderst in Reaktion auf *Niklas Luhmanns* Monographie zur Automation der Verwaltung in den 60er- und *Rüdiger Lautmanns* entscheidungssoziologische Analyse der Justiz in den 70er-Jahren.[11] Auch für viele europäische Höchst- und Verfassungsgerichte ist betont worden, dass sich der Prozess und die Logik rechtlicher Begründung wesentlich von der eigentlichen Entscheidungsfindung unterscheiden.[12]

---

schaft, 6. Aufl., Berlin 1991, S. 348 f.; *K. Engisch*, Einführung in das juristische Denken, 12. Aufl., Berlin 2018, S. 77–80.

11 *N. Luhmann*, Recht und Automation in der öffentlichen Verwaltung, 2. Aufl., Berlin 1997 [Erstveröffentlichung 1966], S. 51 ff.; *H. Koch/H. Rüßmann*, Juristische Begründungslehre, München 1982, S. 115 ff.; *H. Koch*, Die Begründung von Grundrechtsinterpretationen, EuGRZ 1986, 345 (354 f.); *H. Trute*, in: E. Schmidt-Aßmann/W. Hoffmann-Riem (Hrsg.), Methoden der Verwaltungsrechtswissenschaft, Baden-Baden 2004, 293 ff.; *W. Hoffmann-Riem*, ebd., 9 (20 f.); *ders.*, »Außerjuridisches« Wissen, Alltagstheorien und Heuristiken im Verwaltungsrecht, VERW 2016, 1 (20); *ders.*, Innovation und Recht – Recht und Innovation, Tübingen 2016, S. 98 ff.; *Kischel*, Die Begründung (Fn. 3), S. 9 ff.; *K. Gräfin von Schlieffen*, Subsumtion als Darstellung der Herstellung juristischer Urteile, in: G. Gabriel/R. Gröschner (Hrsg.), Subsumtion. Schlüsselbegriff der juristischen Methodenlehre, Tübingen 2012, S. 379 (381 ff.); *A. Guckelberger/H. Kube*, E-Government: Ein Paradigmenwechsel in Verwaltung und Verwaltungsrecht?, VVDStRL 2019, 289 (319 f.); ähnlich *R. Alexy*, Theorie der juristischen Argumentation, 2. Aufl., Warschau 1991, S. 282: Unterscheidung zwischen Entdeckungsprozess und Rechtfertigungsprozess; *B. Schlink*, Die Entthronung der Staatswissenschaft durch die Verfassungsgerichtsbarkeit, Der Staat 1980, 73: Findung und Rechtfertigung; *W. Scheuerle*, Finale Subsumtionen: – Studien über Tricks und Schleichwege in der Rechtsanwendung, AcP 1967, 305 (308 f.); *Campos Zamora*, Das Problem der Begründung (Fn. 4), S. 200; ein anderes Begriffsverständnis zu Grunde legend *M. Jestaedt*, in: C. Engel/W. Schön (Hrsg.), Das Proprium der Rechtswissenschaft, Tübingen 2007, S. 241 (276).

12 Zur sog. Leseberatung und Entscheidungsgestaltung des BVerfG *U. Kranenpohl*, Hinter dem Schleier des Berufsgeheimnisses, Wiesbaden 2010, S. 98–100, 308–330; *A. Kaiser*, Herstellung und Darstellung von Entscheidungen des Bundesverfassungsgerichts, in: J. Masing /M. Jestaedt/O. Jouanjan/D. Capitant (Hrsg.), Entscheidungen und Entscheidungsprozesse der Rechtsprechung, Tübingen 2020, S. 1–15; zu EuGH und EGMR *T. Groß*, ebd., 71 (77 ff.); zum EuGH *U. Everling*, Zur Begründung der Urteile des Gerichtshofs der Europäischen Gemeinschaften, EuR 1994, 127 ff.; zum Conseil constitutionnel *T. Hochmann*, Entscheidungen und Entscheidungsprozesse der Rechtsprechung – Europa, in: J. Masing/M. Jestaedt/O. Jouanjan/D. Capitant (Hrsg.), Entscheidungen und Entscheidungsprozesse der Rechtsprechung, Tübingen 2020, S. 17 (23): Es gebe „sehr wohl juristische Debatten im Verfassungsrat", dieser achte aber darauf, „dass diese in der Entscheidung selbst nicht mehr durchscheinen." Ähnlich konstatiert für den Conseil d'État *B. Latour*, Die Rechtsfabrik – Eine Ethnographie des Conseil d'Etat, Göttingen 2016, S. 192, der Urteilstext sei „so trocken und kurz wie möglich" und kön-

II. Herstellungsmängel

Die Rechtstheorie streitet seit *Ronald Dworkin* wieder herzlich über die Existenz einzig richtiger Entscheidungen[13] und viele Personen in Justiz und Verwaltung werden sich dieser regulativen Idee zumindest als bewusster Fiktion verpflichtet fühlen. Systemisch operiert die Rechtspraxis ebenfalls im Grundsatz nach der Logik richtig-falsch und zieht sich nicht auf eine bloße Vertretbarkeitskontrolle zurück. Dies ist aber weniger rechtstheoretischen Überzeugungen geschuldet, denn praktischen Bedürfnissen eines nach Instanzenzügen geordneten Rechtssystems: Die hierarchisch gegliederte Autorität der Rechtsprechung soll eine einheitliche Rechtsauslegung gewährleisten, Orientierungskraft spenden und damit der Rechtssicherheit dienen.[14] Von diesem Grundsatz wird nur abgewichen, wo die anzuwendenden Normen ihrem Zweck nach keine eindeutige Regel aufstellen wollen oder wo staatliche Überprüfungsinstanzen an die Ränder ihrer Kompetenzen gelangen. So kontrollieren rechtsaufsichtsbefugte Stellen und Verwaltungsgerichte Verwaltungshandeln grundsätzlich in voller tatsächlicher und rechtlicher Hinsicht und reduzieren diese Kontrolldichte nur ausnahmsweise zu einem differenzierten Fehlermaßstab bei Letztent-

---

ne die richterliche Argumentation „niemals ausreichend erhellen". Vergleichend zum Stil höchstrichterlicher Entscheidungen *H. Kötz*, Über den Stil höchstrichterlicher Entscheidungen, RabelsZ 1973, 245–263.

13 *R. Dworkin*, Taking Rights Seriously, Cambridge Mass. 1978, S. 81, 279 und passim; hierzu *U. Neumann*, Wahrheit im Recht: Zur Problematik und Legitimität einer fragwürdigen Denkform, Baden-Baden 2004, S. 37 ff.; *S. Beck*, in: Schuhr (Hrsg.), Rechtssicherheit durch Rechtswissenschaft, Tübingen 2014, 11 ff.; *H.-H. Trute*, in ders./T. Gross/H. C. Röhl/C. Möllers (Hrsg.), Allgemeines Verwaltungsrecht – Zur Tragfähigkeit eines Konzepts, Tübingen 2008, S. 211 (215 ff.); *T. Herbst*, Die These der einzig richtigen Entscheidung Überlegungen zu ihrer Überzeugungskraft insbesondere in den Theorien von Ronald Dworkin und Jürgen Habermas, JZ 2012, 891 ff.; *U. Stelkens*, Die Idee der einzig richtigen, sich aus dem Gesetz ergebenden Entscheidung und ihre Bedeutung für die deutsche Rechtswissenschaft, in: van Oostrom/Weth (Hrsg.), Festschrift für Maximilian Herberger, Saarbrücken 2016, S. 895 ff.

14 *Neumann*, Wahrheit im Recht (Fn. 13), S. 58; vgl. *K. Röhl*, Fehler in Gerichtsentscheidungen, Die Verwaltung Beiheft 5, Berlin 2002, 67 (74); *J. Schuhr*, Zur Vertretbarkeit einer rechtlichen Aussage, JZ 2008, 603 (609); *M. Eichberger/J. Buchheister*, in: F. Schoch/J.-P. Schneider/W. Bier (Hrsg,), VwGO, 25. EL (2013), § 137 Rn. 92; *M. Jestaedt*, Autorität und Zitat. Anmerkungen zur Zitierpraxis des Bundesverfassungsgerichts, in: S. Detterbeck et. al. (Hrsg.): Recht als Medium der Staatlichkeit: Festschrift für Herbert Bethge zum 70. Geburtstag, Berlin 2009, 513 (514): „Richtersprüche sind denn auch nicht *Wahr*sprüche, sondern *Macht*sprüche".

scheidungskompetenzen der Verwaltung. Die Revisionsinstanz überprüft, ob die Rechtsauslegung durch die Vorinstanz „richtig" oder „falsch" erfolgte, wobei auch eine vertretbare, von der Revisionsinstanz aber nicht präferierte Interpretation in diesem Sinne falsch ist.[15] Das BVerfG nimmt schließlich bei Verfassungsfragen eine Vollprüfung für sich in Anspruch. In Abgrenzung zum Kompetenzbereich der Fachgerichtsbarkeit zieht es sich bei der Urteilsverfassungsbeschwerde durch die Heck'sche Formel und die Mephisto-Formel auf Prüfungen spezifischen Verfassungsrechts zurück und betrachtet die fachgerichtliche Rechtsanwendung und Auslegungsergebnisse zurückgenommen durch diese Lupe.[16]

Nun ist sich die Rechtswissenschaft einig darin, dass die Auslegung und Anwendung auch vollständig revisibelen Rechts nicht logisch aus Rechtsnorm und Tatbestand ableitbar ist.[17] Es existieren auch Optionenräume außerhalb von Ermessensermächtigungen.[18] Dementsprechend können sich auch Begründungen nicht in zwingenden Deduktionen erschöpfen.[19] Ein juristisches Entscheidungsergebnis und die Begründung dieses Ergebnisses lässt sich also nicht mit mathematischer Genauigkeit falsifizieren, was den entscheidenden Personen Möglichkeitsräume öffnet, in denen sie sich ohne Ansehensverlust positionieren können. Wo man sich nun im Raum positioniert, dafür sind auch außerjuridische Einflussfaktoren mitursächlich, seien es Vorverständnisse, Intuitionen, Emotionen oder unbewusste Sinnesregungen. Für den administrativen Bereich legte *Herbert A. Simon*

---

15 *Eichberger/ Buchheister*, VwGO (Fn. 14), § 137 Rn. 92.

16 *K. Schlaich/S. Korioth*, Das Bundesverfassungsgericht, 12. Aufl., München 2021, Rn. 292 ff. m.w.N.

17 *Luhmann*, Recht und Automation (Fn. 11), S. 54 ff.; *J. Brüggemann*, Die richterliche Begründungspflicht, Berlin 1971, S 47 f.; *Larenz*, Methodenlehre der Rechtswissenschaft (Fn. 10), S. 155; *K. Larenz/C. Canaris*, Methodenlehre der Rechtswissenschaft, 3. Aufl., Heidelberg 1995, S. 26; *Alexy*, Theorie der juristischen Argumentation (Fn. 11), S. 17; *Kischel*, Die Begründung (Fn. 3), S. 5, 8; *Müller/Christensen*, Juristische Methodik I (Fn. 4), Rn. 471; vgl. auch *W. Hoffmann-Riem*, "Außerjuridisches" Wissen, Alltagstheorien und Heuristiken im Verwaltungsrecht, Die Verwaltung 2016, 1 (1 ff.).

18 *W. Hoffmann-Riem*, Innovation und Recht – Recht und Innovation, Tübingen 2016, S. 99.

19 *H. Coing*, Die juristischen Auslegungsmethoden und die Lehren der allgemeinen Hermeneutik, Wiesbaden 1959, S. 22; *Kischel*, Die Begründung (Fn. 3), S. 8; vgl. *F. Brecher*, Scheinbegründungen und Methodenehrlichkeit im Zivilrecht, in: Festschrift für Arthur Nikisch, Tübingen 1958, 227 (235 ff.); *Alexy*, Theorie der juristischen Argumentation (Fn. 11), S. 43 f.; *K. Hesse*, Grundzüge des Verfassungsrechts der Bundesrepublik Deutschland, 20. Aufl., Heidelberg 1995, Rn. 76: „Fiktion und Lebenslüge der Juristen"; *Jestaedt*, Autorität und Zitat (Fn. 14), S. 514.

frühzeitig die begrenzte Rationalität des Entscheidungsprozesses dar[20] und auch die Forschung zum Entscheidungsverhalten der US-Justiz ist längst den Kinderschuhen entwachsen.

Immer neue Studien meinen den Einfluss unliebsamer Faktoren auf die Urteilspraxis feststellen zu können. Sie erkennen Auswirkungen der Ethnie[21] und anderer rechtlich irrelevanter Umstände[22] angeklagter Personen auf das von US-Bundesgerichten verhängte Strafmaß und stellen generell rolleninduzierte Wahrnehmungsverzerrungen bei Juristen fest.[23] Manche dieser Untersuchungen werden sehr kontrovers beurteilt und in ihren Ergebnissen angegriffen,[24] in ihrer Gesamtheit muss ihre Lektüre aber doch allzu idealistische Rollenbilder in Justiz und Verwaltung irritieren. Für das Anliegen dieses Beitrags bleibt festzuhalten, dass all dies, falls es denn geschieht, im Verborgenen geschieht und keinen Niederschlag in den Entscheidungsgründen findet.

---

20 *H. Simon*, Administrative Behavior: A Study of Decision-Making Processes in Administrative Organizations, 4. Aufl., New York 1997 [Erstveröffentlichung 1947], S. 92 ff.; generell mit vielen Beispielen zur begrenzten menschlichen Entscheidungsrationalität: T. Arntz, Systematische Urteilsverzerrungen richterlicher Entscheidungsfindung, JR 2017, 253–264; *C. Coglianese/A. Lai*, Algorithm Vs. Algorithm, Duke Law Journal 2022, 1281 (1288 ff.); *D. Nink*, Justiz und Algorithmen, Berlin 2021, S. 45 ff.

21 *D. Steffensmeier/S. Demuth*, Ethnicity and Sentencing Outcomes in U.S. Federal Courts: Who is Punished More Harshly?, American Sociological Review 2000, 705 (705 ff.); *C. Yang*, Free at Last? Judicial Discretion and Racial Disparities in Federal Sentencing, Journal of Legal Studies 2015, 75.

22 *A. J. Wistrich/J. J. Rachlinski/C. Guthrie*, Heart Versus Head: Do Judges Follow the Law or Follow Their Feelings?, Texas Law Review 2014, 855; *H. Spamann/L. Klöhn*, Justice Is Less Blind, and Less Legalistic, than We Thought: Evidence from an Experiment with Real Judges, Journal of Legal Studies 2016, 255; nicht bestätigt in *D. Klerman/H. Spamann*, Law Matters – Less Than We Thought, Legal Studies Research paper 2022, 19 (19).

23 *Z. Eigen/Y. Listokin*, Do Lawyers Really Believe Their Own Hype, and Should They? A Natural Experiment, Journal of Legal Studies 2012, 239; *C. Engel/A. Glöckner*, Role-Induced Bias in Court: An Experimental Analysis, Journal of Behavioral Decision Making 2013, 272; *H. Spamann*, Extension: Lawyers' Role-Induced Bias Arises Fast and Persists despite Intervention, Journal of Legal Studies 2020, 467.

24 Dies gilt insb. für die populäre Studie, nach welcher das Entscheidungsverhalten von Richtern von dem Umstand abhängt, ob diese zeitnah pausiert und eine Mahlzeit zu sich genommen haben: *L. Danziger/J. Levav/L. Avnaim-Pesso*, Extraneous factors in judicial decisions, PNAS 2011, 6889. Darstellung der Kritik an der Studie bei *K. Chatziathanasiou*, Der hungrige, ein härterer Richter? Zur heiklen Rezeption einer vielzitierten Studie, JZ 2019, 455.

III. Darstellungsmodalitäten

Nach *Paul Kirchhof* soll eine Begründung „Rationalität sprachlich vermitteln".[25] Es handelt sich bei der menschlichen Entscheidungsbegründung also um einen kommunikativen Akt, der verfassungsrechtlich vorgegeben wird und gesetzlich ausgestaltet meist bestimmte Mindestbestandteile enthalten muss, der inhaltlich aber nicht vollständig determiniert wird und gewisse Gestaltungsfreiräume – in staatsrechtlich-unorthodoxem Duktus könnte man auch sagen: Kreativität – belässt.[26]

Dabei wird die Abfassung der Begründung in Reinform dem tatsächlichen Zeitpunkt der inhaltlichen Festlegung regelmäßig nachfolgen. Kaum einmal wird die entscheidende Stelle einfach „darauf losschreiben". Schon der Aufbau von Verwaltungsakten und Gerichtsentscheidungen mit vorangestelltem Tenor und anschließender Begründung im „Urteilsstil" widerspricht so einer Logik.[27] Die Begründung kann nun nicht einfach das komplette Seelenleben der entscheidenden Person im Hinblick auf die konkrete Entscheidung offenlegen. Zwar fordern manche einen Grundsatz der *Begründungswahrheit* ein, nach welchem die Begründung die subjektiv-wirklichen Gründe des Entscheidungsträgers in rechtlicher Hinsicht wiederzugeben habe und keine vorgeschobenen Erwägungen oder bloße Begründbarkeitsoptionen liefern dürfe.[28]

---

25 *P. Kirchhof*, in: J. Isensee/P. Kirchhoff (Hrsg.), Handbuch des Staatsrechts der Bundesrepublik Deutschland – Band II Verfassungsstaat, 3. Aufl., Heidelberg 2004, § 20 Deutsche Sprache Rn. 27; aufgreifend *Kischel*, Die Begründung (Fn. 3), S. 338; *ders.*, in: H. Kube/G. Morgenthaler/R. Mellinghoff/U. Palm/T. Puhl/C. Seiler (Hrsg.), Leitgedanken des Rechts I, Heidelberg 2013, § 34 Rn. 1, 19.

26 Vgl. zu staatlichem Informationshandeln *T. Mast*, Staatsinformationsqualität, Berlin 2020, S. 171 f.

27 Vgl. auch § 39 Abs. 1 Satz 2 VwVfG: „Gründe mitzuteilen, die die Behörde zu ihrer Entscheidung *bewogen haben*" (Hervorhebung hier).

28 *Kischel*, Die Begründung (Fn. 3), S. 357 f.; *ders.*, Leitgedanken des Rechts I (Fn. 25) § 34 Rn. 1, 19; *W. Hoffmann-Riem*, in ders./E. Schmidt-Aßmann/A. Voßkuhle (Hrsg.), Grundlagen des Verwaltungsrechts Band I, 2. Aufl., München 2012, § 10 Rn. 31 f.; *ders.*, Innovation und Recht – Recht und Innovation: Recht im Ensemble seiner Kontexte, Tübingen 2016, S. 101: „Eine nur äußerlich eindrucksvolle, aber die wirkliche Vorgehensweise verdeckende Fassade kann nicht rechtsstaatliches Leitbild sein." A.A. *D. Roth-Isigkeit*, Die Begründung des vollständig automatisierten Verwaltungsakts, DÖV 2020, 1018 (1021 f.). Bzgl. § 39 I 2 VwVfG, dessen Wortlaut freilich so eine Begründungswahrheit mindestens anklingen lässt: *P. Stelkens* in: ders./Bonk/Sachs (Hrsg.), VwVfG (Fn. 4), § 39 Rn. 47; *M. Schuler-Harms*, in: F. Schoch/J. Schneider (Hrsg.), VwVfG, München 2020, § 39 Rn. 51, 53 f.

Selbst wenn man diesen Grundsatz anerkennt, ist sein Appell aber auf eine Rechtsentscheidung gemünzt und daher nach überwiegender Ansicht gegenständlich auf die *rechtlichen* Erwägungen der Person begrenzt.[29] Zu einer ersten Verengung des Begründungsumfangs kommt es also, indem etwaige soziologische, psychologische und anderen außerjuridische Entscheidungsmotive außenvor belassen werden. Zu einer zweiten Verengung kommt es, indem sodann aus sämtlichen rechtlichen Erwägungen jene herausgestellt werden, die letztlich als *entscheidungserheblich* gelten sollen.

Auch insoweit ist über seine normative Kraft indes noch nichts gesagt, denn unauthentische Begründungen können in vielen Schattierungen auftreten. Sie müssen keiner Unredlichkeit, sondern können auch schierer Unfähigkeit geschuldet sein. So scheint unsere Fähigkeit zur Introspektion recht beschränkt. Erkenntnisse der Psychologie und Neurobiologie deuten darauf hin, dass Menschen kaum Einblick in ihre kognitiven Prozesse höherer Ordnung haben und stattdessen kognitive Reaktionen auf Stimuli mit für plausibel erachteten Kausaltheorien zu erklären versuchen.[30] Insbesondere gehen einige Neurobiologen davon aus, dass unsere moralische Haltung nicht kausal für unsere Entscheidungen ist, sondern diese nachgelagert rechtfertigt.[31] Auch unser Gedächtnis ist fehleranfällig und täuscht uns mitunter.[32] Begründende Personen können danach schlicht nicht wissen, welche unbewussten Faktoren ihre Entscheidung mitbestimmt haben.

---

29 Vgl. *H. Trute*, Methoden der Verwaltungsrechtswissenschaft (Fn. 11), S. 301 f.; *Wischmeyer*, Regulierung intelligenter Systeme (Fn. 3), 1 (59); befürwortend *Koch/ Rüßmann*, Juristische Begründungslehre (Fn. 11), S. 1; *H. Koch*, Die Begründung von Grundrechtsinterpretationen, EuGRZ 1986, 345 (355); *R. Alexy*, Theorie der juristischen Argumentation (Fn. 11), S. 32 f.; kritisch *W. Hoffmann-Riem*, in: ders. (Hrsg.), Sozialwissenschaften im Öffentlichen Recht, München 1981, S. 10 ff.; ders., GVwR I (Fn. 29), § 10 Rn. 31 f.; empirisch *R. Lautmann*, Justiz – die stille Gewalt, Wiesbaden 2011 [Erstveröffentlichung 1972], S. 205 ff.

30 *R. Nisbett/T. Wilson*, Telling More Than We Can Know: Verbal Reports on Mental Processes, Psychological Review 1977, 231; *P. Johansson et al.*, Failure to detect mismatches between intention and outcome in a simple decision task, Science 2005, 116; *C. Petitmengin/A. Remillieux/B. Cahour/S. Carter-Thomas*, A gap in Nisbett and Wilson's findings? A first-person access to our cognitive processes, Consciousness and Cognition 2013, 654.

31 *C. Funk/M. Gazzaniga*, The functional brain architecture of human morality Current Opinion in Neurobiology 2009, 678 (680).

32 *E. Loftus*, Creating False Memories, Scientific American 1997, 70; *M. Steffens/S. Mecklenbräuker*, False memories: Phenomena, theories, and implications, Journal of Psychology 2017, 12 (12 ff.); *H. Welzer*, Das kommunikative Gedächtnis, 4. Aufl., München 2017, S. 19 ff.; *D. Myers/J. Wilson*, in: D. Myers (Hrsg.), Psychologie, 3. Aufl., Heidelberg 2014, S. 356 ff.

Besonders delikat wird es, wenn bewusste Taktiererei hinzukommt. Nach der Alltagserfahrung der allermeisten Personen, die professionelle Einblicke in Justiz und Verwaltung erhalten haben, werden die dortigen Amtsträger die aus ihrer subjektiven Sicht „richtige" Begründung angeben. Auch für das deutsche Gerichtswesen existiert aber durchaus ethnographische Forschung, die die taktischen und auf Selbstschutz gerichteten Erwägungen bei der Abfassung der Entscheidungsbegründung hervorhebt.[33] Hiernach soll es durchaus vorkommen, dass mehrere als vertretbar eingeschätzte Begründungen staatlich identifiziert und zwischen diesen sodann aus außerjuridischen Erwägungen ausgewählt wird. In solchen Fällen scheint es also zu einer Wechselwirkung zwischen Entscheidungsherstellung und -begründung insofern zu kommen, als das Wissen darum, die ausgegebene Entscheidung in einer den rechtlichen Anforderungen genügenden Weise begründen zu müssen, bereits auf den Entscheidungsprozess ausstrahlt.[34] Authentisch wird man solche Begründungen aber kaum mehr bezeichnen können. Das Entstehende ist kein Kondensat, keine Essenz, sondern im besten Falle eine Selektion, im schlechteren Falle ein Aliud.[35]

C. Herstellung und Darstellung automatisierter Entscheidungen

Bei automatisiert erstellten Entscheidungen, auch solchen die unter Einsatz künstlicher Intelligenz operieren, stehen der Herstellungsprozess und die Darstellung in einem epistemisch wesentlich anderen Verhältnis zueinander.

---

33 *Lautmann*, Justiz – die stille Gewalt (Fn. 29), S. 205 ff.
34 *W. Hoffmann-Riem*, in: E. Schmidt-Aßmann/W. Hoffmann-Riem (Hrsg.), Methoden der Verwaltungsrechtswissenschaft, Baden- Baden 2004, S. 9 (22 f.); *ders.*, in: GVwR I (Fn. 29), § 10 Rn. 33; *ders.*, Innovation und Recht – Recht und Innovation (Fn. 29), S. 99; ähnlich *Luhmann*, Recht und Automation in der öffentlichen Verwaltung (Fn. 11), S. 66; *Schlüter*, Das Obiter dictum, 1973, S. 97; *Koch*, EuGRZ 1986, 345 (355); *Alexy*, Theorie der juristischen Argumentation (Fn. 11) S. 282; *Christensen/Kudlich* (Fn. 10), S. 124 f.; *K. Gräfin von Schlieffen* (Fn. 11), S. 384; *T. Wischmeyer*, in: M. Eifert (Hrsg.), Digitale Disruption und Recht, Baden-Baden 2020, S. 73 (79); empirisch *Lautmann*, Justiz – die stille Gewalt (Fn. 29), S. 218–223.
35 Optimistischer *Kischel*, Die Begründung (Fn. 3), S. 13: minus statt aliud.

I. Ansätze

Viele Ansätze werden diskutiert, um unter KI-Einsatz zustande gekommene Entscheidungen zu erklären. Gemeint sind hier keine Systemtransparenz im Sinne der Einsicht in den Programmcode[36] oder generellen Funktionsbeschreibungen. Diese eignen sich nicht dazu, eine konkrete Entscheidung des Systems verständlich werden zu lassen und deren Qualität überprüfbar zu halten.[37]

Als übergeordnete Kategorien seien hier lediglich zwei genannt: Erstens existieren Ansätze, menschlich interpretierbare Informationen über die *herangezogenen Faktoren* und deren Gewichtung bereitzustellen.[38] Hierbei kann die Erklärbarkeit vereinfacht werden, indem nicht das gesamte Modell in seiner globalen Verhaltensweise (Model-Centric Explanations), son-

36 Hierzu *J. A. Kroll/J. Huey/S. Barocas/E. W. Felten/J. R. Reidenberg/D. G. Robinson/H. Yu*, Accountable Algorithms, University of Pennsylvania Law Review 2017, 633 (657 ff.); *A. Tutt*, An FDA forAlgorithms, Administrative Law Review 2017, 83 (110 f.); *L. Edwards/M. Vaele*, Slave to the Algorithm? Why a 'Right to an Explanation' Is Probably Not the Remedy You Are Looking For, Duke Law & Technology Review 2017, 18 (43, 65 f.); *M. Martini/D. Nink*, Wenn Maschinen entscheiden... – vollautomatisierte Verwaltungsverfahren und der Persönlichkeitsschutz, NVwZ – Extra 10/2017, 1 (11); *Martini*, Blackbox Algorithmus (Fn. 4), S. 181 f.; *K. Zweig*, Algorithmische Entscheidungen: Transparenz und Kontrolle, 2019, S. 8 f., abrufbar unter https://www.kas.de/de/analysen-und-argumente/detail/-/content/al gorithmische-entscheidungen-transparenz-und-kontrolle (zuletzt abgerufen: 14.09.2022); *Wischmeyer*, Regulierung intelligenter Systeme (Fn. 3), 1 (53); *T. Wischmeyer*, in: ders./T. Rademacher (Hrsg.), Regulating Artificial Intelligence, Heidelberg 2020, 75 (86 Rn. 23); *Nink*, Justiz und Algorithmen, (Fn. 20), S. 339.
37 *Wischmeyer*, Regulierung intelligenter Systeme (Fn. 3), 1 (53); *F. Doshi-Velez/M. Kortz/R. Budish/C.Bavitz/S. Gershman/D. O'Brien/K. Scott/S. Schieber/J. Waldo/D. Weinberger/A. Welle/A. Wood*, Accountability of AI Under the Law: The Role of Explanation, v3 (2019), S. 4, abrufbar unter https://arxiv.org/abs/1711.01134 (zuletzt abgerufen: 14.09.2022) *M. Kaminsky*, in: W.Barfield (Hrsg.), The Cambridge Handbook of the Law of Algorithms, Cambridge 2021, 121 (127 ff.).
38 Vgl. *S. Wachter/B. Mittelstadt/L. Floridi.*, Why a Right to Explanation of Automated Decision-Making Does Not Exist in the General Data Protection Regulation, International Data Privacy Law 2017, 76 (78 f.); *K. Atkinson/T. Bench-Capon/D. Bollegala*, Explanation in AI and law: Past, present and future, Artificial Intelligence 2020, 4 f.; *C. Busch*, Algorithmic Accountability, 2018, S. 57 f., abrufbar unter https://www.abida.de/de/blog-item/gutachten-algorithmic-accountability (zuletzt abgerufen: 14.09.2022); *Doshi-Velez/Kortz/Budish/Bavitz/Gershman/O'Brien/ Scott/Schieber/Waldo/Weinberger/Welle/Woo*, Accountability of AI Under the Law: The Role of Explanation (Fn. 37), S. 4; *Wischmeyer* (Fn. 36), S. 87 f.

dern lediglich die für den konkreten Input lokal relevant gewordenen Faktoren erklärt werden (Subject-Centric Explanations).[39]

In Verwandtschaft zu letzteren zielen zweitens *kontrafaktische Erklärungsansätze* auf die Offenlegung (nur) der Faktoren, die geändert werden müssten, um das Ergebnis (in der gewünschten Weise) zu beeinflussen. Sie zeigen mithin hypothetische Szenarien auf und ermöglichen dadurch, das eigene Verhalten anzupassen oder die Entscheidung anzufechten, ohne den Entscheidungsprozess in all seinen Details exakt nachzeichnen zu können.[40]

II. Authentizität

Insofern betont insbesondere *Thomas Wischmeyer*, dass intelligente Systeme und ihre Entscheidungen nicht per se intransparenter sind als ihre menschlichen Pendants.[41] Während nämlich der Mensch tatsächlich eine „black box" ist, dessen Begründungsauthentizität absehbar nicht kontrolliert werden kann,[42] ist diese bei algorithmischen Entscheidungssystemen,

---

39 *Edwards/Vaele*, Slave to the Algorithm? (Fn. 37), 18 (55 ff.); *A. Deeks*, The Judical Demand for Explainable Artificial Intelligence, Columbia Law Review 2019, 1829 (1835 ff.); *Doshi-Velez/Kortz/Budish/Bavitz/Gershman/O'Brien/Scott/Schieber/Waldo/Weinberger/Welle/Woo*, Accountability of AI Under the Law: The Role of Explanation, (Fn. 37), S. 13.

40 Dazu *Wachter/Mittelstadt/Russell*, Counterfactual Explanations without Opening the Black Box (Fn. 4), 841 (860 f.); *Deeks*, The Judical Demand for Explainable Artificial Intelligence (Fn. 40), 1829 (1836 f.); *Doshi-Velez/Kortz/Budish/Bavitz/Gershman/O'Brien/Scott/Schieber/Waldo/Weinberger/Welle/Woo*, Accountability of AI Under the Law: The Role of Explanation, (Fn. 37), S. 5, 14; *Wischmeyer*, Digitale Disruption und Recht (Fn. 36), S. 91; (noch) skeptisch *A. Páez*, Artificial Explanations: The Epistemological Interpretation of Explanation in AI, Synthese 2009, 131 (143 ff.).

41 *Wischmeyer*, Regulierung intelligenter Systeme (Fn. 37), 1 (8, 44 f., 54); *ders.* Regulating Artificial Intelligence (Fn. 36), S. 78; dem folgend *Nink*, Justiz und Algorithmen (Fn. 20), S. 337 f.; aus dem englischsprachigen Raum *J. Kleinberg/J. Ludwig/S. Mullainathan/C. R. Sunstein*, Algorithms as discrimination detectors, PNAS 2020, 30096 (30097); *Coglianese/Lai*, Algorithm Vs. Algorithm (Fn. 21), 1281 (1286 f., 1313).

42 Vgl. *Kischel*, Die Begründung (Fn. 3), S. 10; *C. Ernst*, Algorithmische Entscheidungsfindung und personenbezogene Daten, JZ 2017, 1026 (1029); *Scheuerle*, Finale Subsumtionen (Fn. 11), 305 (340 Fn. 129): „die (psychischen) Fakten des (tatsächlichen) Zustandekommens der Entscheidung [sind] hinter richterlichen Stirnen wohltuend verborgen und hoffentlich durch keinen technischen „Fortschritt" je ans Licht zu zerren."; *A. Posner*, How Judges Think, Cambridge Mass.

für die ein Erklärungstool existiert, lediglich von der korrekten Programmierung (und Anwendung) des Erklärungstools abhängig und als solche überprüfbar. Zwar wird auch ein Mensch in seiner Entscheidungsbegründung regelmäßig Faktoren anführen und gewichten und mitunter auch auf kontrafaktische Argumente zurückgreifen[43] (ohne dass damit notwendigerweise ein obiter dictum geäußert würde[44]). Bei alldem kann man sich aber nie sicher sein, ob all dies eine bloße Fassade darstellt, ob im Hintergrund andere Faktoren wirkten und die behaupteten kontrafaktischen Gegebenheiten bei ihrem Vorliegen doch nicht als ausschlaggebend betrachtet worden wären.

In gewisser Weise kommt es bei automatisierten Erklärungsprogrammen demgegenüber zu einer *Ent-Differenzierung*: Die so erzeugten Darlegungen sind zwar nicht identisch mit den Herstellungen, häufig werden sie von zweiten Systemen erstellt, die an die eigentlichen Entscheidungssysteme anknüpfen ohne notwendigerweise selbst vollständigen Einblick in deren Programmabläufe zu haben.[45] Sie können in ihrem Zuschnitt und ihrer Verständlichkeit auch unterschiedlich geeignet sein. Aber während unser menschliches Gedächtnis uns mitunter täuscht und wir uns auch sonst nicht immer verstehen, haben KI-Systeme ein prinzipiell fehlerfreies Gedächtnis, unterliegen keinen kognitiven Verzerrungen oder sozialen Zwängen. Darauf aufsetzende Erklärungsprogramme glätten nicht taktisch, sparen nichts aus Selbstschutzerwägungen aus, sondern liefern soweit technisch möglich die nackte Wahrheit. Sie profitieren davon, dass sich intelligente Systeme durch eine *Plastizität* auszeichnen, die ihnen er-

---

2008: „judges' decision-making methods are often and inevitably opaque because they involve telescoped rather than step-by-step thinking".

43 *T. Miller*, Explanation in artificial intelligence: Insights from the social sciences, Artificial Intelligence 2019, Kapitel 1.2 Ziffer 1, Kapitel 2.3 m.w.N.

44 Eine staatliche Stelle kann etwa einen rechtlichen Maßstab aufzeigen und dann darlegen, inwiefern die betroffene Person diesem nicht genügt, welche nicht gegebenen Aspekte bei ihrem Vorliegen mithin zu einer anderen Entscheidung geführt hätten.

45 Die Vorteile dieses Ansatzes hervorhebend *Doshi-Velez/Kortz/Budish/Bavitz/Gershman/O'Brien/Scott/Schieber/Waldo/Weinberger/Welle/Woo*, Accountability of AI Under the Law: The Role of Explanation, (Fn. 37) S. 16 f.; *L. Edwards/M. Vaele*, Slave to the Algorithm? (Fn. 37), 18 (64 f.); sehr kritisch demgegenüber *C. Rudin*, Stop explaining black box machine learning models for high stakes decisions and use interpretable models instead, Nature Machine Intelligence 2019, 206–215; vgl. auch *Wischmeyer*, Regulierung intelligenter Systeme (Fn. 3), 1 (61): „Langfristiges Ziel ist hier, intelligente Systeme so zu programmieren, dass sie selbst Auskunft über die ihre Entscheidung „tragenden" Gründe geben und diese in einer für menschliche Empfänger verständlichen Form aufbereiten können."

laubt, „sich leichter und präziser als menschliche Entscheider bzw. die tradierten Modi der Verhaltenssteuerung programmieren [zu] lassen".[46] Im besten Fall können die gespeicherten Inputs, Zwischenschritte und Outputs exakt wiedergegeben werden, ohne kognitiven Unzulänglichkeiten oder strategischen Glättungen zu unterliegen.[47] Dem Resultat ist dann eine höhere „Methodenehrlichkeit"[48] zu attestieren. Zwar mögen auch Fehlfunktionen von Erklärungstools auftreten, die im Ausgangspunkt menschlichen Begründungsdefiziten entsprechen. Etwaige Programmfehler können aber, nachdem sie erkannt wurden, ausgemerzt werden, menschliche Denkmuster kaum. Eine gelogene Begründung einer Erklärungssoftware – erinnert sei an die geheime Volkswagen-Software, die in Testszenarien andere Werte als im Normalbetrieb ausgab ("Abgasskandal") – wäre eine Lüge der Programmierer, die im Code der Erklärungssoftware niedergeschrieben und damit entdeckbar wäre.

Wenn es dann doch zu *Re-Differenzierungen* kommt, ist dies anders als bei menschlichen Begründungen nicht subjektintern bedingt, sondern dem Zweck geschuldet, die Verständnishorizonte der Erklärungsempfänger zu berücksichtigen. Im Ausgangspunkt ähnlich einer menschlichen Rechtsbegründung wird auch für KI-Erklärungsansätze mit Blickverengungen und Komplexitätsreduzierungen gearbeitet.[49] Jede Erklärung, ob menschlich oder maschinell getätigt, unterliegt einem Zielkonflikt zwi-

---

46 *T. Wischmeyer*, AöR 143 (2018), 1 (45); vgl. auch *Luhmann* (Fn. 11), S. 49; *C. Ernst*, Algorithmische Entscheidungsfindung und personenbezogene Daten, JZ 2017, 1026 (1027 f.).

47 *Doshi-Velez/Kortz/Budish/Bavitz/Gershman/O'Brien/Scott/Schieber/Waldo/Weinberger/ Welle/Woo*, Accountability of AI Under the Law: The Role of Explanation (Fn. 37), S. 18; *Coglianese/Lai*, Algorithm Vs. Algorithm (Fn. 21), 1281 (1309); *W. Hoffmann-Riem*, Recht im Sog der digitalen Transformation, Tübingen 2022, S. 54.

48 Zum Begriff *F. Brecher*, in: Festschrift für Arthur Nikisch, Tübingen 1958, S. 277 ff.; *W. Scheuerle*, Finale Subsumtionen (Fn. 11), 429 (436); *Brüggemann*, Die richterliche Begründungspflicht (Fn. 17), S. 72 ff.; *H. Haferkamp*, in: K. P. Berger/G. Borges/H. Herrmann/A. Schlüter/U. Wackerbarth (Hrsg.), Zivil- und Wirtschaftsrecht im Europäischen und Globalen Kontext – Festschrift für Norbert Horn zum 70. Geburtstag, Berlin 2006; *H. Hamann/L. Hoeft*, Die empirische Herangehensweise im Zivilrecht. Lebensnähe und Methodenehrlichkeit für die juristische Analytik?, AcP 2017, 311 ff.

49 *Doshi-Velez/Kortz/Budish/Bavitz/Gershman/O'Brien/Scott/Schieber/Waldo/Weinberger/ Welle/Woo*, Accountability of AI Under the Law: The Role of Explanation (Fn. 37), S. 13; *de Vries*, Nordic Yearbook of Law and Informatics 2020–2021 (Fn. 2), S. 149.

schen Verständlichkeit und Genauigkeit.[50] Gut gestaltete Begründungsprogramme, die sich einer hohen Verständlichkeit verschreiben, liefern als Resultate aber im besten Sinne Kondensate, kein aliud.

D. *Funktionalitätsvergleich auf hoher Generalisierungsebene*

Im Folgenden soll der Versuch unternommen werden, die Verwirklichungschancen der Begründungsfunktionen auf einer hohen Generalisierungsebene im menschlichen wie maschinellen Kontext zu vergleichen. Hierbei müssen zunächst die unterschiedlichen *Gegenstände* menschlicher und maschineller Begründungen berücksichtigt werden. Während entscheidende Personen Gründe dafür angeben, weswegen sie die entsprechende Entscheidung aus dem Recht herleiten, beschränken sich Methoden der „Explainable AI" regelmäßig darauf, Entscheidungen rein tatsächlich erklärbar zu machen. Ihre Erklärungen sind vor allem tatsächliche Beschreibungen, welche Datenbereiche bzw. Inputfaktoren eine Rolle für eine Klassifizierung gespielt haben. Aktuelle Anwendungsfälle automatisierter Entscheidungssysteme würden allenfalls Aussagen zu einzelnen Tatbestandsvoraussetzungen oder Rechtsfolgenbestandteilen, etwa der Zuverlässigkeit einer Person oder der adäquaten Forderungs- oder Strafhöhe treffen. Sie stellen aber keine Rechtfertigung dafür dar, weswegen die getroffene Entscheidung sich aus dem Recht ergibt, also rechtlich richtig bzw. vertretbar ist (insbesondere auf welcher Rechtsgrundlage sie beruht, welche Tatbestandsvoraussetzungen diese hat oder welche methodisch rückgebundenen Argumente für oder gegen sie gesprochen haben).

Etwaige Versuche, die „Explainable AI" um juristische Erklärungszusammenhänge zu erweitern, könnten auf dem aktuellen Stand der Technik kaum mit einer auf juristischem Wissen gründenden Argumentation verglichen werden.[51] Es wird zwar mitunter für möglich gehalten, irgendwann eine KI zu entwickeln, die Strukturen in menschlichen Rechtstex-

---

50 *Edwards/Vaele*, Slave to the Algorithm? (Fn. 37), 18 (59); *Wischmeyer* (Fn. 36), S. 88 Rn. 26; *H. Asghari/N. Birner/A. Burchardt/D. Dicks/J. Faßbender/N. Feldhus/F. Hewett/V. Hofmann/M. C. Kettemann/ W. Schulz/J. Simon/J. Stolberg-Larsen/T. Züger*, What to explain when explaining is difficult?, 2022, S. 7 f, abrufbar unter: https://graphite.page/explainable-ai-report/ (zuletzt abgerufen: 15.09.2022).
51 *M. Herberger*, Künstliche Intelligenz, NJW 2018, 2825 (2828); *Nink*, Justiz und Algorithmen (Fn. 20), S. 228; Darstellung eines Ansatzes bei *V. Herold*, in: J. Taeger (Hrsg.), Rechtsfragen digitaler Transformationen, Oldenburg (Oldenburg) 2018, S. 453 (458 f.).

ten erfassen und mittels Sprachtaktiken und gelernten Reaktionsmustern rechtliche Fragen klären und passende Begründungen produzieren kann.[52] Dabei würde eine rechtliche Begründung aber lediglich *simuliert*.[53] *Thomas Wischmeyer* bemüht insofern das Bild der KI-basierten Rechtsargumentation als eines schlechten Sachbearbeiters „der die Rechtsmaterie nicht ‚verstanden' hat und sich daher mit der Lektüre ähnlicher Bescheide behilft, um daraus mit einer gewissen Trefferquote die zutreffenden Textbausteine zu kopieren."[54] Um solche Ansätze soll es im Folgenden nicht gehen.

Des Weiteren können die Eigenheiten von einzelnen Rechtsbereichen, Anwendungsfällen oder Erklärungsansätzen im vorliegenden Rahmen nicht berücksichtigt werden. Die daraus resultierenden Ungenauigkeiten bitte ich zu entschuldigen; sie sind der Preis dafür, im Rahmen eines Kolloquiums die Eigenschaften eines Meta-Prozesses skizzieren zu können. Mir scheinen sich jedenfalls sämtliche Begründungsfunktionen im Mensch-Maschinen-Vergleich spezifisch zu unterscheiden.[55]

I. Selbstkontrolle

Bei Menschen erfolgt eine *Selbstkontrolle* durch das Begründungserfordernis bereits ex ante während des Abfassungsprozesses disziplinierend und dient der Selbstvergewisserung der Rechtmäßigkeit.[56] Der Herstellungsprozess wird hierdurch angeleitet oder wenigstens irritiert.

---

52 *J. Wagner*, Legal Tech und Legal Robots in Unternehmen und den diese beratenden Kanzleien, BB 2017, 898 (902 f.); *A. Adrian*, Der Richterautomat ist möglich – Semantik ist nur eine Illusion, Rechtstheorie 2017, 77 (95 ff.; 112 ff.); Darstellung bei von *A. von Graevenitz*, „Zwei mal Zwei ist Grün" – Mensch und KI im Vergleich, ZRP 2018, 238 (240); *Wischmeyer*, Digitale Disruption und Recht (Fn. 34), S. 88 f.

53 Vgl. *Adrian*, Der Richterautomat ist möglich (Fn. 53), 77 (79 und passim); *von Graewnitz*, „Zwei mal Zwei ist Grün" (Fn. 53), 238; *Nink*, Justiz und Algorithmen (Fn. 20), S. 228.

54 *Wischmeyer*, Digitale Disruption und Recht (Fn. 34), S. 87 f.; ähnlich *V. Herold*, Rechtsfragen digitaler Transformationen (Fn. 51), S. 462; vgl. auch *Nink*, Justiz und Algorithmen (Fn. 20), S. 337: „Wozu der Vorgang dient, welchen Sinn dies hat, was daraus folgt, ist für die Maschine weder erkennbar noch relevant."

55 Meines Erachtens zu stark nivellierend *F. Doshi-Velez et. al.*, Accountability of AI Under the Law: The Role of Explanation (Fn. 37), S. 18: „the significance of the decision, the relevant social norms, the extent to which an explanation will inform future action – are likely to be the same"; *T. Wischmeyer*, in: Regulating Artificial Intelligence (Fn. 37), S. 78.

56 *Kischel*, Die Begründung (Fn. 3), S. 40 f., 43.

Demgegenüber werden automatisiert erstellte Begründungen aktuell, soweit ersichtlich, nicht mit den eigentlichen ML-Prozessen dergestalt rückgekoppelt, dass gerade die Begründung dem Programm als Kontrollmaßstab dient. Automatisiert ablaufende Entscheidungsprozesse müssen auch nicht dazu angehalten werden, sich vorschnell festzulegen. Automatisierte Begründung sind zwar den Programmierern sowohl vor dem eigentlichen Programmeinsatz in der Trainingsphase sowie ex post nützlich (Selbstkontrolle i.w.S.): Aufgrund der hohen Begründungsauthentizität ist es möglich, Fehler und Ungewolltes zu erkennen und auszumerzen.[57] Die Art der Erklärung, die für die Entwickler interessant ist, unterscheidet sich aber meist erheblich von denen, die für Betroffene und interessierte Dritte adäquat wäre.

II. Befriedung

Hinsichtlich der *Chance, einen Rechtsstreit zu befrieden* als empirischer Frage hat die menschliche Begründung einen Trumpf und einen Malus. Zwar kann bereits der Umstand, dass das gefundene Ergebnis rechtlich rückgebunden ist, befrieden. Dennoch dürfte tendenziell abträglich sein, dass der menschliche Entscheidungsfindungsprozess nicht nachvollziehbar ist und Raum für allerlei Spekulation belässt. Andererseits können Menschen bei der Abfassung ihrer Begründungen aus der Gesamtheit ihrer Erfahrungen schöpfen und damit maßgeschneidert den Kontext, die Bedürfnisse des Einzelfalls und den Erwartungshorizont ihres Gegenübers berücksichtigen.[58] Sie können auch Verständnis für die Notlage oder Unzufriedenheit einer beteiligten Person artikulieren, ohne dieser Recht zu geben.

Die Befriedungsfunktion steht und fällt bei KI-gestützten Systemen damit, ob der gewählte Erklärungsansatz den Betroffenen verständlich macht, weswegen eine konkrete Entscheidung getroffen wurde. Auch sie unterliegen der Adressatenproblematik und müssen sich um eine kontext-

---

57 Vgl. *Martini*, Blackbox Algorithmus (Fn. 4), S. 190.
58 *Miller*, Explanation in artificial intelligence (Fn. 44), Kapitel 1.2 Ziffer 4, Kapitel 4, Kapitel 5 m.w.N.; *Doshi-Velez/Kortz/Budish/Bavitz/Gershman/O'Brien/Scott/Schieber/Waldo/Weinberger/Welle/Woo*, Accountability of AI Under the Law: The Role of Explanation (Fn. 37), S. 18; vgl. *Kischel*, Die Begründung, (Fn. 3), S. 340 ff., 379 ff.; *Mast*, Staatsinformationsqualität (Fn. 27), S. 282 ff., 308 ff.

spezifische, benutzerfreundliche Art und Weise der Erklärung bemühen.[59] Rein technische Informationen oder Hinweise auf relevant gewordene „Datenbereiche" genügen dem jedenfalls nicht. Solche müssten zunächst von menschlichen Experten interpretiert und sodann den betroffenen Laien übersetzt werden. Ohne eine solche Übersetzungsleistung könnten hochkomplexe Erklärungen Betroffene überwältigen und eher abschrecken. Aber selbst in den Fällen, in denen eine benutzerfreundliche Erklärung in natürlicher Sprache gelingt, dürften automatisierte Entscheidungen von manchen als unheimlich empfunden und daher kaum von dieser befriedet werden. Falls das Bewusstsein um deren gesteigerte Authentizität zunimmt, liegen gegenläufige Prozesse nahe. Was die Möglichkeiten der Eigenwerbung und Kritikantizipation anbelangt, bleiben automatisiert erstellte Begründungen deutlich hinter ihren menschlichen Pendants zurück, solange diese keine entsprechende Empathie entwickeln.[60]

III. Ausrichtung zukünftigen Verhaltens

Was die *Ausrichtung zukünftigen Verhaltens* anbelangt, erlauben begründete Einzelfallentscheidungen im Ausgangspunkt entsprechende Verhaltensausrichtungen. Allerdings kann man sich in den Fällen, in denen Menschen kontrafaktisch argumentieren, realiter nicht absolut sicher sein, ob im Falle des Vorliegens der verneinten Aspekte nicht doch ein anderer Weg für dasselbe Ergebnis eingeschlagen worden wäre.

Demgegenüber ist bei Entscheidungen deterministischer Systeme eine Verhaltensausrichtung vollumfänglich möglich. Bei ML-Systemen ermöglichen kontrafaktische Erklärungen zwar, die tatsächliche Konsistenz zwischen unterschiedlichen Entscheidungen desselben Systems zu überprüfen.[61] Allerdings erlaubt der Umstand, dass zu einem bestimmten Zeitpunkt ein bestimmter Input zu einem Ergebnis geführt hätte, aufgrund

---

59 Überblick m.w.N. bei *Miller*, Explanation in artificial intelligence (Fn. 44), Kapitel 5.3; *K. Sokol/P. Flach*, Explainability Fact Sheets: A Framework for Systematic Assessment of Explainable Approaches, FAT* 2020, 56 (59 ff.).

60 Darstellung erster Ansätze *Miller*, Explanation in artificial intelligence (Fn. 44), Kapitel 5.3.

61 *Doshi-Velez/Kortz/Budish/Bavitz/Gershman/O'Brien/Scott/Schieber/Waldo/Weinberger/ Welle/Woo*, Accountability of AI Under the Law: The Role of Explanation (Fn. 37), S. 5; *Coglianese/Lai*, Algorithm Vs. Algorithm (Fn. 21), 1281 (1307).

der ständigen Weiterentwicklung des ML-Systems keine sichere Prognose, ob dies auch zukünftig der Fall sein wird.[62]

IV. Rechtsschutz

Unter formeller Betrachtung wird Rechtssicherheit bei menschlichen Entscheidungen dadurch geleistet, dass nicht irgendwelche implizit gebliebenen Erwägungen der entscheidenden Stelle, sondern die Entscheidungsbegründung den Maßstab der weiteren Überprüfung im Instanzenzug bildet. Allerdings kann neben der nicht völlig auszuräumenden Möglichkeit, dass verdeckt gebliebene Diskriminierungen zu einer Entscheidung geführt haben, auch nicht ausgeschlossen werden, dass eine Stelle ihre Entscheidung unter Strapazierung des tatsächlichen Geschehens „rechtsmittelfest" formuliert.[63] „In der Praxis orientiert die Darstellung sich allerdings häufig vorrangig nur an dem Ziel, die Unangreifbarkeit der Entscheidung vor der Kontrollinstanz zu sichern".[64] Jedenfalls denkbar sind damit Situationen, in denen die entscheidende Stelle die Position derjenigen Seite stärkt, die sie im Recht sieht und die Chancen zur höherinstanzlichen Abänderung im Interesse der anderen Seite schmälert.

Sowohl die Faktorenerörterung als auch kontrafaktische Erklärungen erlauben bei KI-basierten Entscheidungen eine Überprüfung anhand der rechtlichen Vorgaben im Instanzenzug. Anders als bei menschlichen Begründungen kann bei automatisiert erstellten Begründungen taktische Kosmetik ausgeschlossen werden, was die Rechtsschutzfunktion stärkt. Demgegenüber wird die Rechtsschutzfunktion geschwächt, wenn

---

62 Vgl. *R. Binns*, Analogies and Disanalogies Between Machine-Driven and Human-Driven Legal Judgement, CRCL online-first 2020, 1 (5 f.), abrufbar unter: https://journalcrcl.org/crcl/article/view/5 (zuletzt abgerufen: 15.09.2022); *K. Kaminski*, Gründe geben. Maschinelles Lernen als Problem der Moralfähigkeit von Entscheidungen, in: K. Wiegerling/M. Nerurkar/C. Wadephul, Datafizierung und Big Data, Heidelberg 2020, 151 (157); *Wischmeyer*, Regulating Artificial Intelligence (Fn. 37), S. 82 Rn. 15. Daran ändert auch der „rückblickende Charakter" von ML-Systemen, der daraus folgt, dass Prognosen stets anhand des benutzten Datenmaterials erfolgen, nichts, vgl. *Herold*, Rechtsfragen digitaler Transformationen (Fn. 51), S. 462 f.

63 Vgl. *Jestaedt*, Autorität und Zitat (Fn. 14), S. 516; *C.-O. Bauer/F. Graf Westphalen/G. Otto/H.-G. Weiss/G. Heine*, Das Recht zur Qualität, Heidelberg 1996, S. 376.

64 *Hoffmann-Riem*, GVwR I (Fn. 29), § 10 Rn. 32; empirisch *Lautmann*, Justiz – die stille Gewalt (Fn. 29), S. 206.

bei künstlichen neuronalen Netzwerken kontrafaktische Erklärungen versagen, etwa weil nicht sämtliche Entscheidungsschritte zwischen Input und Output nachvollzogen werden können.[65] Im Unterschied zum Menschen, bei dem die einzelnen Gedankenschritte ebenfalls im Dunkeln verbleiben, aber die hiernach verfasste Begründung auf ihre Stringenz und Folgerichtigkeit überprüft werden kann, kann ein „Explainable AI"-Einsatz aufgrund seiner authentischeren Beziehung zum eigentlichen Herstellungsprozess keine Stringenz oder Folgerichtigkeit darstellen, wo diese im Entscheidungsprozess nicht erkennbar sind. Da gerichtlich primär das *Ergebnis* des automatisierten Entscheidungsvorgangs überprüft wird,[66] führen entsprechende Dunkelfelder zwar nicht dazu, dass Rechtsschutz per se verstellt wäre; ohne genau nachvollziehen zu können, inwiefern die herangezogenen Kriterien zu dem Ergebnis geführt haben, lassen sich aber etwa Diskriminierungen kaum nachweisen.[67] Dies gilt umso mehr, als uns menschliche Ausflüchte und Täuschungsmotive noch vergleichsweise intuitiv sind, während Fehlfunktionen eines automatisierten Systems maximal unintuitiv ausfallen können.

V. Entlastung des Justizsystems

Menschliche Begründungen *entlasten das Justizsystem* potentiell in doppelter Hinsicht. Zum einen sinkt die Wahrscheinlichkeit, dass das Rechtschutzsystem überhaupt angerufen wird, wenn eine Entscheidung verständlich und akzeptabel erscheint.[68] Zum anderen ermöglicht die Begründung anfechtenden wie kontrollierenden Personen, „sich auf eine bestimmte Anzahl zweifelhafter Teile des Gedankenganges zu beschränken",

---

65 Ein weiterer Kritikpunkt betrifft die Möglichkeit, dass ein sog. Rashomon-Effekt auftritt, bei dem unterschiedliche kontrafaktische Erklärungen widersprüchlich ausfallen. Hierzu *de Vries*, Nordic Yearbook of Law and Informatics 2020–2021 (Fn. 2), S. 151 ff.

66 Nach der h.M. genügt es etwa für die materielle Rechtmäßigkeit eines Verwaltungsakts, dass dieser objektiv die gesetzlichen Voraussetzungen erfüllt. Unerheblich ist demgegenüber, ob er sachlich zutreffend begründet ist, *Stelkens*, VwVfG (Fn. 4), § 39 Rn. 30 m.w.N.

67 *Roth-Isigkeit*, Die Begründung des vollständig automatisierten Verwaltungsakts (Fn. 4), 1018 (1024 f.), vgl. § 114 Satz 2 VwGO.

68 *Kischel*, Die Begründung (Fn. 3), S. 58.

sie sind nicht gezwungen, „die Entscheidung uneingeschränkt und in allen Teilen infragezustellen."[69]

Bei *automatisiert erstellten Begründungen* ist eine tendenziell größere Übersetzungsleistung notwendig um diese im Rechtssystem aufzugreifen und zu verarbeiten, als bei von Juristinnen und Juristen erstellten Begründungen. Die statistischen Korrelationen, auf denen ML-Systeme aufbauen, stimmen nicht notwendigerweise mit denjenigen Aspekten überein, die juristisch in die Entscheidungsbegründung miteingeflossen wären.[70] Weiter geschwächt wird die Entlastungsfunktion, wenn bei künstlichen neuronalen Netzwerken nicht sämtliche Entscheidungsschritte zwischen Input und Output nachvollzogen werden können. In dem Falle kann sich eine rechtliche Überprüfung nicht am automatisierten Entscheidungsweg orientieren, sondern muss das gefundene Ergebnis „von der Pike auf" eigenständig konstruieren.

VI. *Akzeptanz- und Vertrauenswürdigkeit*

Die Möglichkeit, Entscheidungen öffentlich zu diskutieren und ein gesundes Maß an Misstrauen auf seine Berechtigung hin abzutasten, ist demokratisch positiv.[71] Hier kommt menschlichen Entscheidungen der Vorteil zu, offensiv für sich werben und sich als interessengerecht und vernünftig ausweisen zu können.[72] Andererseits dürfte die nicht ausräumbare Möglichkeit von vorgeschobenen oder sonstig unaufrichtigen Entscheidungsbegründungen die *Akzeptanz- und Vertrauenswürdigkeit* aus Sicht Betroffener unterminieren. Die Vertrauenssoziologie deutet darauf hin, dass institutionelles Vertrauen davon lebt, dass effektive Misstrauens- und Sanktionsmechanismen bestehen.[73]

---

69 *Kischel*, Die Begründung (Fn. 3), S. 58; *T. Wischmeyer*, Regulierung intelligenter Systeme (Fn. 3), 1 (57 f., 60); vgl. *Campos Zamora*, Das Problem der Begründung richterlicher Entscheidungen (Fn. 4) S. 195.

70 *Herold*, Rechtsfragen digitaler Transformationen (Fn. 52), S. 462; *Nink*, Justiz und Algorithmen (Fn. 20), S. 228.

71 *Kischel*, Die Begründung (Fn. 3), S. 59 f.

72 Vgl. *T. Würtenberger*, Akzeptanz durch Verwaltungsverfahren NJW 1991, 257 (259).

73 Vgl. *T. Strulik*, Nichtwissen und Vertrauen in der Wissensökonomie, Frankfurt am Main 2004, S. 88 ff.; *R. Lepsius*, in: S. Hradil (Hrsg.), Differenz und Integration: die Zukunft moderner Gesellschaften, Frankfurt am Main 2004, S. 289 f.; *M. Endreß*, Vertrauen, Bielefeld 2015, S. 59 ff.; *S. Marschall*, Lügen und Politik im "postfaktischen Zeitalter", APuZ 2017, 17 (19); vgl. *H. Jäckel*, in: P. Haungs

An die Stelle der Zweifel an der menschlichen Aufrichtigkeit treten bei automatisierten Entscheidungsbegründungen Technikaversionen in Justiz und Bürgerschaft. Durch deren Einsatz verschiebt sich Macht hin zu den entwickelnden und betreibenden Personen und Unternehmen. Wer also sein Vertrauen v.a. auf die richterliche Kompetenz stützt, dem dürfte negativ aufstoßen, dass sich bei automatisierten Begründungen Macht hin zu den entwickelnden und betreibenden Personen und Unternehmen verschiebt. Andererseits bietet die Technologie – sofern sie die hohen Zuverlässigkeitshürden für einen staatlichen, insb. gerichtlichen Einsatz nähme[74] – vielzählige Möglichkeiten, Entscheidungen durch nichtstaatliche Experten oder im Wege von „Probedurchläufen" auch durch Laien überprüfen zu lassen und gesellschaftlichen Akteuren damit unmittelbare Kontrollen zu erlauben.[75]

E. Fazit

Eine um normative Kraft bedachte Verfassungsauslegung muss den Blick ab und an vom Sollen aufs Sein schwenken. Die Digitalisierung der Ge-

---

(Hrsg.), Politik ohne Vertrauen?, Baden-Baden 1990, S. 33 f.; nach *E. Schmidt-Aßmann*, in: ders./W. Hoffmann-Riem/A. Voßkuhle (Hrsg.), Grundlagen des Verwaltungsrechts Band II, 2. Aufl., München 2012 § 27 Rn. 106 spiegeln sie den „Ernst exekutivischer Gesetzesbindung" wider.

74 Allgemein hierzu *Kroll/Huey/Barocas/Felten/Reidenberg/Robinson/Yu*, Accountable Algorithms (Fn. 37), 633 (703); vgl. frühzeitig *D. Citron*, Technological Due Process, Washington University Law Review 2008, 1249 (1298 ff.); optimistischer hinsichtlich der Position der Judikative *Deeks*, The Judical Demand for Explainable Artificial Intelligence (Fn. 40), 1829 (1837 f.). Das BVerfG fordert im Hinblick auf Wahlcomputer – wenn auch mit der wenig überzeugenden Lösung eines Papierprotokolls – die „Möglichkeit einer zuverlässigen Richtigkeitskontrolle" (BVerfGE 123, 39 (73); kritisch *T. Mast*, Schöne neue Wahl – Zu den Versprechen der Blockchain-Technologie für demokratische Wahlen, JZ 2021, 237 (243)). Der Saarländische Verfassungsgerichtshof knüpfte an diese Erwägungen im Hinblick auf die Verwertbarkeit von Geschwindigkeitsmessgeräten an, NJW 2019, 2456 (2458); *J. Mysegades*, Eine Lanze für den SaarlVerfGH – zugleich eine Erwiderung auf *B. Krenberger*, Anm. zu AG Waldbröl: Polizeiliche Verfolgungsfahrt als Fahrzeugrennen? Entscheidungsbesprechung, NZV 2019, 317, sowie *C. Krumm*, VerfGH Saar: Fehlen von Rohmessdaten bei Geschwindigkeitsmessung – Recht auf faires Verfahren, NJW 2019, 2460 und *E. Peuker*, Verfassungsrechtlich verfahren: Zum „Blitzer-Urteil" des saarländischen VerfGH, NZV 2019, 443, NZV 2020, 119 ff. m.w.N.

75 *Kroll/Huey/Barocas/Felten/Reidenberg/Robinson/Yu*, Accountable Algorithms (Fn. 37), 633 (702 f.).

sellschaft und des Staates beeinflusst das sich ständig neu ausrichtende Pendel der verfassungsrechtlichen Wirklichkeitsgestaltung vielfältig in positiver und negativer Weise. Die verfassungsrechtliche Legitimität einer Begründung hängt dabei von ihrer tatsächlichen Funktionalität ab. Zwar dürften menschliche Entscheidungen in Exekutive und Judikative in der überwiegenden Zahl der Fälle nicht nur primär rechtsgeleitet hergestellt, sondern auch authentisch und rechtmäßig begründet sein. Dennoch gedeihen Demokratie und Rechtstaatlichkeit dort besser, wo Vertrauen gegen Kontrollierbarkeit ausgetauscht werden kann. Sich der funktionalen Vor- und Nachteile hergebrachter menschlicher Praktiken gegenüber ihren digitalen Surrogaten bewusst zu machen, kann im besten Falle sowohl die bisherigen Praktiken irritieren als auch technologische Weiterentwicklungen anleiten. Denn wer das Alte mit dem Neuen vergleicht, erhält von beiden ein besseres Bild.

III. Transparency in Health Care

Too Much Transparency Is Not Always a Good Thing?

Paul Nolan

A. Introduction

The roots of Western medicine stem from Ancient Greece where Hippocrates introduced numerous medical terms universally used by physicians, including symptom, diagnosis, therapy, trauma and sepsis.[1] There was the creation of empirical medicine grounded in ethical vows. Whilst most clinicians are familiar with the Hippocratic Oath, they are less likely to be familiar with the medical texts of that time. Many now view the Greek physician–patient relationship as paternalistic, in which the physician concealed diagnostic or prognostic information from the patient.[2]

With the requirement of informed consent so prevalent in recent decades, has that paternalistic concealment been largely obliterated or is there some remaining scope for a balancing exercise between the right to be informed and the risk that too much information may, inadvertently or otherwise, lead to harm. The Hippocratic Oath amongst other things adopts the Latin maxim *'primum non nocere'* which translates to 'First, do no harm'. It is followed later by, 'Then try to prevent it'. Is a clinician who prevents harm due to information overload necessarily acting in the patient's best interests? The question is open.

It is sometimes said: "A little knowledge is a dangerous thing. So is a lot".[3] It is also said that: "Knowledge without practice is useless and practice without knowledge is dangerous".[4] Regardless of which is right or wrong, there are certain situations where too much information (and in the situation about to unfold involving Artificial Intelligence in healthcare) too much transparency is not always a good thing. Human beings are

---

1 *C. F Kleisiaris/C. Sfakianakis/I. V. Papathanasiou*, Health care practices in ancient Greece: The Hippocratic Ideal, Journal of medical ethics and history of medicine 2014, available at: https://www.ncbi.nlm.nih.gov/pmc/articles/PMC4263393/ (last access: 30.09.2022).

2 *S. H. Miles*, Hippocrates and informed consent, The Lancet 2009, 1322–1323.

3 Albert Einstein, German-born physicist and founder of the theory of relativity 1879–1955; a variation on a quotation of Alexander Pope, English poet, 1688–1744.

4 Confucius, Chinese philosopher, 551–479BC.

individuals whose capacity to understand varies greatly. What may seem straightforward and intelligible to one person, is beyond comprehension to the next. Within those extremities there is a wide cognitive spectrum. Within the complexity of AI in medicine, the need for informed consent, and the requirements for AI transparency, it may be that therapeutic privilege will play an increasing role in assisting clinicians and, ultimately, patients to achieve optimal healthcare outcomes.

B. *Current AI Developments in Healthcare*

Artificial Intelligence (AI) technologies, such as machine learning (ML), are gaining importance in healthcare.[5] Healthcare is a priority area of AI development, with both governments and private sector pouring significant investments into the field. AI-enabled medical applications have been developed that promise to improve diagnosis;[6] assist in the treatment and prediction of diseases;[7] improve clinical workflow; enable high quality direct-to-consumer services,[8] such as wearable monitoring devices[9]; aid

---

5 For current paragraph, see generally: *R. Matulionyte/P. Nolan/F. Magrabi/A. Beheshti*, Should AI-enabled medical devices be explainable, International Journal of Law and Information Technology 2022, available at https://papers.ssrn.com/sol3/papers.cfm?abstract_id=4140234 (last access: 20.10.2022).

6 *G. Litjens/C. I. Sánchez/N. Timofeeva/M. Hermsen/I. Nagtegaal/I. Kovac/C. Hulsberge -van de Kaa/P. Bult/B. van Ginneken/J. van der Laak*, Deep learning as a tool for increased accuracy and efficiency of histopathological diagnosis, Scientific reports 2016, 1; *N. Zhang/G. Yang/Z. Gao/C. Xu/Y. Zhang/R. Shi/J. Keegan/L. Xu/H. Zhang/Z. Fan/D. Firmin.*, Deep learning for diagnosis of chronic myocardial infarction on nonenhanced cardiac cine MRI, Radiology 2019, 606.

7 *A. Cheerla/O. Gevaert*, Deep learning with multimodal representation for pan-cancer prognosis prediction, Bioinformatics 2019, i446 -i454; *M. Roberts/D. Driggs/M. Thorpe/J. Gilbey/M. Yeung/S. Ursprung/A. I. Aviles-Rivero/C. Etmann/C. McCague/L. Beer/J. R. Weir-McCall/Z. Teng/J. H. F. Rudd/E. Sala/C. Schönlieb*, Machine learning for COVID-19 detection and prognostication using chest radiographs and CT scans: a systematic methodological review, arXiv 2020, available at https://europepmc.org/article/ppr/ppr347321 (last access: 20.10.2022)

8 *T. P.Quinn/S. Jacobs/M. Senadeera/V. Le/S. Coghlan.*, The three ghosts of medical AI: Can the black box present deliver?, (2022) Artificial Intelligence in Medicine 2022, 124; *A. Rajkomar/J. Dean/I. Kohane*, Machine learning in medicine, New England Journal of Medicine 2019, 1347.

9 *N. D. Lane/S. Bhattacharya/P. Georgiev/C. Forlivesi/F. Kawsar*, An early resource characterization of deep learning on wearables, smartphones, and internet-of-things devices, in: Proceedings of the 2015 international workshop on internet of things towards applications, New York 2015, p. 7.

in genome interpretation[10] and biomarker discovery[11]; and in automated robotic surgery[12]. Deep learning, a sub-set of machine learning, has already achieved near-human performance in medical image classification, such as the diagnosis of diabetic retinopathy.[13] Gradually, AI-enabled medical devices are gaining regulatory approval and being released to the market. The US Food and Drug Administration (FDA) has approved hundreds of AI-enabled medical devices and this number will continue to increase sharply.[14]

C. AI and The Black Box

The feature of AI that poses specific challenges to the evaluation of liability and regulation is its 'black box' nature.[15] Unless specifically programmed

---

10 *J. Zou/M. Huss/A. Abid/P. Mohammadi/A. Torkamani/A. Telent* A primer on deep learning in genomics, Nature genetics 2019, 12.

11 *S. M. Waldstein/P. Seeböck/R. Donner/A. Sadeghipour/H. Bogunović/A. Osborne/U. Schmidt-Erfurt*, 'Unbiased identification of novel subclinical imaging biomarkers using unsupervised deep learning, Scientific reports 2020, 1; *L. Li/F. Wu/G. Yang/L. Xu/T. Wong/R. Mohiaddin/D. Firmin/J. Keegan/X. Zhuang*, Atrial scar quantification via multi-scale CNN in the graph-cuts framework, Medical image analysis 2020, available at https://www.sciencedirect.com/science/article/pii/S1361841519301355 (last access: 30.09.2022).

12 *A. I. Chen/M. L. Balter/T. J. Maguire/M. L. Yarmush*, Deep learning robotic guidance for autonomous vascular access, Nature Machine Intelligence 2020, 104.

13 *Quinn/Jacobs/Senadeera/Lea/Coghlan*, The Three Ghosts of Medical AI (n. 8); *V. Gulshan/L. Peng/M. Coram/M. C. Stumpe/D. Wu/A. Narayanaswamy/S. Venugopalan/K. Widner/T. Madams/J. Cuadros/R. Kim/R. Raman/P. C. Nelson/J. L. Mega/D. R. Webster*, Development and validation of a deep learning algorithm for detection of diabetic retinopathy in retinal fundus photographs, Jama 2016, 2402; *R. Sayres/A. Taly/E. Rahimy/K. Blumer/D. Coz/N. Hammel/J. Krause/A. Narayanaswamy/Z. Rastegar/D. Wu/S. Xu/S. Barb/A. Joseph/M. Shumski/J. Smith/A. B. Sood/G. S. Corrado/L. Peng/D. R. Webster*, Using a deep learning algorithm and integrated gradients explanation to assist grading for diabetic retinopathy, Ophthalmology 2019, 552.

14 https://www.fda.gov/medical-devices/software-medical-device-samd/artificial-intelligence-and-machine-learning-aiml-enabled-medical-devices (last access: 14.06.2022) (The list is not meant to be an exhaustive or comprehensive resource of AI/ML-enabled medical devices. Rather, it is a list of AI/ML-enabled devices across medical disciplines, based on publicly available information).

15 *W. Nicholson Price II.*, Black Box Medicine, Harvard Journal of Law and Technology 2015, 420; *W. Nicholson Price II.*, Medical Malpractice and Black-Box Medicine, Big Data, Health Law, and Bioethics 2017, available at https://papers.ssrn.com/sol3/papers.cfm?abstract_id=2910417 (last access: 01.10.2022).

to do so by AI designers and engineers, an algorithm does not provide a rationale or explanation for its output and remains opaque (thus, 'black box'). The black box nature is amplified by an evolutionary nature of AI which is especially characteristic of ML based techniques such as deep learning or neural networks. Its very purpose is to learn, that is, change conclusions based on new data with which the algorithms are furnished. As will be seen below, opacity and evolution pose challenges when analysing the tort of negligence.

The 'black box' phenomenon is something that is troubling the medical profession — one which has the notion of trust as its bedrock.[16] ML systems specifically, and AI systems in general, are so structurally complex and can process such vast amounts of data that 'there is no straightforward way to map out the decision-making processes of these complex networks of artificial neurons.'[17] Black box AI in healthcare is problematic from several perspectives.

The medical profession is built on trust. The functioning of contemporary medicine relies fundamentally on trust.[18] Doctors interact with their patients in a personal and physical way, and they are privy to sensitive information about their patients. Intrinsically, trust is what imbues the clinician-patient relationship with its singularity and importance. For medical AI to be successful, it must be trusted by governments, health professionals, and the public. The quality of medical advice depends on medical reasoning being open to clarification, scrutiny, and evaluation.

Optimal healthcare delivery also depends on a satisfactory dialogue between experts, which can afford the clinician added information about a patient or a condition. This in turn could usefully feed back into the initial clinician–patient dialogue about prognosis and treatment options. AI systems that lack sufficient understanding, arguably do not allow for

---

16 See: *Breen v Williams* (1996) 186 CLR 71 where Brennan J at para 81 held that '[T]he relationship of doctor and patient is one where the doctor acquires an ascendancy over the patient and the patient is in a position of reposing trust in the doctor'.

17 Y. *Bathaee*, The Artificial Intelligence Black Box and the Failure of Intent and Causation, Harvard Journal of Law and Technology 2018, 891.

18 R. *Rhodes*, The Professional Responsibilities of Medicine, in: R. Rhodes/L. P. Francis/A. Silvers (eds.), The Blackwell Guide to Medical Ethics, Hoboken 2007; S. *Nundy/T. Montgomery/ R. M. Wachter*, Promoting Trust Between Patients and Physicians In The Era Of Artificial Intelligence, Journal of the American Medical Association 2019, 497; J. *Hatherley*, Limits Of Trust In Medical AI, Journal of Medical Ethics 2020, 478.

the satisfactory development of this knowledge and discovery process.[19] Further, an ability (or inability) to explain decisions in a clear manner will impact on how clinicians will utilise the information gleaned from AI systems when treatment plans are put in place.[20] In other words, an inability to adequately explain the AI system will inhibit trust from two perspectives: 1) the clinician not understanding the AI and being reserved about its capabilities and ultimate decisions; and 2) it follows that if the clinician does not have adequate understanding and trust in the AI system, this will filter down to the patient. If a clinician is unsure about how the AI system functions and, earnestly, discloses that to a patient, then the patient's confidence in the system will hardly be galvanised.

Some scholars warn that black box algorithms can hamper patient autonomy in clinical decision making.[21] A patient must be able to make their own autonomous decision about treatment options. That can only be achieved when they have both the decision and the reasons for it explained to them. That is a fundamental requirement of medical care, with or without AI systems. An AI system, by reason of its opacity or unexplainability, precludes a patient from being fully informed of how a particular recommendation or decision was arrived at. That, in turn, compromises their ability to decide whether to accept or reject the AI recommendation. This may provide an ethical reason to oppose the introduction of black box AI systems in that it would violate the right to informed consent.[22]

Being mindful of the problems discussed above, AI-enabled medical devices are expected to comply with a number of ethical principles and policy recommendations. AI ethical guidelines,[23] including healthcare-spe-

---

19 C. *Rudin*, Stop Explaining Black Box Machine Learning Models for High Stakes Decisions and Use Interpretable Models Instead, Nature Machine Intelligence 2019, 206; For over-reliance on AI, see: *D. Lyell/E. Coiera*, Automation Bias and Verification Complexity: A Systematic Review, Journal of the American Medical Informatics Association 2017, 423.

20 D. *Lyell/E. Coiera/J. Chen/P. Shah/F. Magrabi*, How Machine Learning Is Embedded to Support Clinician Decision Making: An Analysis of FDA-Approved Medical Devices, BMJ Health and Care Informatics 2021 available at https://pubmed.n cbi.nlm.nih.gov/33853863/ (last access: 20.10.2022).

21 T. *Grote/P. Berens*, On the Ethics of Algorithmic Decision-Making in Healthcare, Journal of Medical Ethics 2020, 205, R. J. *McDougall*, Computer Knows Best? The Need for Value-Flexibility in Medical AI, Journal of Medical Ethics, 156 (158).

22 See generally, H. R. *Sullivan/S. J. Schweikart*, Are Current Tort Liability Doctrines Adequate for Addressing Injury Caused By AI?, American Medical Association Journal of Ethics 2020, 160; *McDougall*, Computer Knows Best? (n. 21).

23 See e.g. OECD, Principles on AI (2019) https://www.oecd.org/going-digital/ai/ principles/; European Commission, Ethics Guidelines for Trustworthy AI (2019)

cific AI ethical guidelines,[24] require AI-enabled medical devices to respect such principles as benevolence, privacy and protection of data, safety, fairness, accountability and responsibility, avoidance of bias, governance, and others.

A sought-after principle is that of transparency and/or explainability, which is found in most ethical AI guidelines.[25] It mandates that AI in healthcare should be transparent and/or explainable.

While there is no consensus on what an AI explainability principle means, it generally requires that outputs generated by AI should be explainable and interpretable by different stakeholders, such as healthcare providers. The term 'transparency' has been used interchangeably or as

---

https://ec.europa.eu/digital-single-market/en/news/ethics-guidelines-trustworth y-ai; G20, AI Principles (2019) https://www.g20-insights.org/wp-content/upload s/2019/07/G20-Japan-AI-Principles.pdf; Australia's AI Ethics Framework (2022) https://www.industry.gov.au/data-and-publications/australias-artificial-intelligence -ethics-framework/australias-ai-ethics-principles (last access: 01.10.2022).

24 The Royal Australian and New Zealand College of Radiologists: Standards of Practice for Artificial Intelligence (2020), https://www.ranzcr.com/college/docu ment-library/standards-of-practice-for-artificial-intelligence; Royal College of Physicians and Surgeons (Canada) (2020), https://www.royalcollege.ca/rcsite/healt h-policy/initiatives/ai-task-force-e; International Medical Device Regulators Forum (SaMD) (Sept 2017), https://www.imdrf.org/sites/default/files/docs/imdrf/final/ technical/imdrf-tech-170921-samd-n41-clinical-evaluation_1.pdf; World Health Organisation (WHO), Ethics and Governance of Artificial Intelligence for Health, https://www.who.int/publications/i/item/9789240029200 (last access: 01.10.2022).

25 See: Australia's AI Ethics Framework (2022), 'There should be transparency and responsible disclosure so people can understand when they are being significantly impacted by AI and can find out when an AI system is engaging with them.' https://www.industry.gov.au/data-and-publications/australias-artificial-intellige nce-ethics-framework/australias-ai-ethics-principles; OECD – Recommendation of the Council on AI (2022) para 1.3 https://oecd.ai/en/dashboards/ai-principles /P7; European Commission – Ethics Guidelines for Trustworthy AI (2019) 14–19 https://www.aepd.es/sites/default/files/2019-12/ai-ethics-guidelines.pdf (last access: 01.10.2022); *J. Morley/C. C. V. Machado/C. Burr/J. Cowls/I. Joshi/M. Taddeo/L. Florid*, The Ethics Of AI In Health Care: A Mapping Review, Social Science & Medicine 2020 available at https://www.sciencedirect.com/science/article/abs/pi i/S0277953620303919 (last access: 20.10.2022); *A. Jobin/M. Ienca/E. Vayena*, 'The Global Landscape Of AI Ethics Guidelines, Nature Machine Intelligence 2019, 389.

a synonym of 'explainability',[26] while in other cases these concepts are clearly delineated.[27]

There is debate as to the level of transparency that should surround medical AI. That is, exactly how much of the AI system do clinicians and patients really need to understand before they can comfortably make an informed decision as to its use. Enabling patients to understand how AI determined diagnosis and treatment options are arrived at is crucial but also complicated. Clinicians also must be able to provide clear and cogent explanations of diagnoses and treatment options. This is something that bears upon the principle of informed consent, namely, before a patient can fully consent to something, they should at the very least have knowledge of all material matters.[28] Similarly, clinicians should be able to provide the explanations sought. Current ML systems lack explainability. In healthcare, if AI makes a decision that will impact on a patient, then all material risks need to be recognised, explained, and understood. Obviously, that will include knowing how the AI arrived at a given decision, which needs to be explained in layperson's terms and not replete with technical jargon.

D. Drugs and Other Medical Black Boxes

Strictly speaking, AI is not the only black box in medicine. In an article researching the ability of AI to improve the prediction and treatment of sepsis in hospital patients, Sendak noted that "[T]he human body is in many ways "a black box," in which the causes and mechanisms of illnesses often elude explanation".[29]

---

26 *Quinn/Jacobs/Senadeera/Lea/Coghlan*, The Three Ghosts of Medical AI: Can the Black Box Present Deliver? (n. 8); *A. Poon/J. Sung*, Opening the Black Box of AI-Medicine, Journal of Gastroenterology and Hepatology 2021, 581.

27 *G. Yang/Q. Ye/J. Xia*, Unbox the Black Box for the Medical Explainable AI via Multi-modal and Multi-centre Data Fusion: A Mini-Review, Information Fusion 2022, 29 (31).

28 *G. I. Cohen*, Informed Consent and Medical Artificial Intelligence: What to Tell the Patient?, Georgetown Law Journal 2019, 1425; *J. Amann/A. Blasimme/E. Vayena/D. Frey/V. I. Madai*, Explainability for Artificial Intelligence in Healthcare: A Multidisciplinary Perspective', 2020 available at https://bmcmedinformdecismak. biomedcentral.com/articles/10.1186/s12911-020-01332-6 (last access: 20.10.2022)

29 *M. Sendak/M. C. Elish/M. Gao/J. Futoma/W. Ratliff/M. Nichols/C. O'Brien*, "The human body is a black box" supporting clinical decision-making with deep learning, in: Proceedings of the 2020 conference on fairness, accountability, and transparency, 2020, pp. 99–109.

Electroconvulsive therapy (ECT) is a safe and effective treatment for certain psychiatric disorders. ECT is most commonly used to treat severe depression (major depression). It is often the fastest and best treatment available for this illness. ECT is also sometimes used to treat other psychiatric disorders, such as mania and psychosis. During ECT, a small amount of electrical current is passed through the brain while the patient is under general anaesthesia. This current causes a seizure that affects the entire brain, including the parts that control mood, appetite, and sleep. It causes chemical and cellular changes in the brain that relieve severe depression. Since the introduction of ECT in 1938, the mechanism of action of this highly effective treatment has intrigued psychiatrists and neuroscientists who do not yet fully understand exactly how it works.[30]

Certain drugs also remain to be fully explained, for example, lithium. Doctors don't know exactly how lithium works to stabilise the mood of a patient, but it is thought to help strengthen nerve cell connections in brain regions that are involved in regulating mood, thinking and behaviour. Another is acetaminophen (paracetamol). Despite competing explanations for how acetaminophen works, we know that it is a safe and effective pain medication because it has been extensively validated in numerous randomised controlled trials (RCTs).[31]

The point to be made is that despite being largely unknown or a black box, these drugs and treatments are regularly used in the healthcare system. That is because they have undergone RCTs which have historically been the gold-standard way to evaluate medical interventions. It should be no different for AI systems.

E. Informed Consent

The law of negligence is premised upon the general rule that those whose acts or omissions might injure another should exercise reasonable care to avoid such an occurrence. The elements that are required to be made out in an action for negligence can be stated as follows: the existence of a duty of care; a breach of that duty by a negligent act or omission; and damage suffered as a consequence. Fundamental to these, but often considered

---

30 T. G. Bolwig, How does electroconvulsive therapy work? Theories on its mechanism, The Canadian Journal of Psychiatry 2011, pp. 13–18.

31 K. Toussaint/X. C. Yang/M. A. Zielinski/K. L. Reigle/S. Nagar/R. B.Raffa, What do we (not) know about how paracetamol (acetaminophen) works?, Journal of clinical pharmacy and therapeutics 2010, 617–638.

separately, is the requirement of a causal connection between breach and damage.

In the context of healthcare, one area that has gained increasing attention over the past decades when looking at the tort of negligence is the principle of informed consent. That is, an analysis must proceed on the legal acceptance that people have the right to decide for themselves whether or not they will undergo medical treatment. This includes being warned of material risks associated with said treatment. It is apposite to look at several judicial decisions.

I. Rogers v Whitaker

In the Australian High Court case of *Rogers v Whitaker*,[32] the salient facts were as follows: the patient had injured her right eye in a childhood accident and an ophthalmic surgeon advised her that an operation on the eye would not only improve its appearance but would likely also substantially restore sight to it. The operation was not successful, but it was performed with the requisite care and skill. Unfortunately, the patient suffered sympathetic ophthalmia post-operatively and, as a result of inflammation arising from that, lost all sight in the left eye. The patient was rendered almost totally blind.

In Australia, it had been accepted that the standard of care to be observed by a professional person is that of the ordinary skilled person exercising and professing to have that special skill. The question in *Rogers* was whether the observance of that standard of care required information regarding the risk associated with the aftermath of surgery to be given to the patient. The eye surgeon gave evidence that it had not occurred to him to mention sympathetic ophthalmia to the patient.

There was a body of evidence from other medical practitioners to similar effect. However, there was also evidence from other specialists that they would have given a warning to the patient. The state of the evidence may have signalled to the Court that the old rule was unsustainable. In England, the approach to the resolution of similar problems had been determined by a case which lends its name to the *Bolam* rule. The case of *Bolam v Friern Hospital Management Committee*[33] involved a patient who

---

32 *Rogers v. Whitaker* (1992) 175 CLR 479 (High Court of Australia delivered judgment on 19 November 1992).

33 *Bolam v Friern Hospital Management Committee* (1957) 1 WLR 582.

was injured whilst receiving electroconvulsive therapy ('ECT') without the prior administration of a relaxant drug. Evidence as to the accepted practice varied as between doctors, leading the Court to formulate a rule that has since been stated as follows:

> A doctor is not negligent if he acts in accordance with a practice accepted at the time as proper by a responsible body of medical opinion even though other doctors adopt a different practice. In short, the law imposes the duty of care; but the standard of care is a matter of medical judgment.[34]

It followed from this rule that so long as an acceptable number of medical practitioners adopted the practice in question, that would avail the practitioner a complete defence. It can be observed that the *Bolam* rule is directed to accepted practice in the actual provision of treatment, whereas *Rogers v Whitaker* was concerned with medical advice addressing the risks involved in treatment. In cases decided after *Bolam*, some judges held the view that the rule should only apply in matters involving negligent treatment or surgery, but not where the issue was the sufficiency or adequacy of the advice or information given. In *Rogers v Whitaker* the High Court decided that the rule should be restricted in that way.[35]

In relation to diagnosis and treatment, the Court accepted that the *Bolam* rule would continue to be influential, the reason being that whether a diagnosis or a method of treatment was negligent would depend largely upon medical standards, something known best by doctors. The issue of whether a risk is relevant to a patient, and about which they should be warned, is different. The High Court held that this was a question for the courts themselves. The High Court held:

> *"The law should recognize that a doctor has a duty to warn a patient of a material risk inherent in the proposed treatment; a risk is material if, in the circumstances of the particular case, a reasonable person in the patient's position, if warned of the risk, would be likely to attach significance to it or if the medical practitioner is or should reasonably be aware that the particular patient, if warned of the risk, would be likely to attach significance to it. This duty is subject to the therapeutic privilege."*[36]

---

34 *Sidaway v Governors of Bethlem Royal Hospital* (1985) AC 871, 881 (per Lord Scarman).
35 *Rogers v Whitaker* (1992) 175 CLR 479, 489–490.
36 *Ibid.*

Important to this ruling was the notion that an individual has autonomy and is entitled to make informed decisions about their life. Therefore, a patient must be informed of material risks. The High Court held that it would be reasonable for a person with one functioning eye to be concerned about the possibility of injury to it, particularly in the context of an elective procedure.

In *Rogers*, the Court did not entirely rule out the exercise of therapeutic judgment on the part of a doctor as to what information should be given to certain patients and how it is to be conveyed. The qualification the Court made to the duty owed to patients to give information about risks, was where there was a danger that the provision of all information would harm an unusually nervous, disturbed, or volatile patient.

II. *Montgomery v Lanarkshire Health Board*

In *Montgomery*,[37] the United Kingdom Supreme Court considered liability in negligence for failure to disclose material risks to patients as part of the process of informed consent. Nadine Montgomery was awarded £5.2 million compensation following birth complications. She was of small stature and had gestational diabetes and had expressed anxieties about vaginal delivery. Her obstetrician failed to warn of shoulder dystocia and her son was born with cerebral palsy. The Court found that had her son been born by elective caesarean section, it is more probable than not that he would have been born uninjured.[38] In a joint judgement, Lords Kerr and Reed (with whom the other justices agreed[39]) distinguished between cases concerning errors in treatment and diagnosis where the test set down in *Bolam* will continue to apply, and cases concerning the disclosure of risk and treatment alternatives which, it was held, are not purely a matter of professional judgement and cannot be decided by reference to a responsible body of medical opinion.[40] *Montgomery* galvanises a position that has been

---

37 *Montgomery v Lanarkshire Health Board* (2015) SC11 [2015] 1 AC 1430 (Judgment delivered by UK Supreme Court on 11 March 2015).

38 *Ibid*. at para 22.

39 Lady Hale's judgement makes additional observations about the context of childbirth. Unless stated otherwise, references in this article to Montgomery are to Lords Kerr and Reed's joint judgement.

40 Montgomery (2015) UKSC 11, at paragraph 86.

adopted in practice.[41] The Supreme Court declared that Lord Scarman in *Sidaway* had represented substantially the correct position, subject to the *Rogers v Whitaker* 'refinement'.[42]

Setting out a revised test, Lords Kerr and Reed stated:

> *"The doctor is therefore under a duty to take reasonable care to ensure that the patient is aware of any material risks involved in any recommended treatment, and of any reasonable alternative or variant treatments. The test of materiality is whether, in the circumstances of the particular case, a reasonable person in the patient's position would be likely to attach significance to the risk, or the doctor is or should reasonably be aware that the particular patient would be likely to attach significance to it."*[43]

What can be distilled from these decisions of superior Courts is that a patient must be warned of material risks, and this is a subjective test. That is, what is significant to the individual patient in a particular case.[44] As noted though, this provision of information must be balanced: "On the one hand, physicians must provide all the information a patient needs to make an informed decision. On the other hand, complex medical information, including all aspects that are somehow relevant to the treatment, would rather prevent informed consent than promoting it".[45]

---

41 *Ibid.* at para 70 citing General Medical Council, Good Medical Practice (2013). See also para 78 citing GMC, Consent: Patients and Doctors Making Decisions Together (2008), para 5.

42 *Ibid.* at para 86–87.

43 *Ibid.* at para 87.

44 The issue of informed consent was looked at by OLG Hamm, judgment of June 18, 2013 – 26 U 85/12. It was held that, *"...the patient should recognize the "type and severity" of the intervention through the informational discussion. To do this, the risks do not have to be presented to him in all conceivable forms, but a "general picture of the severity and direction of the specific risk" ("broadly") is sufficient. However, jurisprudence recognizes that the patient must also be made aware of rare and even extremely rare risks, where these risks, if they materialize, are a heavy burden on the lifestyle and, despite their rarity, are specific to the procedure but surprising to the layperson are"*, available at https://openjur.de/u/645241.html (last access: 20.10.2022).

45 *B. Buchner/M. Freye*, Informed Consent in German Medical Law: Finding the right path between patient autonomy and information overload, 2022 available at https://papers.ssrn.com/sol3/papers.cfm?abstract_id=4088631 (last access: 20.10.2022).

F. Therapeutic Privilege

There is an 'assumption that the physician cares not only for the patient's physiological health but for his psychological and moral wellbeing.'[46] The duty to have regard to the best interests of the patient and her welfare taken as a whole may clash with the patient's right to choose treatment based on adequate information. To consider provision of information solely in terms of the rights of the patient (and therefore the correlative duty of the health care professional) discounts the 'ethical and social dimension of medical treatments' and may potentially harm the relationship.[47]

Multiple studies that have attempted to determine and quantify the anxiety-generating effect of informed consent provide mixed results about whether a more detailed consent process is physiologically or psychologically harmful to a patient.[48]

Clearly, there are medical situations in which the information involved in planning is of such a nature that the decision-making capacity of a patient is overwhelmed by the sheer complexity or volume of the information they are confronted with. In such cases a patient cannot attain the understanding necessary for informed decision making, and informed consent is therefore not possible.[49]

When faced with these complex clinical contexts, physicians may wonder about the most appropriate ethical conduct. Is it the right time to tell a depressed patient about their cancer? Should they talk about a possible side effect or a risk when it could potentially lead the patient to refuse a medically necessary treatment? Should they discuss a prognosis when they know

---

46 B. *Barber*, Informed Consent in Medical Therapy and Research, New Brunswick 1980.

47 N. J. *Hanna*, Challenging medical decision-making: professional dominance, patient rights or collaborative autonomy?, Oxford Journal of Legal Studies 1998; 143.

48 D. D.*Kerrigan*/R. S.*Thevasagayam*/T. O. *Woods*/I. Mc *Welch*/W. E. *Thomas*/A. J. *Shorthouse*/A. R. *Dennison.*, Who's afraid of informed consent? BMJ 1993, 298; J. J. *Goldberger*/J. *Kruse*/M. A. *Parker*/A. H. *Kadish*, Effect of informed consent on anxiety in patients undergoing diagnostic electrophysiology studies, American Heart Journal 1997, 119; N. *Casap*/M. *Alterman*/G. *Sharon*/Y. *Samuni*, The effect of informed consent on stress levels associated with extraction of impacted mandibular third molars, Journal of Oral and Maxillofacial Surgery 2008, 878; Z. N. *Kain*/S. M. *Wang*/L. A. *Caramico*/M. *Hofstadter*/L. C. *Mayes*, Parental desire for perioperative information and informed consent: a two-phase study, Anesthesia & Analgesia 1997, 299.

49 J. *Bester*/C. M. *Cole*/E. *Kodish*, The limits of informed consent for an overwhelmed patient: clinicians' role in protecting patients and preventing overwhelm, AMA Journal of Ethics 2016, 869.

that it might precipitate an anxiety reaction? Should they withhold certain facts, or present them in a more favourable light? In other words, can they lie to their patients? The physician's judgement is based on clinical context as well as personal and professional values.[50]

In a clinical setting, reporting information without regard for the special conditions of each particular doctor – patient encounter reflects neither the spirit nor the letter of this conception of the truth. An honest medical relationship requires that the doctor consider the limits inherent in the therapeutic process and the circumstances and limitations of each patient. A relationship based on meaningful dialogue permits the doctor to determine these limits and adjust the conversation to the specific capacities and needs of each patient. This process may allow the doctor to consider responsibility and duty, demonstrating the complexity of the role.

Consider the following example: Patient A has been diagnosed with a form of cancer. A sophisticated AI system has recommended a course of drug treatment that is quite particular and unique to Patient A, given all the circumstances and data that is relied upon. It might be aptly described as 'personalised' treatment.

Patient A's prognosis will be much better with the treatment, but there are contraindications as with all chemotherapy. Clinician X knows that this is a treatment regime that will assist but is unable to understand how the AI system arrived at its decision due to the black box effect, let alone explain it in meaningful laypersons terms to the Patient.

What do they do? Save the patient from themselves at risk of compromising their autonomy on the basis of therapeutic privilege? Or admit that they cannot explain the decision adequately and risk not receiving consent for what will be a necessary life-preserving treatment? Time may be of the essence.

In consultations, where everything transpires in a single interview, given the avalanche of information, an informed decision is probably highly improbable for a significant number of patients. Unable to make a personal decision, the patient is often reduced to blindly trusting the doctor, which happens to varying degrees with any expert. Last, to assume that the patient's decision is based firmly on a complete understanding of the issues and without outside influence is neither realistic nor achievable and ultimately significantly underestimates the finitude of human beings.

---

50 *C. Richard/Y. Lajeunesse/M. T. Lussier*, Therapeutic privilege: between the ethics of lying and the practice of truth, Journal of Medical Ethics 2010, 353.

G. Variables Influencing the Sliding Scale of Capacity to Decide and Consent

As clinical medicine and the involvement of AI is evolving, medical ethics will face the challenge of keeping pace with the development and clinical application of new technologies and therapies. The doctrine of informed consent in specific clinical contexts may need to be looked at through this new prism. Informed consent has become so central and important to the way clinicians practice that there may be situations in which patients' ability to provide informed consent may be compromised or overlooked, particularly where complex information is involved.

I. Patient-related factors

One set of variables is patient related. An obvious case is a patient who is unconscious and lacks capacity to make even the most basic decisions. Others include patients under the influence of alcohol or drugs, young children, and patients with decreased cognitive function. There are also subtle cases where capacity is unclear. Some patients don't have the educational or intellectual ability to understand the choices before them, particularly if the choices are scientifically complex like with AI. Similarly, language and cultural barriers may also impose limits on capacity.

II. Information-related factors

If we are looking at a sliding scale, the more complex, scientifically advanced, and intellectually demanding information becomes, the greater the difficulty for patients to provide consent. Put simply, on one end of the scale is comprehensible, straightforward information about the AI involved in the process and its risks and benefits that is clear and easily understandable. As we move up the sliding scale, the information becomes more voluminous and more complex. If we keep going up the scale, we get to a point where people who ordinarily have capacity to make their own decisions find it all impossible to fully understand. There may be exceptions but for most patients, a full understanding—and truly informed consent—will be impossible.[51]

---

51 *Bester/Cole/Kodish*, The limits of informed consent (n. 49), 869.

III. *Communication-related factors*

Dumping an indigestible barrage of complex information about AI on a patient would challenge their understanding. The clinician's capacity to communicate complex information is therefore an important variable that impinges on the capacity to provide consent.

IV. *Emotional overwhelm*

It is reasonable that a patient may be emotionally overwhelmed by the illness experience and by the implications and complexity of decisions they are faced with. Being emotionally overwhelmed may make informed consent very difficult to achieve. Informed consent may still be possible in this case but is more difficult to attain as the patient's ability to make decisions is compromised.

V. *Informational overload*

A patient's ability to provide informed consent can easily be overwhelmed by the complexity, uncertainty, or sheer volume of information involved in the decision, as may occur with newer technologies such AI. In short, the information required to provide informed consent is of such complexity, volume, or uncertainty that it makes it impossible for a patient to make an informed choice because the patient is overwhelmed. They're in effect incapacitated for the decision in question.

H. *Conclusion*

There can be no escaping that AI in healthcare has well-arrived and will continue to exponentially increase. It is trite to say that it is a complex integration. Understanding it poses difficulties to those that design and construct it, let alone the hospitals and clinics that deploy it, the clinicians and others who use it, and the patients who trust and rely upon it.

Where does this leave consent in terms of AI healthcare? The clinical dilemma arises because of the tension between legal constraints and ethical practice. There must be an analysis on a case-by-case basis. Patients will still need to be given a broad overview but not to an intricate technical level.

Clinical validation develops a heightened importance and trust is essential – both in the AI system and in the clinician.

With the development and introduction of AI, arguably there should not be a hardline insistence on obtaining informed consent from patients who are clearly overwhelmed with information due to transparency requirements. Steps should be taken to provide the assistance that patients in each specific situation require. If this necessitates a tailored multi-factorial approach beyond the scope of this paper, then so be it. Too much information may be too much for the wrong patient.

AI-D des Hippokrates

David Schneeberger

A. Einleitung

Ὄμνυμι Ἀπόλλωνα ἰητρὸν, καὶ Ἀσκληπιὸν, καὶ Ὑγείαν, καὶ Πανάκειαν, καὶ θεοὺς πάντας τε καὶ πάσας, ἵστορας ποιεύμενος, ἐπιτελέα ποιήσειν κατὰ δύναμιν καὶ κρίσιν ἐμὴν ὅρκον τόνδε καὶ ξυγγραφὴν τήνδε. Die Verständigung zwischen Ärztin und Patientin stößt – wie dieses Zitat aus dem Text des hippokratischen Eides metaphorisch illustrieren soll – mitunter aufgrund des fehlenden gemeinsamen Vokabulars oft auf Kommunikationsschwierigkeiten.

Ohne eine verständliche Aufklärung über die Diagnose oder Behandlungsoptionen bleibt die Entscheidungsgewalt in den Händen der Ärztin. Um solchen Informations- und daraus resultierenden Machtasymmetrien zwischen Ärztin und Patientin vorzubeugen, zielt die moderne Medizin anstatt paternalistischer Bevormundung auf eine partnerschaftliche Entscheidungsfindung ab.[1] Damit eine Patientin ihr Recht auf Selbstbestimmung ausüben kann, müssen ihr alle Informationen vermittelt werden, die notwendig sind, um eine fundierte Entscheidung zu treffen (sog. *informed consent*). Eine Zustimmung zur Behandlung kann nur dann gültig erfolgen, wenn ihr die Tragweite ihrer Entscheidung bewusst ist.[2] Fehlt es daran, ist die Behandlung rechtswidrig, selbst wenn sie medizinisch indiziert ist und sorgfaltsgemäß durchgeführt wird.[3]

Dieses Konzept der partnerschaftlichen Entscheidungsfindung zwischen Ärztin und Patientin wandelt sich jedoch durch die Verbreitung von Künstlicher Intelligenz (KI), insbesondere in der Unterform des Machine Learning (ML). Denn da ML-Systeme u.a. in der Diagnose, z.B. von Hautkrankheiten oder diabetischer Retinopathie,[4] bei der Prävention von

---

1 *M. Neumayr* in: M. Neumayr/R. Resch/F. Wallner, Gmundner Kommentar zum Gesundheitsrecht, 2. Aufl., Wien 2022, Einleitung ABGB Rn. 36.
2 *F. Wallner*, Medizinrecht, 2. Aufl., Wien 2022, Rn. 481.
3 *Neumayr* (Fn. 1), Einleitung ABGB Rn. 32.
4 *E. Topol*, Deep Medicine. How Artificial Intelligence can Make Healthcare Human Again, New York 2019, S. 41 ff.; siehe auch die Beiträge in A. Manzei-Gorsky/C. Schubert/J. von Hayek (Hrsg.), Digitalisierung und Gesundheit, Baden-Baden

Krankheiten, z.B. durch die Feststellung von für Krankheiten indikative Biomarker, sowie im Bereich der Medikamentenentwicklung oder Gensequenzierung zunehmend Einsatz finden,[5] treten sie metaphorisch als dritte Partei an die Seite der Ärztin und Patientin und sind somit prototypisch für die verstärkte Dominanz der Naturwissenschaften in der Medizin.[6] In Form von „verkörperten" KI-Systemen, d.h. Robotik, sind auch bspw. chirurgische Roboter, sozial oder physisch assistierende Roboter sowie Pflegedienstroboter bereits im Einsatz.[7]

Vor allem aufgrund verschiedener technischer Eigenschaften (einiger) der verwendeten Modelle, die eine Interpretation des Entscheidungsprozesses erschweren (sog. „Black-Box-Problematik"),[8] ergibt sich ein Spannungsverhältnis zwischen der Aufklärung[9] als Bedingung für Selbstbestimmung und dem Einsatz intelligenter Medizinprodukte. Den Ausgangspunkt der Überlegungen bildet der Einsatz von ML-Modellen in einem *decision-support*-Szenario (z.B. Empfehlung einer Diagnose oder einer Behandlungsmethode). Das Aufklärungsgespräch verbleibt dabei in der Hand der Ärztin, während das ML-Modell und sein Output zum Gegenstand der Aufklärung werden. Die Einführung eines vollautomatisierten „Dr. Robot" oder eine automatisierte Aufklärung[10] ist dabei zum gegenwärtigen Stand auch aus rechtlichen Gründen – ärztliche Tätigkeit ist auf-

---

2022. Ein weiterer Anwendungsbereich liegt in der Immunologie z.B. bei der Bekämpfung der COVID-19-Pandemie, *L. J. Catania*, AI for Immunology, Boca Raton, 2021.

5 *D. Roth-Isigkeit*, Unionsrechtliche Transparenzanforderungen an intelligente Medizinprodukte, GesR 2022, 278 (279); *C. Katzenmeier*, Big Data, E-Health, M-Health, KI und Robotik in der Medizin, MedR 2019, 259 (259). Daneben existieren auch Monitoringsysteme, Modelle zur Spracherkennung oder Systeme, die bei der Recherche unterstützen, siehe *D. Linardatos*, Intelligente Medizinprodukte und Datenschutz, CR 2022, 367 (368).

6 *Katzenmeier*, Data (Fn. 5), 270 f.

7 *E. Fosch-Villaronga/H. Drukarch*, AI for Healthcare Robotics, Boca Raton, 2022, S. 24 f.

8 *A. D. Selbst/S. Barocas*, The Intuitive Appeal of Explainable Machines, Fordham Law Review 2018, 1085 (1094 ff.).

9 Zur Einordnung der Aufklärung als eine Form von „Transparenz", vgl. *A. Kiseleva/D. Kotzinos/P. de Hert*, Transparency of AI in Healthcare as a Multilayered System of Accountabilities, Frontiers in Artificial Intelligence 2022, 1 (11 ff.).

10 *C. Rahn*, Ärztliche Aufklärung durch Künstliche Intelligenz, Hamburg 2022.

grund des Arztvorbehalts auf Menschen beschränkt[11] – unwahrscheinlich und daher nicht Gegenstand der Betrachtungen.

B. *Medizinische Aufklärung*

I. *Rechtsgrundlagen*

Die österreichische Rechtsordnung kennt zwei Grundlagen für die ärztliche Aufklärungspflicht: zum einen gesetzliche Regelungen, wobei die Aufklärungspflicht nicht umfassend geregelt ist und in der Rechtsordnung verstreut nur einige wenige Bestimmungen existieren, zum anderen den Behandlungsvertrag zwischen der Patientin und der behandelnden Ärztin bzw. dem Krankenanstaltenträger.[12] Die Rechtslage mit einer fehlenden Regelung der Aufklärung im Allgemeinen ähnelt damit der deutschen vor 2013, als die Grundsätze der Aufklärung in § 630c Abs. 2 S. 1 BGB und § 630e BGB kodifiziert wurden.[13]

Die Thematik der Aufklärung über „intelligente Medizinprodukte" hat einen hohen Überschneidungsgrad mit dem Medizinprodukterecht, geregelt in der MPVO,[14] und dem geplanten Artificial Intelligence Act (AIA), der diese teilweise ergänzt. Medizinprodukte, die aufgrund ihrer Risikoklasse einer *ex-ante*-Konformitätsprüfung aufgrund harmonisierter Rechtsvorschriften wie der MPVO unterliegen, fallen als Hochrisikosysteme unter den AIA (Art. 6 Abs. 1 AIA i.V.m. Anhang II Z. 11, 12).[15] Daneben be-

---

11 G. *Ganzger/L. Vock*, Artificial Intelligence in der ärztlichen Entscheidungsfindung, JMG 2019, 153 (157 f.); *Linardatos*, Medizinprodukte (Fn. 5), 368 f; *Roth-Isigkeit*, Transparenzanforderungen (Fn. 5), 282.

12 M. *Memmer*, Aufklärung, in: G. Aigner/A. Kletečka/M. Kletečka-Pulker/M. Memmer (Hrsg.), Handbuch Medizinrecht für die Praxis, Wien 2022, I.3.

13 C. *Katzenmeier*, Aufklärungspflicht und Einwilligung, in: A. Laufs/C. Katzenmeier/V. Lipp (Hrsg.), Arztrecht, 8. Aufl., München 2021, Kap V. Rn. 3 f; C. *Katzenmeier* in: W. Hau/R. Poseck (Hrsg.), BeckOK BGB, 62. Edition, München 2022, § 630e BGB Rn. 1.

14 Software fällt dabei unter die Definition des Medizinprodukts gem. Art. 2 Abs. 1 MPVO, K. *Helle*, Intelligente Medizinprodukte, MedR 2020, 993 (994); D. *Schneeberger/K. Stöger/A. Holzinger*, The European Legal Framework for Medical AI, in A. Holzinger/P. Kieseberg/A. M. Tjoa/E. Weippl (Hrsg.), CD-MAKE 2020, Cham 2020, S. 209 (216 f.).

15 *Roth-Isigkeit*, Transparenzanforderungen (Fn. 5), 283. Software-Produkte, die Informationen liefern, die zu Entscheidungen für diagnostische oder therapeutische Zwecke herangezogen werden, fallen zumindest in die Risikoklasse IIa (Regel 11 Anhang VIII MPVO), S. *Jabri*, Artificial Intelligence and Healthcare, in: T.

steht aufgrund der Verarbeitung von Gesundheitsdaten typischerweise eine Anwendbarkeit der DSGVO, wobei Art. 22 DSGVO und die damit verbundenen „speziellen" Informationspflichten und das Auskunftsrecht im medizinischen Kontext häufig nur eine eingeschränkte Rolle spielen, da Vollautomatisierung bereits an berufsrechtliche Grenzen stößt.[16]

II. Aufklärungsformen

Auch wenn häufig nur von „Aufklärung" gesprochen wird, lässt sich diese nach ihrem Gegenstand und ihrer Funktion in zwei Hauptformen unterteilen: erstens die Selbstbestimmungsaufklärung, die, indem sie das notwendige Wissen verschafft, die Grundlage für die Entscheidung der Patientin zur Einwilligung oder Ablehnung einer Behandlung bildet; zweitens die Sicherungsaufklärung, die, nachdem die Patientin in die konkrete ärztliche Maßnahme eingewilligt hat, zum Tragen kommt. Diese stellt einen Teil der ärztlichen Behandlung dar, soll die bestmögliche Mitwirkung der Patientin bewirken und dient damit der Sicherstellung des Heilerfolgs.[17] Der Fokus dieses Beitrags liegt auf der Selbstbestimmungsaufklärung.

Im Rahmen der Selbstbestimmungsaufklärung ist der Patientin jenes Wissen zu vermitteln, das notwendig ist, um abschätzen zu können, worin sie einwilligt bzw. welche Folgen die Ablehnung einer Behandlung nach sich zieht. Sie ist über die Diagnose, den Therapieverlauf sowie alternative Methoden und über die Risiken der in Aussicht genommenen Maßnahme aufzuklären. Die Selbstbestimmungsaufklärung lässt sich demnach in die Diagnoseaufklärung, die Verlaufsaufklärung sowie die Risikoaufklärung unterteilen.[18]

Wischmeyer/T. Rademacher (Hrsg.), Regulating Artificial Intelligence, Cham 2020, S. 307 (323).

16 *Roth-Isigkeit*, Transparenzanforderungen (Fn. 5), 282; *K. Stöger*, Explainability und „informed consent" im Medizinrecht, in P. Leyens/I. Eisenberger/R. Niemann (Hrsg.), Smart Regulation, Tübingen 2021, S. 143 (144 ff.).

17 *D. Engljähringer*, Ärztliche Aufklärungspflicht vor medizinischen Eingriffen, Wien 1996, S. 7 ff; *H. Jesser-Huß*, Zivilrechtliche Haftung und Fragen der Aufklärung, in: R. Resch/F. Wallner (Hrsg.), Handbuch Medizinrecht, 3. Auflage, Wien 2020, IV. Rn. 78; *M. Kletečka-Pulker/M. Grimm/M. Memmer/L. Stärker/J. Zahrl*, Grundzüge des Medizinrechts, Wien 2019, 54 f; *Memmer*, Aufklärung (Fn. 12), I.3.2; *Neumayr* (Fn. 1), Einleitung ABGB Rn. 35; *K. Prutsch*, Die ärztliche Aufklärung. Handbuch für Ärzte, Juristen und Patienten, 2. Aufl., Wien 2004, S. 136.

18 *S. Laimer*, Ausmaß und Grenzen der Selbstbestimmungsaufklärung, RdM 2022, 250 (251); *Memmer*, Aufklärung (Fn. 12), I.3.2.1.

1. Diagnoseaufklärung

Bei der Diagnoseaufklärung muss die Ärztin die Patientin über den erhobenen Befund informieren.[19] Als Ausgangspunkt für das Selbstbestimmungsrecht ist die Patientin darüber aufzuklären, dass sie überhaupt krank ist und an welcher Krankheit sie leidet.[20] Sie hat erst stattzufinden, wenn die Diagnose gesichert ist, da eine bloße Verdachtsdiagnose möglicherweise zu Verunsicherung führt.[21]

In der Literatur ist bereits die Frage umstritten, ob über den Einsatz eines ML-Systems, z.B. zur Diagnose, aufgeklärt werden muss. Dies ist m.E. in Hinblick auf Art. 22 DSGVO und die damit verknüpften Informationspflichten in Art. 13–14 DSGVO umso eher zu bejahen, je mehr die Diagnoseentscheidung in die „Hände der Maschine" gelegt wird. Wenn eine Ärztin nur noch als „Sprachrohr" einer automatisierten Diagnose fungiert und keine überprüfende Funktion wahrnimmt, ist eine Information über den Einsatz von KI datenschutzrechtlich notwendig. Faktisch würde dieses *rubber stamping* jedoch, wie bereits erwähnt, gegen berufsrechtliche Grenzen verstoßen. Ist die ML-Diagnose nur eine „zweite Meinung", d.h. nur ein Faktor unter vielen, und hat somit nur geringen Anteil an der Diagnose, ist eine solche Bekanntgabe schwieriger zu argumentieren.[22]

Da es sich bei ML zum gegenwärtigen Stand noch um eine nicht weitverbreitete „Außenseitermethode"[23] mit noch unbekannten Risiken handelt, sollte m.E., um die Selbstbestimmungsrechte der Patientinnen zu wahren, darüber aufgeklärt werden. Auch aus medizinethischer Sicht wurde gefordert, den KI-Einsatz nicht zu verbergen.[24] Wenn sich KI jedoch als Stand der Wissenschaft eingebürgert hat, ist es wahrscheinlich, dass – wie

---

19 *Memmer*, Aufklärung (Fn. 12), I.3.2.1.1; *Neumayr* (Fn. 1), Einleitung ABGB Rn. 38.

20 *Prutsch*, Aufklärung (Fn. 17), S. 136 f.

21 *Kletečka-Pulker/Grimm/Memmer/Stärker/Zahrl*, Grundzüge (Fn. 17), S. 57 f; *Memmer*, Aufklärung (Fn. 12), I.3.2.1.1.

22 *G. I. Cohen*, Informed Consent and Medical Artificial Intelligence, The Georgetown Law Journal 2020, 1425 (1442).

23 *D. Schneeberger*, KI-Assistenzsysteme in der Medizin, RdM 2021, 138 (142).

24 *F. Ursin/C. Timmermann/M. Orzechowski/F. Steger*, Diagnosing Diabetic Retinopathy With Artificial Intelligence, Frontiers in Medicine 2021, 1 (2); *WHO*, Ethics and Governance of Artificial Intelligence for Health, 2021, S. 48, abrufbar unter https://www.who.int/publications/i/item/9789240029200 (zuletzt abgerufen: 09.12. 2022).

auch bei anderen Verfahren – nicht mehr explizit über die Verwendung einer KI gestützten Diagnosemethode aufgeklärt werden muss.[25]

Dabei darf nur über eine gesicherte Diagnose aufgeklärt werden. Eine Verdachtsdiagnose ist, wenn ausnahmsweise darüber aufgeklärt wird, als eine solche zu benennen.[26] Das Ergebnis eines ML-Modells ist jedoch technisch zwangsläufig eine durch Induktion gewonnene Wahrscheinlichkeitsaussage. Ein ML-Ergebnis muss insofern als Verdacht präsentiert und darf weder der Ärztin noch der Patientin als gesicherte Diagnose „verkauft" werden. Ein solcher „Diagnosevorschlag" muss daher vor der Aufklärung durch zusätzliche (menschliche) Untersuchungen abgesichert werden. Der Ärztin obliegt damit als überprüfende Instanz, als *human-in-the-loop*, eine Kontrollfunktion. Wie hoch der „Verdacht" hinter einer Diagnose ist, lässt sich technisch durch Angabe eines *confidence scores*, d.h. dem „Vertrauen" eines Modells in sein Ergebnis, quantifizieren. Fehlt eine solche Angabe, könnten subsidiär im Rahmen der Evaluierung ermittelte Fehlermetriken wie Genauigkeit angegeben werden.[27]

Die Aufklärung über den Befund impliziert, dass nicht nur über einen Output eines Black-Box-Modells (z.B. „Hautkrebs Stufe IV") aufgeklärt wird. Ein solches „orakelartiges" Ergebnis hat – da die Diagnose nicht näher begründet wird – m.E. nur wenig Mehrwert in Bezug auf die Selbstbestimmung der Patientin. Jedoch darf mit Blick auf die zunehmende Komplexität der Medizin, die eine Aufklärung in allen Details auch ohne den Einsatz von KI häufig „zur Fiktion"[28] werden lässt, die Anforderung an die Aufklärung nicht überspannt werden. Eine ausführliche Erläuterung einer Diagnose ist auch bei rein „menschlichen Diagnosen" nicht geboten. Ärztinnen generieren Diagnosen oft selbst mittels Erfahrung und Intuition und können diese nicht im Detail begründen. Auch z.B. bei Untersuchungen mittels MRT muss die technische Funktionsweise nicht näher erläutert werden. In Hinblick auf die Verständlichkeit der Aufklärung scheint es im Ergebnis argumentierbar, dass grundlegende Informationen über die we-

---

25 *F. Molnár-Gábor*, Artificial Intelligence in Healthcare, in: T. Wischmeyer/T. Rademacher (Hrsg.), Regulating Artificial Intelligence, Cham 2020, S. 337 (349 f.); *Stöger*, Explainability (Fn. 16), 150.

26 *Memmer*, Aufklärung (Fn. 12), I.3.2.1.1.

27 *Stöger*, Explainability (Fn. 16), 147.

28 *W. Eberbach*, Wird die ärztliche Aufklärung zur Fiktion? (Teil 1), MedR 2019, 1; *W. Eberbach*, Wird die ärztliche Aufklärung zur Fiktion? (Teil 2), MedR 2019, 111.

sentliche Funktionsweise und mögliche Fehlerquellen für eine informierte Einwilligung ausreichen.[29]

Im Falle einer Hautkrebsdiagnose wäre dies z.B. die Angabe, dass ein Modell mithilfe von Bilddaten trainiert wurde und so erlernt hat, zwischen verschiedenen Formen von Muttermalen zu unterscheiden. Notwendig könnten auch Angaben zur Performanz des Systems und der erfolgten klinischen Bewertung sein. Somit würde die Diagnoseaufklärung gleichgeschaltet werden mit der h.M. zur Auslegung der „involvierten Logik" in Art. 13–15 DSGVO.[30] Eine Aufklärung i.S.v. „Sie haben Hautkrebs, da die Größe des Muttermals 5 mm überschreitet und die Ränder unscharf sind"[31] ist rechtlich nicht erforderlich. Dieser Fokus auf eine Form von Systemtransparenz spiegelt sich m.E. inzwischen auch in Art. 13 AIA wider, der das Hauptaugenmerk auf Gebrauchsanweisungen für Nutzerinnen legt. Diese müssen u.a. Informationen zu den Merkmalen, Fähigkeiten und Leistungsgrenzen eines Hochrisikosystems enthalten. Diese Angaben erlauben den Ärztinnen das notwendige grobe Verständnis für ein System und somit eine grobe Aufklärung.

2. Verlaufsaufklärung

Dieser Teil der Aufklärung, teilweise als Therapie-, Behandlungs- oder Verlaufsaufklärung bezeichnet, soll der Patientin ein Bild von Wesen und Umfang, von der Schwere und Dringlichkeit der geplanten Maßnahmen sowie Informationen über die Erfolgsaussichten und allfällige Folgewirkungen liefern.[32] Damit werden die therapeutischen Möglichkeiten und ihre Alternativen dargelegt.[33] Die Ärztin muss daher das Für und Wider

---

29 *Stöger*, Explainability (Fn. 16), 147 f; international *R. Matulionyte/P. Nolan/F. Magrebi/A. Beheshti*, Should AI-Enabled Medical Devices be Explainable? 2022, abrufbar unter https://papers.ssrn.com/sol3/papers.cfm?abstract_id=4140234 (zuletzt abgerufen: 09.12. 2022), S. 27 f; *D. Schiff/J. Borenstein*, How Should Clinicians Communicate with Patients About the Roles of Artificially Intelligent Team Members? AMA Journal of Ethics 2019, 138 (140 f.).

30 *D. Schönberger*, Artificial intelligence in healthcare, International Journal of Law and Information Technology 2019, 171, (190); a.A. *K. Astromskė/E. Peičius/P. Astromskis*, Ethical and legal challenges of informed consent applying artificial intelligence in medical diagnostic consultations, AI & SOCIETY 2021, 509 (515 f.).

31 *Linardatos*, Medizinprodukte (Fn. 5), 371 spricht von der „inneren, medizinspezifischen Logik".

32 *Memmer*, Aufklärung (Fn. 12), I.3.2.1.2.

33 *Neumayr* (Fn. 1), Einleitung ABGB Rn. 39.

einer therapeutischen Maßnahme nachvollziehbar vermitteln, sodass die Patientin die Tragweite ihrer Entscheidung überschauen kann.[34]

Wenn auch ML-Systeme bislang primär in der Diagnose Einsatz finden, so existieren auch im Bereich der Therapie bereits erste Anwendungen. Bspw. wurde ein System für die Diagnose und Behandlung von Sepsis auf der Intensivstation konstruiert, das die passende Medikamentendosierung wählt.[35] Erste vollautomatisierte Chirurgieroboter werden experimentell erprobt.[36]

Dabei stellt sich die Frage, ob für die Verlaufsaufklärung eine Erklärung notwendig ist, warum ein Modell z.B. bei Brustkrebs der Option der chirurgischen Behandlung eine höhere Erfolgswahrscheinlichkeit zuweist als anderen Behandlungsalternativen. Denn nach manchen Stimmen wie *J. C. Bjerring* und *J. Busch* reicht eine Darlegung der Vor- und Nachteile nicht aus. Eine Erklärung, warum eine Therapiemethode effizienter ist, wäre daher notwendig.[37] Auf rechtlicher Ebene ist diese Annahme jedoch zu hinterfragen. Denn die Wahl einer Therapiemethode obliegt der Ärztin, solange sie dem Stand der medizinischen Wissenschaft entspricht. Sie muss nicht ungefragt über potentiell mögliche Behandlungsalternativen aufklären.[38] Sie muss z.B. die Wahl oder Dosierung von Medikamenten nicht umfassend rechtfertigen. Selbst wenn eine „entschlossene Patientin" eine bestimmte Maßnahme wünscht, muss die Ärztin zwar die potentiell geringeren Erfolgschancen, nicht aber etwaige Alternativen darlegen.[39]

Festzustellen ist jedoch wiederum, dass beim Einsatz von ML-Systemen, die gegenwärtig noch als „Außenseitermethoden" anzusehen sind, jedenfalls über den Umstand aufzuklären ist, dass ML eingesetzt wird. Notwendig ist der Hinweis, dass es sich um eine neue oder unerprobte

---

34 *Prutsch*, Aufklärung (Fn. 17), S. 139 f.
35 *M. Komorowski/L. A. Celi/O. Badawi/A. C. Gordon/A. Aldo Faisal*, The Artificial Intelligence Clinician learns optimal treatment strategies for sepsis in intensive care, Nat Med 2018, 1716.
36 *H. Saeidi/J. D. Opfermann/M. Kam/S. Wei/S. Leonard/H. Hsieh/J. U. Kang/A. Krieger*, Autonomous robotic laparoscopic surgery for intestinal anastomosis, Science Robotics 2022, abrufbar unter https://pubmed.ncbi.nlm.nih.gov/3508 0901/ (zuletzt abgerufen: 09.12.2022)
37 *J. C. Bjerring/J. Busch*, Artificial Intelligence and Patient-Centered Decision-Making, Philosophy & Technology 2021, 349 (362 f.).
38 *Neumayr* (Fn. 1), Einleitung ABGB Rn. 40.
39 *Neumayr* (Fn. 1), Einleitung ABGB Rn. 40.

Behandlungsmethode handelt und deshalb die Risiken noch nicht voll abschätzbar sind.[40]

Die Aufklärung über „Art und Wesen" einer Behandlung ist, da nur Grundinformationen notwendig sind (z.B. „Medikamentengabe, deren Dosierung durch KI unterstützt wird"), auch bei Black-Box-Modellen möglich. Die notwendige Aufklärung über „den Umfang", die „Schwere einer Behandlung", die „Erfolgsaussichten und Versagerquote" einer Methode, die „mit der Behandlung verbundenen Belastungen", die „Folgen der Behandlung" und die Gefahren der Unterlassung der Behandlung stellen Informationen dar, die nicht durch gängige *eXplainable-AI*-Techniken (XAI),[41] sondern auf empirischem Weg, primär durch die klinische Bewertung, gewonnen werden können. In einigen Fällen dürften die dafür notwendigen Informationen bereits vorliegen, bspw. wenn ein Modell auf Auswahl und Dosierung zwischen verschiedenen, bereits erprobten Medikamenten eingeschränkt ist.

Die notwendigen Angaben korrespondieren dabei teilweise mit der in Anh. I Regel 23.4 MPVO normierten Gebrauchsanweisung für Medizinprodukte. So informiert bspw. die „Zweckbestimmung des Produkts mit einer genauen Angabe der Indikationen, Kontraindikationen, Patientenzielgruppe[n]" bereits über „Art und Wesen" einer Behandlung. Da die MPVO nicht speziell auf „intelligente Medizinprodukte" abgestimmt ist, könnte Art. 13 Abs. 2, 3 AIA die Anforderungen an Gebrauchsanweisungen weiter konkretisieren. So korrespondieren die dort normierten Angaben über das Maß „an Genauigkeit […] für das das Hochrisiko-KI-System getestet und validiert wurde und das zu erwarten ist" mit den „Erfolgsaussichten" einer Methode.[42] Die weiteren notwendigen Angaben zur Behandlung erfordern dabei m.E., wie bereits dargelegt, empirische Evaluierung.

Besteht eine „echte Auswahl", d.h. Methoden, die gleichwertig sind, aber unterschiedliche Risiken und Erfolgschancen haben, sind die Vor- und Nachteile der Alternativen gemeinsam abzuwägen.[43] So bieten sich

---

40 *C. Katzenmeier*, KI in der Medizin – Haftungsfragen, MedR 2021, 859 (861); *G. Spindler*, Medizin und IT, insbesondere Arzthaftungs- und IT-Sicherheitsrecht, in: C. Katzenmeier (Hrsg.), Festschrift für Dieter Hart. Medizin – Recht – Wissenschaft, Berlin 2020, S. 581 (602). Allgemein zu „Außenseitermethoden" *Memmer*, Aufklärung (Fn. 12), I.3.3.2.3.

41 *C. Molnar*, Interpretable Machine Learning, 2. Aufl., München 2022.

42 Siehe auch Anh. I Regel 15.1 MPVO zu diagnostischen Produkten.

43 *Memmer*, Aufklärung (Fn. 12), I.3.2.1.2.2.

Vergleichsstudien an, um die Vor- und Nachteile einer „menschlichen" und einer „KI-Behandlung" zu kontrastieren.[44]

Um die Erfolgsaussichten von Alternativen zu vergleichen, reichen jedoch übliche Performanzmetriken wie Genauigkeit (*accuracy*),[45] die häufig nur anhand des Testdatensatzes und nicht „im Feld" ermittelt werden, nicht aus. Denn die im „Labor" erzielten Vorteile lassen sich vielfach nicht auf die Realität übertragen. Die so ermittelte Genauigkeit kann potentiell einen fehlerhaften Entscheidungsprozess des Modells i.S.e. „Kluger-Hans"-Effekts[46] verbergen. Neben der Genauigkeit müssen der Patientin daher auch andere Performanzangaben wie die *false-positive-* oder *false-negative-*Rate verständlich mitgeteilt werden.[47]

Um einer Patientin eine echte Wahl zu ermöglichen, sind daneben weiterführende Informationen über Vor- und Nachteile, eine verschieden starke Intensität des Eingriffs, die unterschiedlichen Risiken, Schmerzbelastungen und Erfolgsaussichten zu erteilen.[48] So könnte bspw. darüber aufzuklären sein, dass eine automatisierte Operation weniger invasiv ist und die Konvaleszenz rascher erfolgt. Wiederum ist wahrscheinlich, dass sich eine KI-gestützte Behandlung in Zukunft zum medizinischen Standard entwickelt und somit nicht ungefragt über Alternativen zu dieser aufzuklären sein wird.

3. Risikoaufklärung

Als dritte Komponente der Selbstbestimmungsaufklärung fungiert die Risikoaufklärung. Die Ärztin hat über mögliche Gefahren der Behandlung aufzuklären, damit die Patientin eine Vorstellung erhält, welche Komplikationen selbst dann auftreten können, wenn die Behandlung entsprechend *lege artis* und mit größter ärztlicher Sorgfalt durchgeführt wird.[49] Ihr muss die Möglichkeit unvermeidbarer medizinischer Fehlschläge oder Folgeschäden mitgeteilt werden, soweit sie wissenschaftlich bekannt sind

---

44 *Schiff/Borenstein*, Clinicians (Fn. 29), 140 f.

45 *F. Cabitza*, Breeding electric zebras in the fields of Medicine, 2017, https://arxiv.org/abs/1701.04077, S. 5 (zuletzt abgerufen: 09.12.2022).

46 *H. Chang Yoon/R. Torrance/N. Scheinerman*, Machine learning in medicine, J Med Ethics 2021, 1 (2).

47 *P. Hacker/R. Krestel/S. Grundmann/F. Naumann*, Explainable AI under contract and tort law, Artificial Intelligence and Law 2020, 415 (421).

48 *Memmer*, Aufklärung (Fn. 12), I.3.2.1.2.2.

49 *Memmer*, Aufklärung (Fn. 12), I.3.2.1.3.

und einigermaßen ernsthaft in Betracht kommen.[50] Mit der Einwilligung nimmt die Patientin die Verwirklichung dieser Risiken in Kauf.[51] Die Grenzen zwischen der Risikoaufklärung und der Verlaufsaufklärung sind dabei, wie die obigen Ausführungen zu den Erfolgschancen einer Behandlung zeigen, teilweise fließend.

Zunächst ist im Rahmen der Risikoaufklärung über sog. „eingriffsspezifische Gefahren" aufzuklären. Die „Typizität" ergibt sich nicht aus der Komplikationshäufigkeit, sondern aus dem Umstand, dass das Risiko speziell dem geplanten Eingriff anhaftet und auch bei Anwendung allergrößter Sorgfalt und fehlerfreier Durchführung nicht sicher zu vermeiden ist.[52] Bei KI-Systemen muss daher auch über schwer erkenn-, aber erwartbare Fehlleistungen aufgeklärt werden.[53] Da nur auf zum Zeitpunkt der Behandlung bekannte, typische Gefahren hinzuweisen ist, ist m.E. wiederum der Hinweis auf KI als „Außenseitermethode" notwendig, deren Risiken sich noch nicht vollständig abschätzen lassen.

Dabei ist wahrscheinlich, dass bspw. automatisierte Chirurgie andere „typische" Gefahren (z.B. Übertragung von Elektroschocks, unbemerkt abbrechende Instrumententeile)[54] aufweist, über die aufgeklärt werden muss. Damit korrespondierend muss die Patientin im Rahmen der Sicherungsaufklärung darüber aufgeklärt werden, dass z.B. eine unerwartete Bewegung eine Verletzung durch die autonomen Roboterarme hervorrufen könnte.[55]

Hauptquelle für die Risikoaufklärung könnten wiederum die Gebrauchsanweisungen nach der MPVO, primär aber Art. 13 Abs. 2, 3 AIA, darstellen. Diese haben Informationen über „alle bekannten und vorhersehbaren Umstände, die sich auf das erwartete Maß an Genauigkeit [...] auswirken" oder „[...] die zu Risiken für die Gesundheit und Sicherheit oder die Grundrechte führen" können und Informationen zur „Leistung bezüglich der Personen oder Personengruppen, auf die das System bestimmungsgemäß angewandt werden soll", zu enthalten. Daher müsste angege-

---

50 *Engljähringer*, Aufklärungspflicht (Fn. 17), S. 12; *Prutsch*, Aufklärung (Fn. 17), S. 142 f.

51 *Jesser-Huß*, Haftung (Fn. 17), Rn. 83.

52 *Neumayr* (Fn. 1), Einleitung ABGB Rn. 44.

53 E. *Paar*/K. *Stöger*, Medizinische KI, in: Fritz/Tomaschek (Hrsg.), Konnektivität, Münster 2021, S. 85 (89).

54 E. *Silvestrini*, da Vinci Robotic Surgery Complications, 2021, abrufbar unter https://www.drugwatch.com/davinci-surgery/complications/ (zuletzt abgerufen: 09.12.2022).

55 L. *Blechschmitt*, Die straf- und zivilrechtliche Haftung des Arztes beim Einsatz roboterassistierter Chirurgie, Baden-Baden 2017, S. 75.

ben werden, wenn z.B. die Beleuchtung im Raum negativen Einfluss auf ein Bilderkennungssystem haben könnte, wenn ein chirurgisches System bei einer bestimmten Haltung der Patientin zu unerwarteten Schnittbewegungen neigt oder ein System in Bezug auf eine Patientengruppe, z.B. mangels entsprechender Trainingsdaten, eine geringere Performanz aufweist. Unter die „bekannten oder vorhersehbaren Umstände[,][…] die zu Risiken für die Gesundheit" führen können, fallen m.E. auch sog. „patientenspezifische Risiken". Diese ergeben sich spezifisch aus in der Sphäre der Patientin liegenden Faktoren (bspw. körperliche Merkmale wie Alter, Gewicht, Allgemeinkonstitution, anatomische Regelwidrigkeiten).[56] Daher könnte eine Aufklärung darüber notwendig sein, dass z.B. anatomische Anomalien bei einer Behandlung durch ML zu erhöhten Behandlungsrisiken führen.

Unter Umständen hat eine Ärztin auch über die personelle und apparative Ausstattung aufzuklären. Da nicht jeder Patientin eine Behandlung mit den neuesten Apparaten geboten werden kann, muss sie – wenn die neuen Methoden gravierende Vorteile bringen – über diese informiert werden, um ihr die Option zu eröffnen, diese Behandlung, z.B. in einem anderen Krankenhaus, in Anspruch zu nehmen.[57] Zukünftig muss daher darüber aufgeklärt werden, dass eine KI-gestützte Behandlung als neue Methode in einer anderen Praxis angeboten wird oder dass ein Krankenhaus über bessere KI-Modelle verfügt.

Als Zwischenfazit ist festzustellen, dass sich die Aufklärung, die der Patientin Selbstbestimmung ermöglichen soll, in der Praxis häufig auf den Hinweis auf den Einsatz von KI und auf eine verständliche Darlegung der „Gebrauchsanweisung" reduziert. Dies umfasst eine allgemeine Systembeschreibung in Verbindung mit Angaben zur Leistung, die mittels klinischer Bewertung gesichert sein sollte. Eine präzisere Aufklärung, die potentiell den Einsatz von XAI-Techniken notwendig macht, ist nach dieser Interpretation nicht Kernbestandteil der Aufklärung. Diese Interpretation der medizinischen Aufklärung kann jedoch kritisch hinterfragt werden. Eine Reihe von potentiellen Argumenten lassen sich vorbringen.

---

56 *Memmer*, Aufklärung (Fn. 12), I.3.2.1.3.2; *Neumayr* (Fn. 1), Einleitung ABGB Rn. 45.
57 *Memmer*, Aufklärung (Fn. 12), I.3.2.1.3.3.

C. Aufklärung im (technischen) Wandel

I. AIA und Transparenz

Welche Rolle Transparenz oder Interpretierbarkeit im AIA zukommt, ist zum gegenwärtigen Zeitpunkt Gegenstand von Diskussionen. Art. 13 Abs. 1 AIA verlangt zwar, dass „Hochrisiko-KI-Systeme […] so konzipiert und entwickelt [werden], dass ihr Betrieb hinreichend transparent ist, damit die Nutzer die Ergebnisse des Systems angemessen interpretieren und verwenden können", wobei die Transparenz „[…] auf eine geeignete Art und in einem angemessenen Maß gewährleistet [wird], damit die Nutzer und Anbieter ihre in Kapitel 3 dieses Titels festgelegten einschlägigen Pflichten erfüllen können."

Jedoch verzichtet der AIA auf eine nähere Definition der verwendeten Begriffe Transparenz und Interpretierbarkeit. Die konkrete Interpretation und der Bezug zu Termini wie Erklärbarkeit, Rechtfertigung oder Accountability bleibt damit offen.[58] Es ist jedoch kaum zu erwarten, dass Art. 13 Abs. 1 AIA die Verwendung von White-Box-Modellen oder die detaillierte Erklärung einer konkreten Entscheidung erfordert.[59] Vielmehr ist wahrscheinlich, dass die nähere Implementation von „Transparenz" im Ermessen der Nutzerinnen liegt bzw. erst von den Europäischen Normungsorganisationen durch harmonisierte Standards mit Leben erfüllt wird.

Zahlreiche Fragen wirft die *human-in-the-loop*-Regelung gem. Art. 14 AIA auf. Dieser normiert die Einrichtung einer wirksamen menschlichen Aufsicht. Die zuständigen Personen müssen gem. Art. 14 Abs. 3 AIA die Fähigkeiten und Grenzen eines Hochrisikosystems vollständig verstehen und die Ergebnisse richtig interpretieren können. Als zentraler Aspekt sind „[…] insbesondere […] die vorhandenen Interpretationswerkzeuge und -methoden zu berücksichtigen". Diese Maßnahmen, um die Interpretation zu erleichtern, sind auch Teil der Gebrauchsanweisung (Art. 13 Abs. 3 lit. d AIA). Denn nach Art. 29 Abs. 4 AIA müssen die Nutzerinnen ein System anhand der Gebrauchsanweisung überwachen sowie das Vor-

---

58 *D. Bomhard/M. Merkle*, Europäische KI-Verordnung, RDi 2021, 276 (280); *M. Ebers*, Standardisierung Künstlicher Intelligenz und KI-Verordnungsvorschlag, RDi 2021, 588 (590); *P. Hacker/J.-H. Passoth*, Varieties of AI Explanations Under the Law, in A. Holzinger/R. Goebel/R. Fong/T. Moon/K.-R. Müller/W. Samek (Hrsg.), xxAI, Cham 2022, S. 343 (358 ff.).

59 So wurde bspw nach *Roth-Isigkeit*, Transparenzanforderungen (Fn. 5), 284 zugunsten einer Systemtransparenz, abgesichert durch Begleitpflichten, auf eine Erklärung einer konkreten Entscheidung verzichtet.

liegen eines Risikos oder einer Fehlfunktion melden und die Verwendung aussetzen können.

Ähnlich wird in der medizinrechtlichen Literatur aufgrund der ärztlichen Sorgfalt (in Österreich: § 49 ÄrzteG und § 8 Abs. 2 KAKuG) argumentiert, dass Ergebnisse eines ML-Systems wie Diagnosen einer Plausibilitätsprüfung unterzogen werden müssen.[60] Art. 14 AIA reflektiert damit nach *Buchner* den Gedanken, dass automatisierte Systeme akzeptabel sind, wenn sie von Menschen verstanden und hinterfragt, kontrolliert, überstimmt oder abgeschaltet werden können.[61]

Die Rolle der Interpretationswerkzeuge in Bezug auf Art. 14 AIA ist jedoch m.E. noch zu undefiniert. Ist das Ziel die Vermeidung grober Fehler, z.B. offensichtlicher Fehldiagnosen, sind XAI-Methoden potentiell überflüssig. Ist das Ziel die Aufdeckung subtiler Fehler, können diese Fehler mittels XAI-Methoden nicht zuverlässig und rasch genug evaluiert werden, um eine Aufsicht sicherzustellen. Denn wie in der Literatur[62] festgehalten wurde, erlaubt bspw. eine *heatmap*, die die relevanten Regionen z.B. auf einem Röntgenbild hervorhebt, keinen Schluss darauf, ob medizinisch relevante Faktoren für das Ergebnis ausschlaggebend waren und die Diagnose normativ akzeptiert werden kann.[63] Die Folge könnte sein, dass eine Ärztin aufgrund der eigenen (begrenzten) Fachkenntnisse[64] ihr als logisch erscheinende Ergebnisse bestätigt und damit potentiell Fehler vermeidet, aber auch ihren persönlichen Bias einbringt.

Art. 14 AIA deutet m.E. stärker als Art. 13 Abs. 1 AIA an, dass XAI-Methoden eine bedeutende Rolle im Gefüge des AIA spielen. Welche genau dies im Gefüge der *human-in-the-loop*-Regelung ist, z.B. ob Art. 14 AIA die Pflicht, XAI zu implementieren, beinhaltet, bedarf noch einer Klarstellung im Gesetzgebungsprozess.

---

60 *Paar/Stöger*, KI (Fn. 53), 86.
61 *B. Buchner*, Artificial intelligence as a challenge for the law, Int. Cybersecur. Law Rev. 2022, 181 (184).
62 *M. Ghassemi/L. Oakden-Rayner/A. L. Beam*, The false hope of current approaches to explainable artificial intelligence in health care, Lancet Digit Health 2021, E745; a.A. *J. Amann/A. Blasimme/E. Vayena/D. Frey/V. I. Madai*, Explainability for artificial intelligence in healthcare, BMC Medical Informatics and Decision Making 2020, 1 (2 f.); *S. Reddy*, Explainability and artificial intelligence in medicine, Lancet Digit Health 2022, E745.
63 *Roth-Isigkeit*, Transparenzanforderungen (Fn. 5), 280: „Bei komplexen Gewichtungsvorgängen (wie z.B. Diagnosevorschlägen) ist hingegen weitgehend unklar, inwieweit das sichtbar gemachte Ausgabeergebnis des Arbeitsprozesses für Menschen verständlich wäre."
64 *Eberbach*, Aufklärung (Fn. 28), 3.

II. KI-Systeme als „Aspirin 2.0"

Die häufig vorgebrachte Analogie von KI zu Arzneimitteln, Röntgengeräten und anderen Diagnoseinstrumenten, über die rechtlich nicht näher aufgeklärt werden muss bzw. über die eine Ärztin selbst häufig nicht im Detail Bescheid weiß, könnte sich m.E. in Zukunft als unhaltbar erweisen.[65]

Zwar genügt, wie ausgeführt, zum derzeitigen Stand m.E. in Bezug auf Modelle, die auf einen eng begrenzten Zweck, wie Hautkrebserkennung, zugeschnitten sind, eine allgemeine Funktionsbeschreibung, die eine grobe Vorstellung des Modells ermöglicht, als Substrat der Aufklärung.

Zunehmend werden dem technischen Trend entsprechend jedoch komplexe Modelle wie GPT-3 konstruiert, die für verschiedene Zwecke eingesetzt werden. Würde z.B. ein Modell als Teil der Systemmedizin[66] im Rahmen einer Vorsorgeuntersuchung zahlreiche verschiedene Datenquellen wie die Krankenakte, genetische Daten, Umwelteinflüsse aus Sensordaten und die Social-Media-Aktivität einbeziehen, erlaubt eine abstrakte Funktionsbeschreibung keine Vorstellung von der Funktionsweise und dürfte für eine Patientin jeden Bezug zu ihrer Diagnose verlieren. Würde eine Aufklärung über ein System, das über hundert Krankheiten feststellen kann, i.S.v. „Sie werden innerhalb der nächsten Monate mit 96% Wahrscheinlichkeit Schizophrenie ausbilden. Das dafür verwendete Modell wurde mit Daten aus der Krankengeschichte, genetischen und Social-Media-Daten trainiert. Das Modell ist nach Evaluierungen zu 87% genau." eine selbstbestimmte Entscheidung ermöglichen? Im Gegensatz zu anderen Methoden scheint es zweifelhaft, ob die Ärztin in dieser Situation auch nur eine grobe Vorstellung von der Funktionsweise eines solchen Modells aufweist, die zum Inhalt der Aufklärung werden könnte.[67] Im Kontrast zu Röntgengeräten ist das theoretische Grundgerüst von Modellen, wie ein Verweis auf Systeme zur Emotionserkennung zeigt,[68] häufig nur gering ausgeprägt oder umstritten.

Auch können XAI-Methoden in solchen Konstellationen eine Aufklärung nur bedingt effektuieren. So könnte in einem Idealszenario eine sog. lokale *post-hoc*-Technik wie LIME oder SHAP, die z.B. die entscheidenden

---

65 *T. P. Quinn/S. Jacobs/M. Senadeera/V. Le/S. Coghlan*, The three ghosts of medical AI, Artificial Intelligence In Medicine 2022, 1 (5 f.).

66 *Katzenmeier*, Data (Fn. 5), 259 f.

67 *Matulionyte/Nolan/Magrebi/Beheshti*, Devices (Fn. 29), S. 21.

68 *M. Veale/F. Zuiderveen Borgesius*, Demystifying the Draft EU Artificial Intelligence Act, CRi 2021, 97 (107 f.).

Symptome als Merkmale für eine konkrete Diagnose visualisieren oder reihen, eine Diagnoseaufklärung ermöglichen.[69] Dies setzt jedoch m.E. voraus, dass die hervorgehobenen Merkmale und ihr Bezug zur Diagnose (kausal) nachvollziehbar sind. Bei Modellen mit tausenden Merkmalen, wie dem Tippverhalten am Handy und komplexen Interaktionen, z.B. zwischen Genetik und Umwelt,[70] erlauben solche Methoden jedoch nur bedingten Einblick und begrenztes Verständnis für ein Ergebnis. Aufgrund der korrelationsbasierten Natur von ML ist generell fraglich, ob es eine Erklärung geben kann, die sich in das kausale Denken von Ärztin und Patientin einfügt und somit ein Hinterfragen der Diagnose ermöglicht.

III. Stand der Wissenschaft und Black Box

Eine Frage, die eng mit der Aufklärung über Behandlungsalternativen verzahnt ist, ist, ob Black-Box-Modelle zum neuen Stand der medizinischen Wissenschaft werden könnten oder ob ihre Opazität dem entgegensteht. Nach *Hacker et. al.* reicht höhere Genauigkeit dafür nicht aus. Vielmehr würde die Evaluierung der unterschiedlichen Risiken, ob im konkreten Fall die Vorteile einer Methode die Nachteile überwiegen, häufig den Einsatz von lokalen XAI-Methoden implizieren. Denn die fehlende Interpretierbarkeit wäre trotz der größeren Leistung opaker Modelle mit Risiken für die Patientin verbunden. Ein Modell könnte bspw. nicht auf das Vorliegen von *false negatives* oder *false positives* evaluiert werden. Die Verwendung von Black-Box-Modellen könnte daher nur in Sonderfällen gerechtfertigt werden, z.B. wenn die höhere Performanz die Risiken übertreffen würde oder wenn Fehler auch ohne Interpretierbarkeit aufgedeckt werden könnten. Wäre Interpretierbarkeit zur Aufdeckung von Fehlern notwendig bzw. würde sie diese erleichtern, wäre der Einsatz interpretierbarer Modelle durch den Stand der Wissenschaft geboten. Ebenso kann nach *Hacker et al.* ein Black-Box-Modell den Stand der Wissenschaft nicht „anheben" und damit verpflichtend werden, da ein solches Modell, dessen Ergebnisse nicht kritisch hinterfragt werden können, nicht sinnvoll in den medizinischen Arbeitsablauf eingegliedert werden könnte.[71]

---

69 Ähnlich im Datenschutzrecht, *T. Hoeren/M. Niehoff*, Artificial Intelligence in Medical Diagnoses and the Right to Explanation, EDPL 2018, 308 (317 f.).
70 *W. N. Price, II.*, Medical Malpractice and Black Box Medicine, in: I. Glenn/H. Fernandez Lynch/E. Vayena/U. Gasser (Hrsg.), Big Data, Health Law and Bioethics, Cambridge 2018, S. 295 (297).
71 *Hacker/Krestel/Grundmann/Naumann*, AI (Fn. 47), 421 f.

Damit wäre in vielen Fällen der Einsatz von XAI-Methoden notwendig, damit ein Modell zum neuen Stand der Wissenschaft werden könnte. M.E. ist den Autoren jedenfalls darin zuzustimmen, dass nicht grundlos ein Black-Box-Modell verwendet werden sollte, wenn ein ähnlich performantes White-Box-Modell zur Verfügung steht.

IV. *Generierung von klinischer Evidenz*

Auch wenn klinische Bewertung, auf die z.B. in der Risikoaufklärung verwiesen wird, für intelligente Medizinprodukte eine größere Rolle spielen dürfte als XAI-Techniken, sind damit doch Probleme verbunden. Zunächst herrscht ein Mangel an Studien, die klinische Wirksamkeit und nicht Effizienz im „Labor" belegen.[72] Die Qualität existierender Studien gilt als zweifelhaft.[73] Selbst die Anwendbarkeit von randomisierten klinischen Studien auf ML-Systeme wird teilweise hinterfragt.[74] Auch wenn klinische Evidenz existiert, haben Ärztinnen potentiell keinen Zugang dazu, da Studien nicht veröffentlicht werden müssen, wenn Interessen des Geheimnisschutzes dem entgegenstehen.[75]

Ein Verweis auf eine klinische Bewertung als Teil der Aufklärung ist somit gegenwärtig selten realistisch. Konzeptuell können klinische Studien als Validierungsschritt auch nur bedingt die vorhergehende Hypothesenbildung, die bei ML-Systemen häufig fehlt, ersetzen.[76] Bis ausreichend klinische Evidenz vorliegt, könnten XAI-Methoden dazu beitragen, Ärztinnen eine Plausibilitätsprüfung und eine Abschätzung des Risikos zu ermöglichen. Für die Generierung von klinischer Evidenz könnten wiederum Methoden wie *causal inference*,[77] die Kausalitäten und nicht nur Korrelationen modelliert, zur notwendigen Hypothesenbildung beitragen.

---

72 E. *Topol*, High-performance medicine, nature medicine 2019, 44 (45).

73 S. *Scholz*, Evidenzbasierter Einsatz von KI in der Medizin, in: I. Eisenberger/R. Niemann/M. Wendland (Hrsg.), Smart Regulation. Symposium 2021, Tübingen 2022, i.E.

74 *Price*, Malpractice (Fn. 70), S. 301 f.

75 *Scholz*, Einsatz (Fn. 73), i.E.

76 S. *Kundu*, AI in medicine must be explainable, Nat Med 2021, 1328 (1328).

77 M. *Prosperi/Y. Guo/M. Sperrin/J. S. Koopman/J. S. Min/X. He/S. Rich/M. Wang/ I. E. Buchan/J. Bian*, Causal inference and counterfactual prediction in machine learning for actionable healthcare, Nature Machine Intelligence 2020, 369.

V. (X)AI-Entwicklungen

Auch wenn, wie erwähnt, derzeitig gebräuchliche XAI-Techniken nur begrenzt den Anforderungen der medizinischen Aufklärung i.S.e. personalisierten, auf die Patientin zugeschnittenen Gesprächs entsprechen, so ist die technische Entwicklung nicht statisch. Diese Entwicklungen könnten in Hinblick auf den Stand der Medizin dazu beitragen, dass nicht nur bessere intelligente Medizinprodukte, sondern auch interpretierbarere Medizinprodukte zunehmend dem *state of the art* entsprechen.

So ist ein Trend zu beobachten, neben neuen XAI-Verfahren auch einheitliche Evaluierungsmetriken zu konzipieren, die helfen, die „Brauchbarkeit" einer Erklärung, z.B. den Grad der „Kausalität" oder die notwendige Anpassung an das „Zielpublikum", zu evaluieren und zu vergleichen.[78]

Auch sog. „neuro-symbolische" Techniken, die die Ansätze von Expertensystemen, deren Regeln durch fachlichen Input z.B. von Ärztinnen manuell konstruiert werden, mit maschinellem Lernen verbinden und somit potentiell bessere Interpretierbarkeit aufweisen,[79] könnten m.E. dazu beitragen, dass das Ideal einer gemeinsamen, partnerschaftlichen Entscheidungsfindung aufrecht bleibt und die Rolle der Ärztin als Entscheidungsträgerin nicht unterminiert wird.

D. Conclusio

Jonathan Zittrain spricht von der potentiellen „intellektuellen Schuld",[80] die wir uns aufladen, wenn wir zwar wissen, dass ein Produkt funktioniert, aber die Antwort auf das „Warum?" in die Zukunft verschieben. Die zwei Abschnitte dieses Beitrags haben versucht, die Frage, ob wir die Schuld einer „Black-Box-Medizin" in Kauf nehmen sollen, aus zwei unterschiedlichen Blickwinkeln zu betrachten. Sollen wir die Idealvorstellung der Auf-

---

78 *A. Holzinger/G. Langs/H. Denk/K. Zatloukal/H. Müller*, Causability and explainability of artificial intelligence in medicine, WIRE's Data Mining and Knowledge Discovery 2019, 1.

79 Mitteilung der Kommission an das Europäische Parlament, den Rat, den Europäischen Wirtschafts- und Sozialausschuss und den Ausschuss der Regionen. Weißbuch Zur Künstlichen Intelligenz – ein europäisches Konzept für Exzellenz und Vertrauen, COM (2020) 65 final 5.

80 *J. Zittrain*, Intellectual Debt, in: S. Vöneky/P. Kellmeyer/O. Müller/W. Burgard (Hrsg.), The Cambridge Handbook of Responsible Artificial Intelligence, Cambridge/New York/Port Melbourne/New Delhi/Singapore 2022, S. 176.

klärung als Grundbaustein für eine partnerschaftliche Entscheidungsfindung aufgeben? Sollen wir zugunsten des utilitaristischen Lockrufs einer (potentiell) „besseren Medizin für alle" zulassen, dass das persönliche Aufklärungsgespräch[81] durch allgemeine Informationen und standardisierte Aufklärungsbögen[82] zu KI-Systemen abgelöst wird?

Zusammengefasst gilt es, in den Worten der (österreichischen) *Bioethikkommission*, „abzuwägen zwischen den Möglichkeiten neue Diagnosemöglichkeiten zu erhalten [...] und der für ärztliches Handeln fundamentalen dialogischen Komponente, die dem Begründen und Einsichtigmachen – ,telling a story' – großen Wert beimisst."[83] Mit Blick auf den AIA und seine noch zu konkretisierenden Transparenzanforderungen, einer Rechtsprechung, die der Aufklärung eine immer größere Rolle beimisst, und Entwicklungen im XAI-Bereich ist m.E. noch offen, welche intellektuelle Schuld wir zugunsten intelligenter Medizinprodukte rechtlich auf uns nehmen werden.

---

81 *Memmer*, Aufklärung (Fn. 12), I.3.7.1; *Neumayr* (Fn. 1), Einleitung ABGB Rn. 55.

82 *Memmer*, Aufklärung (Fn. 12), I.3.7.3.1; *Neumayr* (Fn. 1), Einleitung ABGB Rn. 54.

83 *Bioethikkommission*, Ärztliches Handeln im Spannungsfeld von Big Data, Künstlicher Intelligenz und menschlicher Erfahrung, 2020, abrufbar unter https://www.bundeskanzleramt.gv.at/dam/jcr:b3a4fdd0-0d89-430e-ae35-3ad5d991a3e4/200617_Stellungnahme_BigData_Bioethik_A4.pdf (zuletzt abgerufen: 09.12.2022), S. 51.

IV. Transparency in the Financial System

Transparenz(alp)traum DeFi?

Christopher Rennig

A. Einleitung

Berührungsangst mit Superlativen existiert in der Kryptoszene nur selten. Deshalb verwundert es nicht, wenn Decentralized Finance (DeFi) – ein auf der Blockchain-Technologie basierendes Finanzsystem, das ohne zentrale Intermediäre auskommen soll – als „the most automated and transparent financial system in human history"[1] bezeichnet wird – nicht mehr, aber auch nicht weniger! Das Überthema der Konferenz[2] gibt Anlass für eine eingehendere Auseinandersetzung mit dieser Aussage: Geht es bei DeFi tatsächlich transparenter zu als in traditionellen, zentralisierten Finanzsystemen? Dem soll vorliegend nach einer Einführung in DeFi (B.) sowohl aus technischer (C.) als auch aus rechtlicher Sicht (D.) nachgegangen werden.

B. Decentralized Finance (DeFi)

Anwendungen, die DeFi zuzuordnen sind, erbringen – mit den Worten der Deutschen Bundesbank – „finanzwirtschaftliche Dienstleistungen in Verbindung mit Krypto-Token in dezentralen Netzwerken und ersetzen dabei Intermediäre wie Banken, Börsen oder Versicherungen."[3] Im Folgenden soll zunächst das der DeFi zugrunde liegende allgemeine Prinzip dargestellt werden (I.), bevor mit dem *liquidity pool-based lending* ein konkreter Anwendungsfall vorgestellt wird (II.).

---

1 Unstoppable Finance, Unstoppable Finance Statement in the Critical EU Vote on DeFi Wallets on Thursday, 30.3.2022, abrufbar unter https://medium.com/@unsto ppablefinance/unstoppable-finance-statement-on-the-critical-eu-vote-on-defi-wallets -on-thursday-e7abb765edac (zuletzt abgerufen: 19.10.2022).
2 Opazität oder Transparenz? – Zweite Konferenz des Forschungsnetzwerks Junges Digitales Recht 2022.
3 *Deutsche Bundesbank*, Monatsbericht Juli 2021, S. 33, abrufbar unter https://www.b undesbank.de/de/publikationen/berichte/monatsberichte/monatsbericht-juli-2021- 869512 (zuletzt abgerufen: 26.09.2022).

I. Allgemeines Prinzip

DeFi ist das Ergebnis einer Innovationsspirale[4], die ihren Beginn in der Konzeption des Distributed Ledger-Prinzips und der Blockchain-Technologie[5], insb. durch die Veröffentlichung des Bitcoin-Whitepapers[6] im Jahr 2008, nahm. Entwickelt wurden auf dieser Grundlage weitere innovative Technologien, darunter insb. Smart Contracts, also Computerprogramme, die bei Eintritt bestimmter Bedingungen vorher festgelegte Maßnahmen garantiert und manipulationssicher ausführen können,[7] sowie Stablecoins, also Kryptowerte, die durch eine Kopplung an andere (staatliche) Währungen oder Vermögenswerte Wertstabilität erreichen sollen, ohne von staatlichen Stellen herausgegeben worden zu sein. Am (vorläufigen) Ende dieser Entwicklungen steht nun DeFi, dass diese aus der Blockchain-Innovationsspirale hervorgehenden Innovationen miteinander verbindet. Einen guten Überblick über die technische Umsetzung von DeFi bietet der sog. DeFi-Stack:[8]

---

4 Der Begriff der Innovationsspirale beschreibt einen Prozess, in dessen Rahmen Innovationen als Grundlage für weitere Innovationen genutzt werden, sei es durch die Verbesserung von Erfolgsmodellen oder die Nutzung von schlechten Erfahrungen aus misslungenen Innovationen, vgl. *C. Rennig*, Finanztechnologische Innovationen im Bankaufsichtsrecht, Tübingen 2022, S. 47. Der Begriff geht zurück auf *R. Merton*, Financial Innovation and Economic Performance, Journal of Applied Corporate Finance 1992, 12 (18 f.).

5 Vgl. für einen prägnanten Überblick über die Blockchain-Technologie *M. Kaulartz*, Blockchain-Technologien, in: F. Möslein/S. Omlor (Hrsg.), FinTech-Handbuch: Digitalisierung, Recht, Finanzen, 2. Aufl., München 2022, § 5; zu Smart Contracts ebd., Rn. 42 ff.

6 *S. Nakamoto*, Bitcoin: A Peer-to-Peer Electronic Cash System, abrufbar unter https://bitcoin.org/bitcoin.pdf (zuletzt abgerufen: 26.09.2022).

7 Statt vieler *F. Möslein*, Smart Contracts im Zivil- und Handelsrecht, ZHR 2019, 254 (259 ff.); *M. Heckelmann*, Zulässigkeit und Handhabung von Smart Contracts, NJW 2018, 504.

8 Abbildung im Wesentlichen übernommen von *F. Schär*, Decentralized Finance: On Blockchain- and Smart Contract-Based Financial Markets, Federal Reserve Bank of St. Louis Review 2021, 153 (156).

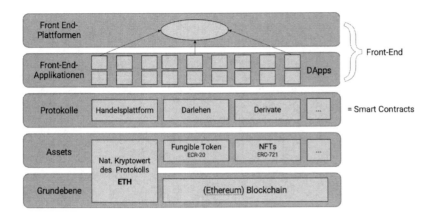

Abbildung 1: Sog. DeFi-Stack

Die Grundebene bildet die Blockchain-Technologie, auf deren Grundlage ein nativer Kryptowert programmiert wird. Im Rahmen von DeFi kommt insb. die Ethereum-Blockchain mit dem nativen Kryptowert Ether (ETH) zum Einsatz. Zudem können andere Kryptowerte auf Grundlage der Blockchain programmiert und transferiert werden. Besondere Bedeutung kommt in DeFi-Systemen sog. Stablecoins – z.B. den jeweils an den US-Dollar gekoppelten DAI, USDC oder USDT – zu, da sie dort als wertstabile Tauschmittel und damit als Geldäquivalent zum Einsatz kommen. Einen weiteren Schub erfahren könnten DeFi-Ökosysteme zudem durch die Einführung elektronischer Zentralbankwährungen, sog. Central Bank Digital Currencies (CBDC).[9] In einem DeFi-Kontext zu sehen sind auch rechtsdogmatische[10] und rechtspolitische[11] Überlegungen zu einer sog. Tokenisierung von Wirtschaftsgütern aller Art und dabei gerade solcher, die nicht ohne Weiteres untereinander austauschbar sind und sich in sog.

---

9 Vgl. zu Diskussionsstand, Umsetzungsmodellen und rechtlicher Einordnung statt vieler *S. Omlor / F. Möslein*, FinTech und PayTech, in: J. Ellenberger/H.-J. Bunte (Hrsg.), Bankrechts-Handbuch, 6. Aufl., München 2022, § 34 Rn. 44 ff.

10 Vgl. dazu z.B. *S. Omlor*, Allgemeines Privatrecht, in: S. Omlor/M. Link (Hrsg., Kryptowährungen und Token, München 2021, S. 257 (295 ff.); *M. Kaulartz/ K. Hirzle/B. Holl*, Tokenisierung durch das Auslobungsmodell, RDi 2022, 324.

11 Zum Beispiel *J. von Buttlar/S. Omlor*, Tokenisierung von Eigentums-, Benutzungs-, Zutritts- und Pfandrechten, ZRP 2021, 169.

Non Fungible Tokens (NFT) verkörpern lassen.[12] Einen ersten Schritt der deutschen Rechtsordnung in diese Richtung stellt das eWpG dar. Dieses erlaubt erstmals die Begebung einer Inhaberschuldverschreibung als Kryptowertpapier, um deren Handelbarkeit über eine Blockchain zu ermöglichen. Je umfassender eine solche Tokenisierung von Wirtschaftsgütern rechtssicher ermöglicht wird, desto umfangreicher können sie auch zur Grundlage von DeFi-Transaktionen werden, mit der Folge einer Annäherung an die Möglichkeiten traditioneller Finanzsysteme (TradFi[13]).

Auf Grundlage der Blockchain-Technologie können auf der Protokollebene Smart Contracts programmiert werden, die eine Programmierung von Wertflüssen oder die Nutzung von DeFi-Anwendungen ermöglichen.[14] Deren Code wird durch die im Rahmen der Blockchain-Technologie genutzten Konsensmechanismen unter Nutzung der Kryptowerte als Tausch- bzw. Anlageinstrument umgesetzt. Ein zentraler Intermediär ist hierzu nicht mehr erforderlich, da dieser durch den Smart Contract ersetzt wird, der die Intermediärsfunktionen übernehmen kann.[15] Um DeFi-Nutzer:innen eine möglichst einfache Interaktion mit dem Code zu ermöglichen, werden für das Front-End sog. DApps (dezentrale Applikation)[16] entwickelt. Einzelne Smart Contracts und DApps sind zudem miteinander kombinierbar.

Entsprechend der mit DeFi verbundenen Dezentralität ist das erklärte Ziel, dass die einmal entwickelten Smart Contracts nicht mehr durch eine zentrale Instanz verändert werden können. Um dennoch die Weiterentwicklung auf Grundlage dezentraler Governancestrukturen zu ermöglichen, werden für eine Vielzahl von Protokollen sog. *governance token* aus-

---

12 Vgl. zu den technischen Grundlagen und den Funktionen von NFT statt vieler *L. M. Guntermann*, Non Fungible Token als Herausforderung für das Sachenrecht, RDi 2022, 200 (201 f.).

13 Bspw. bei *V. Gramlich/M. Principato/B. Schellinger/J. Sedlmeir/J. Amend/J. Stramm/T. Zwede/J. Strüker/N. Urbach*, Decentralized Finance (DeFi) – Foundations, Applications, Potentials, and Challenges, Branch Business & Information Systems Engineering, Fraunhofer Institute for Applied Information Technology FIT, abrufbar unter https://www.fit.fraunhofer.de/en/business-areas/cooperation-systems/blockchain.html (zuletzt abgerufen: 19.10.2022).

14 *F. Möslein/M. Kaulartz/C. Rennig*, Decentralized Finance (DeFi), RDi 2021, 517 (518).

15 Vgl. zur Funktionsübernahme durch den Smart Contract im Rahmen der Kreditvergabe sogleich, B. II.

16 Die Bezeichnung deutet den Unterschied zu Apps an, da der Backend-Code von DApps auf dezentralisierten Servern läuft, vgl. Ethereum, Einführung in DApps, abrufbar unter https://ethereum.org/de/developers/docs/dapps/ (zuletzt abgerufen: 26.09.2022).

gegeben. Deren Inhaber entscheiden durch Mehrheitsentscheidung über sog. *proposals*, also Vorschläge zur Änderung des Codes des zugrundeliegenden Smart Contracts, die von beliebigen Dritten zur Entscheidung gestellt werden können.[17]

II. Speziell: Liquidity pool-based lending am Beispiel von Aave

Als konkretes Anschauungsbeispiel soll an dieser Stelle das dezentral organisierte *liquidity pool-based lending* von Aave dargestellt werden.[18] DeFi-Nutzer:innen wird hier die Möglichkeit eröffnet, Kryptowerte entweder verzinslich zu verleihen oder auf der Gegenseite auf solche Kryptowerte lautende Darlehen aufzunehmen. Die Besonderheit des *liquidity pool-based lending* liegt in der Bereitstellung eines Smart Contracts, der als *liquidity pool* bezeichnet ist. An diesen können Kryptowerte übertragen werden, die sich Kapitalsuchende zeitweise gegen die Zahlung von Zinsen auszahlen lassen können. Der *liquidity pool* erbringt hierbei innerhalb des DeFi-Ökosystems als eine Art technologischer Intermediär im Wesentlichen die Funktionen eines Kreditinstituts: Einerseits werden dort die Kryptowerte einer Vielzahl von Nutzer:innen gesammelt und diese bei Bedarf bspw. gebündelt als Darlehen herausgegeben (sog. Losgrößentransformation), andererseits ermöglicht er das jederzeitige Abziehen der bereitgestellten Kryptowerte, indem gewährte *loans* mit anderen Kryptowerten unterlegt werden (sog. Fristentransformation).[19] Zudem sind die Positionen, die einzelne Nutzer:innen an dem *liquidity pool* halten, selbst tokenisierbar (sog. aToken) und damit handelbar. *Governance token* werden für das Aave-Protokoll in Gestalt des AAVE-Token ausgegeben.

C. DeFi – „the most transparent financial system in history"?

Es sind nun insb. zwei Merkmale, mit denen die Bezeichnung von DeFi als das „transparenteste Finanzsystem aller Zeiten" begründet wird: Einerseits

---

17 *Möslein/Kaulartz/Rennig*, DeFi (Fn. 14), 517 (520).

18 Vgl. für einen detaillierten Überblick über das Aave-Protokoll: https://docs.aave.com/hub/. Die Aave-Protokolle selbst sind einsehbar unter https://github.com/aave (jeweils zuletzt abgerufen: 25.09.2022).

19 Vgl. zu den Funktionen des Finanzsystems und der Bedeutung von Finanzintermediären *C. Rennig*, Finanztechnologische Innovationen, Tübingen 2022, S. 137 ff.

die Open Source-Verfügbarkeit des für den Smart Contract verwendeten Codes, andererseits die Nachverfolgbarkeit sämtlicher Transaktionen, die über eine öffentliche Blockchain abgewickelt werden.[20] Damit verbunden sein soll eine bislang unbekannte freie Verfügbarkeit von historischen und aktuellen Finanzdaten:[21] Über Dienste wie *etherscan.io* lassen sich so nicht nur sämtliche über die Ethereum-Blockchain getätigten Transaktionen minutengenau verfolgen, sondern es ist auch der Kontostand einzelner öffentlicher Adressen innerhalb der Blockchain frei einsehbar. Im Gegensatz dazu sind solche Daten in traditionellen Finanzsystemen entweder überhaupt nicht verfügbar oder auf separat verwalteten Datenbanken verteilt.[22] Mit der freien Einsehbarkeit sämtlicher Transaktionsdaten ist die Hoffnung verbunden, dass sich etwaige systemische Ereignisse, die im schlimmsten Fall zu einem Zusammenbruch des Finanzsystems führen könnten, besser vorhergesehen werden können.[23] Schon die teilweise mit dem Schlagwort „Kryptowinter" betitelten Kursverluste nahezu sämtlicher bekannter Kryptowerte im Mai 2022 legen allerdings nahe, dass diese Hoffnungen nicht überbewertet werden sollten.

Das Versprechen eines erhöhten Grades an Transparenz wird im Hinblick auf seine praktische Umsetzung jedoch zunehmend kritisch beurteilt.[24] Die freie Verfügbarkeit von Daten führe nicht automatisch dazu, dass sie auch genutzt bzw. korrekt interpretiert würden. Dazu kommt, dass trotz der freien Einsehbarkeit von Transaktionen auf der Blockchain darunterliegende Umstände, wie z.B. Abhängigkeiten innerhalb des DeFi-Ökosystems, nicht berücksichtigt werden. Die zu beobachtende Geschwindigkeit von Entwicklungen sowie die Kombinierbarkeit verschiedener Protokolle multipliziert diese Schwierigkeiten nur. Zudem kann die freie Einsehbarkeit der Protokolle einerseits potenziellen Angreifern Gelegenheit bieten, Schwachstellen über längere Zeiträume ungestört auszukundschaften, andererseits den Blockchain-Minern, sich selbst unzulässige Vorteile

---

20 *Schär*, Decentralized Finance (Fn. 8), 153 (169); *D. A Zetzsche/D. W. Arner/ R. P. Buckley*, Decentralized Finance, Journal of Financial Regulation 2020, 172 (181); *Price Waterhouse Cooper*, Decentralised Finance: Defining the future of finance, S. 7, abrufbar unter https://www.pwc.ch/en/insights/digital/defi-defining-t he-future-of-finance.html (zuletzt abgerufen: 26.09.2022).
21 *Schär*, Decentralized Finance (Fn. 8), 153 (169).
22 Ebd.
23 Ebd.
24 *F. Schär*, DeFi Is Transparent, Unless You Look Closely, Coindesk, 13.4.2021, abrufbar unter https://www.coindesk.com/tech/2021/04/13/defi-is-transparent-unl ess-you-look-closely/ (zuletzt abgerufen: 13.07.2022).

zu verschaffen, z.B. durch Front Running.[25] Es lässt sich also zumindest daran zweifeln, dass die technisch hergestellte Transparenz von DeFi einen entscheidenden Vorteil gegenüber traditionellen Finanzsystemen darstellt.

Aus dem Blickwinkel einzelner DeFi-Nutzer:innen bleibt der Nutzen dieser zwei Komponenten ohnehin unklar. Zwar können sie, anders als im Rahmen von TradFi, sämtliche Transaktionen durch Einsichtnahme in die Blockchain stets nachverfolgen. Abgesehen von der damit verbundenen Datenmenge muss der Einzelne zusätzlich in der Lage sein, die richtigen Schlüsse hieraus zu ziehen. Darüber hinaus ist zu befürchten, dass die Nachverfolgbarkeit sämtlicher Transaktionen ein potenziell schädliches Herdenverhalten nach sich ziehen könnte.[26] Zudem ist die Tatsache, dass der Code der Smart Contracts in einer Programmiersprache geschrieben ist, für die allermeisten Nutzer:innen kein Informationsvorteil im Vergleich zum Abschluss eines Finanzgeschäfts im traditionellen Finanzsystem.

Trotz all dieser Zweifel ist noch keine Aussage dazu getroffen, wie sich der Abgleich zwischen der durch technische Instrumente hergestellten und einer durch die Rechtsordnung geforderten Transparenz gestaltet. Ob sich die ersten Impulse, die gegen besondere Transparenzvorteile von DeFi gegenüber TradFi sprechen, auch im Rahmen einer rechtlichen Würdigung bestätigen, soll nun untersucht werden.

D. *Technische Transparenz und rechtliche Transparenzvorgaben – ein Abgleich*

Für Rechtswissenschaftler:innen ist die Transparenz im technischen Sinne nur bedingt interessant. Entscheidender ist die Befolgung von Vorgaben, die im Zusammenhang mit Sachverhalten mit einem Finanzmarktbezug die Herstellung von Transparenz gegenüber Personen verlangt, die Finanzgeschäfte tätigen bzw. Finanzdienstleistungen in Anspruch nehmen wollen. Zu nennen sind hier – nicht abschließend – zivilrechtliche Informationspflichten im Zusammenhang mit Darlehensverträgen (z.B. § 492 II BGB) und Zahlungsdiensten (z.B. § 675d BGB), kapitalmarktrechtliche Pflichten zur Erstellung und Veröffentlichung eines Wertpapierprospekts oder ähnlicher Informationsdokumente sowie geldwäscherechtliche Pflichten. Da DeFi die Revolution gerade solcher Finanzgeschäfte für sich

---

25 *Gramlich et al.*, Decentralized Finance (Fn. 13), S. 8, 32.
26 Vgl. grundlegend zum Herdenverhalten von Kapitalmarktteilnehmern *L. Klöhn*, Kapitalmarkt, Spekulation und Behavioral Finance, Berlin 2006, S. 123 ff.

in Anspruch nimmt, liegt die Frage auf der Hand, wie es im Rahmen von DeFi um die Transparenz im rechtlichen Sinne bestellt ist. Der Schwerpunkt der folgenden Ausführungen soll hierbei auf dem oben vorgestellten *liquidity pool-based lending* liegen. Potenzielle Einfallstore für rechtliche Transparenzvorgaben sind hierbei insb. die zivilrechtlichen Vorschriften zum Verbraucherdarlehensvertrag in den §§ 491 ff. BGB, kapitalmarktrechtliche Informationspflichten sowie geldwäscherechtliche Vorschriften. Letztere sollen vorliegend nur angerissen werden und können aus Platzgründen nicht erschöpfend dargestellt werden.

Vor die Klammer gezogen werden soll aber der Hinweis auf eine entscheidende Vorbedingung, die es im Rahmen der Analyse einer Transparenz im rechtlichen Sinne zu klären gilt: Welche der existierenden Anforderungen müssen bzw. sollten im Zusammenhang mit DeFi überhaupt zur Anwendung kommen? Schließlich verlassen DeFi-Nutzer die traditionellen, bankenbasierten Finanzsysteme aufgrund einer selbstverantwortlichen Entscheidung und damit zugleich den der Rechtsordnung bekannten Bereich. Muss das Recht auf solche Entscheidungen zwingend dergestalt reagieren, dass es DeFi-Nutzer:innen durch die Ausweitung seines ursprünglich angedachten Anwendungsbereichs mit seinen Schutzmechanismen in ihre „Abenteuer" folgt? Diskutiert werden soll diese Frage – die sich nicht nur in Bezug auf Transparenzanforderungen, sondern darüber hinaus ganz allgemein stellt – hier unter dem Stichwort des „Prinzips der Selbstverantwortung", also dem Prinzip, dass jede:r für sein / ihr eigenes Verhalten verantwortlich ist und dessen Folgen zu tragen hat.[27] Dieses Prinzip hat in den im Folgenden in den Blick genommenen Rechtsgebieten jeweils einen unterschiedlichen Stellenwert, der herausgearbeitet und in rechtliche Schlussfolgerungen übersetzt werden soll.

I. Geldwäscherecht

Die Anwendung des Geldwäscherechts auf die Krypto-Ökonomie sorgte insb. im Hinblick auf die durch den Entwurf einer überarbeiteten „Transfer of Funds"-Verordnung[28] vorgeschlagene Anwendung der sog. „Travel Rule" der Financial Action Task Force on Money Laundering (FATF)

---

27 *K. Riesenhuber*, Das Prinzip der Selbstverantwortung, in: ders. (Hrsg.), Das Prinzip der Selbstverantwortung, Tübingen 2011, S. 1 m.w.N.

28 Vorschlag für eine Verordnung des Europäischen Parlaments und des Rates über die Übermittlung von Angaben bei Geldtransfers und Transfers bestimmter Kryptowerte (Neufassung), COM(2021) 422 final, 20.7.2021.

für rege Diskussionen.[29] Das in Deutschland im GwG kodifizierte und maßgeblich durch europäisches Sekundärrecht beeinflusste Rechtsgebiet soll zu einer Transparenz über die Herkunft von Geldern und Zahlungsflüsse führen. Diese Transparenz dient wiederum mindestens der Verhinderung und Erschwerung schwerwiegender, einem eigenen Unrechtscharakter unterliegender Straftaten der Geldwäsche und der Terrorismusfinanzierung.[30] Damit dient das Rechtsgebiet ausschließlich öffentlichen Interessen und bezweckt gerade keinen Individualschutz, sodass die Übertragbarkeit der geldwäscherechtlichen Zielsetzungen auf das DeFi-Ökosystem einer Disposition des Einzelnen nach dem Prinzip der Selbstverantwortung nicht offensteht. Entsprechend leuchtet es ein, dass z.B. durch die Konzeption von Know Your Customer-Vorgaben (KYC) ein Level an Transparenz hergestellt werden soll, das mit zentralisierten Finanzsystemen vergleichbar ist. Die Nachvollziehbarkeit von Transaktionen durch deren Aufzeichnung auf öffentlichen Blockchains reicht hierzu ersichtlich nicht aus, denn die Pseudonymisierung erschwert eine Identifizierung von Transaktionsparteien erheblich.

II. Kapitalmarktrechtliche Informationspflichten

Das Transparenz auf dem Gebiet des Kapitalmarktrechts ein hoher Stellenwert zukommt, ist schon daran erkennbar, dass für dieses Rechtsgebiet auf europäischer Ebene eine Transparenz-Richtlinie[31] existiert. Dem-

---

29 Vgl. nur Ledger, Why the EU's Transfer of Funds Regulation (TFR) is a Threat to Financial Freedom, 30.3.2022, abrufbar unter https://www.ledger.com/blog -why-the-eus-transfer-of-funds-tfr-regulation-is-a-threat-to-financial-freedom (zuletzt abgerufen: 19.10.2022); Bitkom, Position Paper on the Transfer of Funds Regulation (TFR), 13.6.2022, abrufbar unter https://www.bitkom.org/Bitkom/Pu blikationen/Bitkom-on-the-Transfer-of-Funds-Regulation-TFR (zuletzt abgerufen: 19.10.2022); A. *Raden*, Internet der Dinge und Transfer of Funds Regulation, Editorial RDi 6/22, abrufbar unter https://rsw.beck.de/zeitschriften/rdi/single/20 22/06/07/internet-der-dinge-und-transfer-of-funds-regulation (zuletzt abgerufen: 19.10.2022).
30 *J. Kaetzler*, in: U. Zentes/S. Glaab (Hrsg.), GwG – Geldwäschegesetz, Geldtransfer-VO, relevante Vorgaben aus AO, KWG, StGB, VAG, ZAG sowie Exkurs zu Finanzsanktionen, 2. Aufl., München 2020, § 1 Rn. 4.
31 RL 2004/109/EG des Europäischen Parlaments und des Rates vom 15.12.2004 zur Harmonisierung der Transparenzanforderungen in Bezug auf Informationen über Emittenten, deren Wertpapiere zum Handel auf einem geregelten Markt zugelassen sind, und zur Änderung der Richtlinie 2001/34/EG.

entsprechend sehen kapitalmarktrechtliche Rechtsakte eine Vielzahl von Melde-, Aufklärungs- und Informationspflichten vor, die an dieser Stelle nicht erschöpfend dargestellt werden können. Auf den ersten Blick könnte vermutet werden, dass im Bereich dieser Pflichten durchaus Raum für selbstverantwortliches Handeln der Anleger besteht, was die Ausweitung des kapitalmarktrechtlichen Anwendungsbereichs auf innovative DeFi-Geschäftsmodelle nicht um jeden Preis erforderlich machen würde. Tatsächlich dient z.B. die Prospektpflicht auch dazu, die Anleger im eigenen Interesse zu einer sachkundigen Investitionsentscheidung zu befähigen.[32] Gerade die Summe aus diesen Einzelinteressen dient jedoch zusätzlich dem staatlichen Interesse an einem effizienten und funktionsfähigen Kapitalmarkt.[33] Der dem Prinzip der Selbstverantwortung offenstehende Individualschutz ist so mit öffentlichen Interessen verbunden, die nicht vollständig zur Disposition des Einzelnen stehen können: Das öffentliche Interesse erfordert, dass jedenfalls auf eine informierte Entscheidung potenzieller Anleger:innen hinzuwirken ist. Ob diese Anlagegeschäfte auf Grundlage dieser Informationen tätigen, unterliegt dagegen ihrer Verantwortung.[34]

Ansatzpunkt für das Bestehen kapitalmarktrechtlicher Informationspflichten im Zusammenhang mit dem *liquidity pool-based lending* sind insb. die *governance token*, die bei Aave in Gestalt von AAVE-Token ausgegeben werden. Auch im übrigen DeFi-Ökosystem kommt ihnen für die Verwaltung und Pflege der verwendeten Protokolle große Bedeutung zu. Noch nicht ausdiskutiert ist, ob das öffentliche Angebot solcher *token* eine Pflicht zur Erstellung eines Wertpapierprospekts nach Art. 3 der Prospekt-VO[35] auslöst. Dafür müsste es sich bei *governance token* um übertragbare Wertpapiere i.S.d. Art. 2 lit. a Prospekt-VO handeln, wobei dort im We-

---

32 Im Zusammenhang mit der Prospekthaftung *M. Habersack*, Prospekthaftung, in: M. Habersack/P. Mülbert/M. Schlitt (Hrsg.), Handbuch der Kapitalmarktinformation, 3. Aufl., München 2020, § 28 Rn. 1.

33 *O. Seiler/B. Geier*, Grundlagen des Kapitalmarktrechts, in: J. Ellenberger/H.-J. Bunte (Hrsg.), Bankrechts-Handbuch, 6. Aufl., München 2022, § 83 Rn. 73; *M. Habersack*, Prospekthaftung (Fn. 32), § 28 Rn. 1.

34 In diese Richtung auch *C. Hofmann*, Das Prinzip der Selbstverantwortung im Bank- und Kapitalmarktrecht, in: K. Riesenhuber (Hrsg.), Das Prinzip der Selbstverantwortung, Tübingen 2011, 423 (432).

35 VO (EU) 2017/1129 des Europäischen Parlaments und des Rates vom 14.6.2017 über den Prospekt, der beim öffentlichen Angebot von Wertpapieren oder bei deren Zulassung zum Handel an einem geregelten Markt zu veröffentlichen ist und zur Aufhebung der Richtlinie 2003/71/EG.

sentlichen auf Art. 4 I Nr. 44 MiFID II[36] verwiesen wird. Der europäische Wertpapierbegriff umfasst die Kategorien von Wertpapieren, die auf dem Kapitalmarkt gehandelt werden können, mit Ausnahme von Zahlungsinstrumenten, wie Aktien oder Schuldverschreibungen. Aus dem Wertpapierbegriff der MiFID II werden bis zu vier Eigenschaften eines Wertpapiers abgeleitet, die kumulativ vorliegen müssen: Standardisierung, Übertragbarkeit, Handelbarkeit sowie eine Vergleichbarkeit mit den in Art. 4 I Nr. 44 MiFID II genannten idealtypischen Wertpapieren.[37] Da der europäische Wertpapierbegriff keine Verbriefung erfordert, steht er einer Erfassung von Kryptowerten durchaus offen gegenüber.[38]

Governance token erfüllen die Merkmale der Standardisierung, der Übertragbarkeit sowie der Handelbarkeit am Kapitalmarkt. Insb. ist der AAVE-Token über Krypto-Handelsplattformen handelbar.[39] Bedenken bestehen allerdings hinsichtlich der Vergleichbarkeit zu idealtypischen Wertpapieren. Denn wenn man hiermit eine Verbindung mit investorenähnlichen Erwartungen meint, z.B. im Hinblick auf eine Beteiligung an den Zahlungsflüssen eines Unternehmens, ist dies für *governance token* nicht ohne Weiteres zu begründen. Soweit ersichtlich partizipieren deren Halter nicht an Zahlungsflüssen, die sich aus dem zugrundeliegenden Protokoll ergeben. Auch wenn die aus der Inhaberschaft von AAVE-Token ergebenden Rechte an die Stimmrechte erinnern, die mit Aktien verbunden sind, findet eine ökonomische Verwertung von AAVE-Token ausschließlich durch eine Partizipation an der Wertentwicklung und den Verkauf auf einschlägigen Handelsplattformen statt, während eine Art Dividenden-Zahlung – soweit ersichtlich – gerade nicht vorgesehen ist. Somit lassen sich *governance token* nach geltendem Recht nicht unter den Wertpapierbegriff

---

36 RL 2014/65/EU des Europäischen Parlaments und des Rates vom 15.5.2014 über Märkte für Finanzinstrumente sowie zur Änderung der Richtlinien 2002/92/EG und 2011/61/EU.

37 *P. Hacker/C. Thomale*, Crypto-Securities Regulation: ICOs, Token Sales and Cryptocurrencies under EU Financial Law, European Company and Financial Law Review 2018, 645 (663 ff.).

38 Vgl. zur Offenheit des Wertpapierbegriffs für innovative Entwicklungen am Kapitalmarkt *C. Rennig*, Prospektpflicht für Stock Token? – Europäischer Wertpapierbegriff und digitale Innovationen am Kapitalmarkt, BKR 2021, 402; zur Erfassung sog. *security token* als Wertpapier im europäischen und amerikanischen Recht *Hacker/Thomale*, Crypto-Securities Regulation (Fn. 37), 645 (657 ff.).

39 Der im Rahmen des Wertpapierbegriffs zugrundeliegende Kapitalmarktbegriff ist weit zu verstehen und geht über geregelte Märkte sowie *multilateral trading* und *organized trading facilities* hinaus, vgl. *Rennig*, Stock Token (Fn. 38), 402 (405) m.w.N.

der MiFID II fassen; eine Prospektpflicht scheidet damit aus.[40] Das Kapitalmarktrecht vermittelt über die mit *governance token* verbundenen Rechte damit keine Transparenz.

III. Verbraucherdarlehensrecht

Um zu der Forschungsfrage dieses Beitrags auch auf dem Gebiet des Verbraucherdarlehensrechts vorzudringen, müssen einige Annahmen vorangestellt werden, die für sich betrachtet keine Selbstverständlichkeit sind: Zunächst muss bei der Nutzung des *liquidity pool-based lending* ein Vertrag im Rechtssinne zwischen Darlehensnehmer:in und einem/einer anderen Rechtsträger:in als Darlehensgeber:in zustande kommen; hierbei gestaltet sich aufgrund der Zwischenschaltung eines Smart Contracts – der trotz seiner Bezeichnung selbst nicht notwendigerweise einen Vertrag im rechtlichen Sinne darstellt[41] – schon die Identifizierung und rechtliche Begründung eines Vertragsschlusses zwischen zwei Rechtsträgern als schwierig. Ferner muss auf Darlehensnehmerseite die Verbraucher- (§ 13 BGB), auf Darlehensgeberseite die Unternehmereigenschaft (§ 14 BGB) vorliegen. Schon aufgrund der mit dem Einsatz der Blockchain-Technologie verbundenen Schwierigkeiten bei der Feststellung, ob DeFi-Nutzer:innen als Verbraucher oder Unternehmer handeln, könnte man die Anwendbarkeit rollenbezogener Schutznormen in Zweifel ziehen.[42] Für die Zwecke der weiteren Ausführungen werden diese Umstände jedoch als gegeben angesehen. Unterstellt wird weiterhin die Anwendbarkeit deutschen Rechts.

Dabei dienen die in §§ 491a, 492 BGB i.V.m. Art. 247 EGBGB vorgesehenen Informations- und Mitteilungspflichten der Herstellung einer möglichst hohen Transparenz zugunsten des Verbrauchers, die es diesem ermöglicht, eine informierte und umfassende Entscheidung über den Abschluss und den Inhalt eines Kreditvertrages zu treffen.[43] Vor diesem Hin-

---

40 So im Ergebnis auch *Möslein/Kaulartz/Rennig*, DeFi (Fn. 14), 517 (526 f.); *Kaulartz*, Blockchain (Fn. 5), Rn. 60.

41 *Möslein*, Smart Contracts (Fn. 7), 254 (270).

42 So *Möslein/Kaulartz/Rennig*, DeFi (Fn. 14), 517 (522). Argumentieren könnte man allerdings genauso gut, dass das Auftreten z.B. als Unternehmer eine feststehende Rechtstatsache ist, deren Feststellung auf einer nachgelagerten Ebene erfolgen muss. Freilich führt dies unweigerlich zu Schwierigkeiten bei der Prüfung, ob z.B. verbraucherschützende Vorschriften anwendbar sind.

43 *K.-O. Knops* in: B. Gsell/W. Krüger/S. Lorenz/C. Reymann (Hrsg.), beck-online. GROSSKOMMENTAR zum BGB (folgt BeckOGK BGB), München (Stand: 1.1.2022), § 491 Rn. 9 m.w.N.

tergrund soll an dieser Stelle das Pferd gewissermaßen von hinten aufge-
zäumt werden: Denn wenn die Transparenz im technologischen Sinne ohnehin die rechtlichen Transparenzvorgaben der §§ 491 ff. BGB erfüllt,
kommt der Frage der Anwendbarkeit dieser Vorschriften auf das *liquidity
pool-based lending* keine entscheidende Bedeutung mehr zu.

1. Erfüllung der Transparenzvorgaben der §§ 491 ff. BGB

Der Herstellung von Transparenz über Kreditkonditionen dienen zunächst
die im Verbraucherdarlehensrecht vorgesehenen Formerfordernisse. So
unterliegt der Darlehensvertrag gem. § 492 I 1 BGB – mindestens – dem
Schriftformerfordernis (§ 126 BGB), während die vorvertraglichen Informationen gem. § 491a I BGB i.V.m. Art. 247 § 2 I 2 EGBGB grds. in Textform bereitgestellt werden müssen. Selbst wenn man annimmt, dass Smart
Contracts durch die Nutzung der Blockchain der Textform des
§ 126b BGB genügen können,[44] erfüllt der Smart Contract mangels eigen-
händiger Unterschrift jedenfalls die Anforderungen der Schriftform nach
§ 126 BGB nicht. Die in § 126 III BGB eröffnete Möglichkeit der Ersetzung
durch die elektronische Form gem. § 126a BGB ist ebenfalls nicht möglich,
da § 492 I BGB ausdrücklich nur die Wahl einer strengeren Form zulässt.[45]
Im Ergebnis dürfte dies in den allermeisten Fällen dennoch nicht zu der
Unwirksamkeit des Vertragsschlusses führen, denn gem. § 494 II 1 BGB
wird der Vertrag auch dann gültig, soweit der Darlehensnehmer das Darlehen empfängt oder in Anspruch nimmt.

Inhaltlich werden Verbraucher im Zusammenhang mit Darlehensverträgen auf vier Ebenen mit Informationen versorgt, angefangen in der Pha-
se einer etwaigen Werbung über vorvertragliche Informations- und Erläu-
terungspflichten bis hin zu einer Erteilung von Informationen im laufen-
den Vertragsverhältnis.[46] Setzt man gedanklich voraus, dass sich aus dem
öffentlich zugänglichen Code des Smart Contracts die in § 491a I BGB
i.V.m. Art. 247 §§ 3, 4 EGBGB genannten Informationen entnehmen las-

---

44 So *Heckelmann*, Smart Contracts (Fn. 7), 504 (507); *D. Paulus/R. Matzke*, Smart
    Contracts und das BGB – Viel Lärm um Nichts?, ZfPW 2018, 431 (457).
45 Davon abgesehen wären die Anforderungen der elektronischen Form bei Smart
    Contracts ebenfalls nicht erfüllt, da dort nicht die erforderliche *qualifizierte* Signa-
    tur vorliegt, vgl. *Paulus/Matzke*, Smart Contracts (Fn. 44), 431 (457).
46 *J. Schürnbrand/C. A. Weber* in: F. J. Säcker/R. Rixecker/H. Oetker/B. Limperg
    (Hrsg.), Münchener Kommentar zum Bürgerlichen Gesetzbuch (folgt: MüKo-
    BGB), 8. Aufl., München 2019, Vor § 491 Rn. 4.

sen könnten, so stellt sich die Frage, ob dies den Transparenzanforderungen genügen würde. Hierbei geht es weniger darum, ob die technisch hergestellte Transparenz tatsächlich genutzt wird. Auch bei gewöhnlichen Darlehensgeschäften wird man regelmäßig davon ausgehen müssen, dass die Informationen durch Darlehensnehmer:innen – wie bei Allgemeinen Geschäftsbedingungen[47] – nicht gelesen werden; dies setzt das Gesetz auch nicht voraus. Vielmehr ist zu prüfen, ob der mögliche Zugriff auf den Code den rechtlichen Anforderungen überhaupt gerecht werden *kann*, ist dieser doch in einer formale Programmiersprache abgefasst, die den wenigsten der potenziellen Darlehensnehmer:innen geläufig sein wird.[48] Entsprechend wird angemerkt, dass eine große Mehrzahl von Personen und selbst etablierte Finanzinstitutionen kaum in der Lage sein werden, den hinter den DApps stehenden Programmiercode zu lesen und – wichtiger – zu verstehen.[49]

Auf Ebene des Vertragsschlusses stehen der Wahl einer Programmiersprache als Vertragssprache keine durchgreifenden rechtlichen Bedenken entgegen.[50] Das allgemeine Vertragsrecht ist grds. gut in der Lage, die mit Smart Contracts einhergehenden Herausforderungen einer sachgemäßen Lösung zuzuführen.[51] Die Beurteilung der Wirksamkeit eines Vertragsschlusses unterscheidet sich jedoch von einer Informationserteilung, die gerade dem Schutz des Darlehensnehmers dienen sollen. Hier dürfte die Ersetzung einer natürlichen Sprache durch eine formale Programmiersprache zumeist den Zweck verfehlen, wenn die zu schützende Person nicht in der Lage ist, die Sprache zu verstehen. Zwar ist insb. aus der in § 491a BGB i.V.m. Art. 247 § 2 EGBGB enthaltenen gesetzlichen Regelung nicht ersichtlich, in welcher Sprache vorvertragliche Informationen erteilt werden müssen. In diesem Zusammenhang zu sehen ist aber, dass diese Informa-

---

47 Siehe den Überblick zu Untersuchungen des tatsächlichen Leseverhaltens *P. Mc-Colgan*, Abschied vom Informationsmodell im Recht allgemeiner Geschäftsbedingungen, Tübingen 2020, S. 88 ff.

48 Aave nutzt bspw. die Programmiersprachen HTML, Solidity, Typescript und Javascript, vgl. *E. Yazdanparast*, List of Programming Languages and Frameworks Used in 41 Crypto Projects, abrufbar unter https://medium.com/coinmonks/list-of-programming-languages-and-frameworks-used-in-41-crypto-projects-2b7223099c57 (zuletzt abgerufen: 19.10.2022).

49 *H. Allen*, DeFi – Shadow Banking 2.0?, S. 10, abrufbar unter https://papers.ssrn.com/sol3/papers.cfm?abstract_id=4038788 (zuletzt abgerufen: 19.10.2022).

50 *Heckelmann*, Smart Contracts (Fn. 7), 504 (506); *M. Kaulartz/M. Heckelmann*, Smart Contracts – Anwendungen der Blockchain-Technologie, CR 2016, 618 (622).

51 *Möslein*, BeckOGK BGB (Fn. 43), Stand: 1.5.2019, § 145 Rn. 72.

tionen in Textform und damit gem. § 126b S. 1 BGB in Form einer *lesbaren* Erklärung erteilt werden müssen. Bezüglich einer Information über das Bestehen eines Widerrufsrechts im Rahmen eines allgemeinen Verbrauchervertrags, die gem. Art. 246a § 4 III 2 EGBGB ebenfalls lesbar sein muss, wurde bereits überzeugend begründet, dass eine im Code des Smart Contracts hinterlegte Information nicht lesbar ist.[52] Diese Ansicht überzeugt gerade dann, wenn man sich bewusst macht, dass die vorvertraglichen Informationen im Verbraucherdarlehensrecht einen spezifischen Zweck verfolgen, wenn sie Verbraucher:innen in die Lage versetzen sollen, unterschiedliche Angebote am Kreditmarkt vergleichen zu können.[53] Unabhängig von der noch zu klärenden Frage, ob die Schutzzwecke der §§ 491 ff. BGB deren Anwendbarkeit auf das *liquidity pool-based lending* begründen (dazu sogleich), dürfte eine Vergleichbarkeit nur dann sinnvollerweise zu erreichen sein, wenn die Informationen in einer natürlichen und damit ohne weitere spezielle Kenntnisse lesbaren Sprache vorgelegt werden. Daran ändert auch die in § 491a III BGB enthaltene Erläuterungspflicht nichts: Abgesehen davon, dass in DeFi-Systemen entsprechende Erläuterungen kaum vorstellbar sind, ist es – abgesehen von Sprachschwierigkeiten – kaum Ziel der gesetzlichen Regelung, dass Verträge von vornherein auf eine solche Erläuterung ausgerichtet sind.

Im Ergebnis ist daher festzuhalten, dass das *liquidity pool-based lending* derzeit noch nicht den sich aus dem Verbraucherdarlehensrecht ergebenden Anforderungen an eine Transparenz entspricht. Obwohl eine formgerechte Erteilung der Informationen in Textform im Bereich des Möglichen zu liegen scheint, fehlt es insb. aufgrund der Verwendung einer formalen Programmiersprache an der erforderlichen Transparenz gegenüber dem zu schützenden Verbraucher.

2. Anwendbarkeit der Transparenzvorgaben der §§ 491 ff. BGB

Kritisch ist die fehlende Beachtung der Transparenzvorgaben jedoch nur dann, wenn die in §§ 491 ff. BGB vorgesehenen Transparenzanforderungen

---

52 So M. *Kloth*, Blockchain basierte Smart Contracts im Lichte des Verbraucherrechts, VuR 2022, 214 (219 f.).

53 Art. 5 Abs. 1, 6 Abs. 1 sowie ErwG 18, 43 zur Verbraucherkreditrichtlinie (RL 2008/48/EG des Europäischen Parlaments und des Rates vom 23.4.2008 über Verbraucherkreditverträge und zur Aufhebung der Richtlinie 87/102/EWG); vgl. dazu B. *Gsell*, Informationspflichten im europäischen Verbraucherrecht, ZfPW 2022, 130 (137).

überhaupt auf DeFi-Sachverhalte anwendbar sind. Dafür müssten die Vorschriften zum Verbraucherschutzrecht direkt oder entsprechend zur Anwendung kommen. Da es sich bei den Stablecoins, auf die im Rahmen des *liquidity-based pool lending* die Darlehensvaluta lautet, nicht um Geld im Rechtssinn handelt,[54] kommt eine direkte Anwendung des Darlehensrechts und damit der §§ 491 ff. BGB jedenfalls nicht in Betracht.[55] Vertreten wird stattdessen eine analoge Anwendung der Vorschriften über Sachdarlehen (§ 607 BGB),[56] was über eine richtlinienkonforme Auslegung der §§ 491 ff. BGB zur Anwendbarkeit des Verbraucherdarlehensrechts führen kann.[57] Da es sich bei Stablecoins aber ebenso wenig um eine Sache i.S.d. § 90 BGB wie um Geld handelt und der wirtschaftliche Zweck des *liquidity pool-based lending* in der Verschaffung von Kaufkraft[58] liegt, erscheint eine analoge Anwendung des § 488 BGB aus dogmatischer Sicht sachnäher, freilich ohne dass dies im Ergebnis einen Unterschied machen würde.

Gerade im Hinblick auf die in §§ 491 ff. BGB niedergelegten Transparenzvorschriften stellt sich allerdings die Frage, ob eine Anwendung im Wege der Gesamtanalogie tatsächlich angezeigt ist. Erforderlich hierfür ist das Vorliegen einer planwidrigen Regelungslücke trotz Bestehen einer vergleichbaren Interessenlage.[59] Dass weder der europäische Gesetzgeber bei Konzeption der Verbraucherkreditrichtlinie[60] noch der deutsche Gesetzgeber bei Richtlinienumsetzung Konstellationen bedacht haben, bei denen Kaufkraft nicht in Form von staatlichem Geld, sondern von privaten Kryp-

---

54 Vgl. statt vieler *Freitag*, BeckOGK BGB (Fn. 43), Stand: 15.3.2021, § 244 Rn. 28 m.w.N.

55 *L. Maute*, Verträge über Kryptotoken, in: P. Maume/L. Maute (Hrsg.), Rechtshandbuch Kryptowerte: Blockchain, Tokenisierung, Initial Coin Offerings, München 2020, § 6 Rn. 152.

56 Ebd.; *Kaulartz*, Blockchain-Technologien (Fn. 5), § 5 Rn. 83.

57 Dafür *J. Schürnbrand/C. A. Weber* in: F. J. Säcker et al., MüKo BGB (Fn. 46), § 491 Rn. 47; *S. Kessal-Wulf* in: J. von Staudingers Kommentar zum Bürgerlichen Gesetzbuch mit Einführungsgesetz und Nebengesetzen, Neubearbeitung 2012, Köln / Berlin 2012, § 491 Rn. 50; dagegen *M. Nietsch* in: B. Gruneald/H. P. Westermann/G. Maier-Reimer (Hrsg.), Erman BGB, 16. Aufl., Köln 2020, § 491 Rn. 2 m.w.N.

58 *M. Renner*, Kreditgeschäft, in: S. Grundmann (Hrsg.), Bankvertragsrecht, Bd. 1: Grundlagen und Commercial Banking, Berlin 2020, S. 781 (783) m.w.N.

59 Zu den Voraussetzungen einer Gesamtanalogie *T. Möllers*, Juristische Methodenlehre, 4. Aufl., München 2021, S. 257 ff.

60 RL 2008/48/EG des Europäischen Parlaments und des Rates vom 23.4.2008 über Verbraucherkreditverträge und zur Aufhebung der Richtlinie 87/102/EWG des Rates.

towerten überlassen wird, ist offensichtlich. Von dem Bestehen einer Regelungslücke im Verbraucherdarlehensrecht ist damit jedenfalls auszugehen.

Interessanter gestaltet sich indes die Suche nach einer vergleichbaren Interessenlage. Die §§ 491 ff. BGB sollen insgesamt einen Schutz der Verbraucher vor den Gefahren bezwecken, die mit der Überschätzung der eigenen finanziellen Leistungsfähigkeit einhergehen.[61] Außerdem soll die im Massenkreditgeschäft häufig zu beobachtende schwächere Position von Verbrauchern ausgeglichen werden,[62] indem z.B. die Vergleichbarkeit zwischen unterschiedlichen Angeboten hergestellt wird.

Vor diesem Hintergrund lassen sich hinsichtlich der vergleichbaren Schutzbedürfnisse bei traditioneller CeFi- (Centralized Finance) und neuartiger DeFi-Kreditvergabe durchaus verschiedene Standpunkte einnehmen. Einerseits kann man die im BGB vorgesehenen Vertragstypen einschließlich der dort vorgesehenen speziellen Schutzmechanismen als die gesetzliche Umschreibung eines „sicheren Hafens" erkennen. Wird dieser Bereich durch privatautonome Gestaltung verlassen, so begeben sich die Vertragsparteien selbstverantwortlich aus dem Schutzbereich dieser schützenden Vorschriften. Andererseits lässt sich auch vertreten, dass bspw. das Verbraucherdarlehensrecht allgemeine Prinzipien des Verbraucherschutzes aufstellt, die zwar nicht direkt erfasst sind, jedoch auch in ähnlichen Konstellationen zur Anwendung kommen müssen. Für diese letzte Sichtweise ließe sich systematisch mit § 512 S. 2 BGB argumentieren, der eine Umgehung der Schutzmechanismen verhindern soll.

Die erste Sichtweise fußt dagegen gerade auf dem Prinzip der Selbstverantwortung. Da das Verbraucherdarlehensrecht dem Schutz von Individualinteressen dient, scheint es eigenverantwortlichen Entscheidungen von Verbrauchern auf den ersten Blick durchaus zugänglich zu sein. Allerdings wird im hier interessierenden zivilrechtlichen Kontext vertreten, dass die Ausübung von Selbstverantwortung das Vorliegen einer ausreichenden Informationsgrundlage voraussetzt.[63] Vorzunehmen wäre eine Aufteilung der in den §§ 491 ff. BGB vorgesehenen Schutzinstrumente: Während eine Herstellung von Transparenz durch die dargestellten Informationspflichten nicht disponibel wäre, wäre die auf Grundlage dieser Informationen getroffene, nunmehr selbstverantwortliche Entscheidung irre-

---

61 *Knops*, BeckOGK BGB (Fn. 43), Stand: 1.1.2022, § 491 Rn. 9.
62 Ebd.
63 *Hofmann*, Selbstverantwortung im Bank- und Kapitalmarktrecht (Fn. 34), 423 (424, 438).

versibel, insb. durch die Nichtgewährung eines Widerrufsrechts aus § 495 BGB.

Fällt aber nicht schon die Bildung einer Informationsgrundlage in den Bereich der Selbstverantwortung? Der Blick auf neueres europäisches Recht scheint eine klare Antwort zu geben: Die Schwarmfinanzierungs-VO[64] deutet an, dass jedenfalls der europäische Gesetzgeber bei Anlagegeschäften im digitalen Raum eine noch höhere Dichte an Informationsinstrumenten zur Anwendung bringt, um Anleger:innen vor Anlageentscheidungen eine ausreichende Informationsgrundlage zu verschaffen.[65] Auch die vorgeschlagene Änderung (im Folgenden: Vorschlag)[66] der allgemeinen Verbraucherrechte-RL (VR-RL[67]) mit ihrer Erweiterung um im Fernabsatzgeschäft abgeschlossene Verbraucherverträge über Finanzdienstleistungen (Art. 3 Abs. 1b i.d.F. des Vorschlags) deutet in diese Richtung. Für solche Verträge werden dort spezifische Informationspflichten des Unternehmers angeordnet (Art. 16a i.d.F. des Vorschlags), ohne hiervon Ausnahmen zuzulassen. Demgegenüber ist ein Widerrufsrecht für solche Finanzdienstleistungen, deren Preis auf dem Finanzmarkt Schwankungen unterliegt, ausgeschlossen – hierunter fallen ausdrücklich auch Geschäfte im Zusammenhang mit Kryptowerten i.S.d. MiCA-VO (Art. 16b II lit. a) i.d.F. des Vorschlags). Wenngleich hierin noch keine abschließende gesetzgeberische Wertung für sämtliche DeFi-Sachverhalte zu sehen ist, so lässt sich doch der Stellenwert erkennen, den gerade der europäische Gesetzgeber Informationspflichten und damit der Transparenz von Finanzdienstleistungen zuschreibt.[68]

---

64 VO (EU) 2020/1503 des Europäischen Parlaments und des Rates vom 7.10.2020 über Europäische Schwarmfinanzierungsdienstleister für Unternehmen und zur Änderung der Verordnung (EU) 2017/1129 und der Richtlinie (EU) 2019/1937.

65 Für einen Überblick über die Informationsinstrumente der ECSP-VO siehe *C. Rennig* in: P. Buck-Heeb/R. Harnos/C. H. Seibt (Hrsg.), Beck'scher Onlinekommentar Wertpapierhandelsrecht, 4. Edition, München 2022, WpHG § 32c Rn. 2 ff.

66 *Europäische Kommission*, Vorschlag für eine Richtlinie des Europäischen Parlaments und des Rates zur Änderung der Richtlinie 2011/83/EU in Bezug auf im Fernabsatz geschlossene Finanzdienstleistungsverträge und zur Aufhebung der Richtlinie 2022/65/EG, Brüssel 2022, abrufbar unter https://eur-lex.europa.eu/legal-content/DE/TXT/?uri=CELEX:52022PC0204 (zuletzt abgerufen: 19.10.2022).

67 RL 2011/83/EU des Europäischen Parlaments und des Rates vom 25.10.2011 über die Rechte der Verbraucher, zur Abänderung der Richtlinie 93/13/EWG des Rates und der Richtlinie 1999/44/EG des Europäischen Parlaments und des Rates sowie zur Aufhebung der Richtlinie 85/577/EWG des Rates und der Richtlinie 97/7/EG des Europäischen Parlaments und des Rates.

68 Vgl. dazu auch *Europäische Kommission*, Vorschlag (Fn. 66), S. 3.

Einfluss auf die Anwendbarkeit der verbraucherschützenden Vorschriften hat zudem die Frage, ob es sich bei Verbraucherschutz um ein Rechtsprinzip des deutschen bzw. europäischen Privatrechts handelt.[69] Will man dies bejahen,[70] so ist hiermit unter anderem eine lückenfüllende Funktion verbunden, die bei durch den Gesetzgeber noch nicht bedachten Sachverhalten eingreifen kann.[71] Um gerade einen solchen Sachverhalt könnte es sich z.B. bei *liquidity pool-based lending* handeln.

Insgesamt lässt sich die Anwendbarkeit der sich aus dem Verbraucherdarlehensrecht ergebenden Transparenzvorschrift damit nicht abschließend beurteilen. Tendenziell spricht wohl gerade die herausragende Bedeutung, die insbesondere der europäische Gesetzgeber Informationspflichten zumisst, für eine Übertragung jedenfalls der Informationspflichten auf eine Kreditvergabe in DeFi-Ökosystemen. Wünschenswert wäre jedoch eine Klarstellung durch den Gesetzgeber. Umso unbefriedigender ist, dass die MiCA-VO das Thema DeFi im Wesentlichen ausklammert und für diese neuartigen Finanzdienstleistungen keine Regelungen enthält. Gefordert wird deshalb, unter anderem von EZB-Präsidentin *Christine Lagard*, schon vor Inkrafttreten der MiCA-VO die Konzeption einer „MiCA 2" zum Zwecke der Lückenschließung.[72]

E. Fazit

DeFi als „the most transparent financial system in human history" – die in dieser Aussage mitschwingende Euphorie ist nach dem Vorstehenden zumindest zu bremsen. Denn nicht nur ist der Nutzen der technischen Komponenten, die zu einem hohen Grad an Transparenz führen soll, zumindest zweifelhaft. Darüber hinaus kann festgehalten werden, dass in DeFi-Ökosystemen aus rechtlicher Sicht keine mit traditionellen, zen-

---

69 Vgl. allgemein zu Rechtsprinzipien *Möllers*, Juristische Methodenlehre (Fn. 59), S. 325 ff.

70 So z.B. durch M. *Tamm*, Verbraucherschutzrecht, Tübingen 2011, S. 950; *dies.*, Verbraucherschutz und Privatautonomie, in: M. Tamm/K. Tonner/T. Brönneke (Hrsg.), Verbraucherrecht, 3. Aufl., Baden-Baden 2020, § 1 Rn. 62.

71 *Tamm*, Verbraucherschutzrecht (Fn. 70), S. 901.

72 Siehe D. *Attlee*, EZB-Präsidentin fordert Regulierung von Krypto-Krediten und Staking, Cointelegraph v. 22.6.2022, abrufbar unter https://de.cointelegraph.com /news/ecb-head-calls-for-separate-framework-to-regulate-crypto-lending (zuletzt abgerufen: 19.10.2022); in diese Richtung auch P. *Maume*, Mehr MiCAR bitte, Editorial RDi 8/22, abrufbar unter https://rsw.beck.de/zeitschriften/rdi/single/202 2/08/04/mehr-micar-bitte (zuletzt abgerufen: 19.10.2022).

tralisierten Finanzsystemen vergleichbare Transparenz herrscht: Zu groß sind noch die Unsicherheiten hinsichtlich der Anwendbarkeit geltender rechtlicher Transparenzanforderungen und deren Erfüllung. Diese Unsicherheiten muss insb. der Gesetzgeber zum Anlass nehmen, für DeFi technisch umsetzbare und an die damit verbundenen Risiken angepasste Transparenzanforderungen zu konzipieren, ohne zugleich die von DeFi ausgehende Innovationswirkung auszuschließen.

Meaningful information on the use of AI in the robo-investing context

Patrick Raschner

A. Background

Due the nature of financial markets as mass markets dealing mainly with intangible goods, algorithmic systems are used at almost every level, including operations, regulatory compliance as well as customer-focused applications.[1] One customer-facing activity in which algorithms have been deployed for many years, leading to questions about the "right" level of transparency (and opacity) *vis-à-vis* clients, is so-called robo-advice.[2] Contrary to what could be assumed at first glance, it is however not only about a "robot" advising on investing in financial products, but about an algorithmic system making investment decisions on behalf of the client.[3] Thus, it might be better framed as "robo-investing",[4] which is also the case in this paper.

---

1 Cf., e.g., *G. Spindler*, Control of Algorithms in Financial Markets – the Example of High Frequency Trading, in: M. Ebers/S. Navas (eds.), Algorithms and Law, Cambridge 2020, 207; *Financial Stability Board*, Artificial intelligence and machine learning in financial services, Market developments and financial stability implications, November 2017, 18 et seq.

2 On the history, e.g., *P. Maume*, Reducing Legal Uncertainty and Regulatory Arbitrage for Robo-Advice, ECFR 2019, 622 (633).

3 More on this in the next paragraph. "Robot advisors" are not only discussed in the investment context, but for instance also in insurance. See, e.g., *European Insurance and Occupational Pensions Authority (EIOPA)*, Artificial intelligence governance principles: towards ethical and trustworthy artificial intelligence in the European insurance sector, A report from EIOPA's Consultative Expert Group, 17 June 2021, 45. This contribution focuses, however, on investing.

4 See, e.g., *H. J. Allen*, Driverless Finance [:] Fintech's Impact on Financial Stability, Oxford 2022, p. 66.

In general, robo-investing[5] comprises three steps.[6] First, it starts with an online questionnaire where a potential customer has to answer various questions regarding his or her investment goals, previous financial knowledge, risk tolerance etc. Second, in light of the responses to this web-questionnaire and on the basis of some finance model,[7] an algorithm (sometimes called "profiling algorithm"[8]) constructs a tailored investment portfolio, which includes different financial products.[9] After the presentation of this initial proposal, a potential customer usually has the option to enter into a contract with the service provider and to transfer the necessary funds so that the proposed investment can be implemented.[10] But this is not the end. Subsequently, the actual robo-investing begins. Another algorithm (accordingly referred to as "quantitative management algorithm"[11]) continuously monitors the initial investment and as the market moves up and down, makes decisions on selling and buying financial products

---

5   It is not the intention of this contribution to provide a detailed explanation, see rather for a more detailed analysis, e.g, *W.-G. Ringe/C. Ruof*, Robo Advice: Legal and Regulatory Challenges, in I. Chiu/G. Deipenbrock (eds.), Routledge Handbook of Financial Technology and Law, London 2021, p. 193 et seqq.; *D. Linardatos*, Technische und rechtliche Grundlagen, in: D. Linardatos (ed.), Rechtshandbuch Robo Advice, München 2020, § 1 marginal no. 22 et seqq.; also, *P. Maume*, Robo-advisors [:] How do they fit in the existing EU regulatory framework, in particular with regard to investor protection?, June 2021, PE 662.928, 11 et seq. Recently, *F. Zunzunegui*, Robo-Advice as a Digital Finance Platform, ECFR 2022, 272 (275).

6   See, e.g., *D. Linardatos*, Robo Advice, in: M. Ebers (ed.), StichwortKommentar Legal Tech, Baden-Baden Forthcoming 2023, marginal no. 2; also, *Better Finance*, Are Robo-Advisors sufficiently intelligent to provide suitable advice to individual investors? A research report by Better Finance, December 2021, 16. Arguably, one can also distinguish between only two phases (e.g., *Maume*, Robo-advisors [n. 5], 16 et seq).

7   Often the "modern portfolio theory", on this, i.a., *M. Bianchi/M. Brière*, Robo-Advising: Less AI and More XAI? Augmenting algorithms with humans-in-the-loop, Working Paper 109–2021 I April 2021, 10.

8   See, e.g., *ESMA*, Final Report Guidelines on certain aspects of the MiFID II suitability requirements, 28 May 2018, ESMA35–43–869, para. 6, referring to some market participants.

9   The investment universe often contains investment funds, esp. Exchange Traded Funds (ETFs). See, e.g., *Maume*, Robo-advisors (n. 5), 13; *Linardatos*, Grundlagen (n. 5), marginal no. 26.

10 More detailed, e.g., *Linardatos*, Grundlagen (n. 5), marginal no. 29 et seq.

11 See reference at n. 8.

included in the portfolio.[12] In this regard, it has to be stressed that this "rebalancing" or risk management process is not fully autonomous; rather "hybrid" systems that combine algorithms with some human control predominate.[13] Altogether, the ongoing re-allocation should increase the client's long-term return.

As for the underlying technical architecture, there are indeed some service providers on the market who state to use "intelligent algorithms" and/or "artificial intelligence" (AI) on their website.[14] This concerns both the customer onboarding process as well as the ongoing rebalancing/asset allocation. In general, however, scepticism seems to be warranted when firms claim that intelligent models are already in use. This is suggested by a recent report of Brussels based *Better Finance*, looking specifically at the client profiling and initial portfolio construction. In a mystery shopping exercise, Better Finance concluded that the systems are generally a far cry from AI today.[15] This finding is also consistent with earlier statements by researchers[16] as well as supervisory authorities.[17]

So although the use of AI in the robo-investing process does not yet seem to have become mainstream, there is an increased discussion that firms will use more powerful systems in the future.[18] Also, supervisors are already discussing potential regulatory measures.[19] In particular, in

---

12 Cf., e.g., *Better Finance*, Robo-Advisors (n.), 16; *R. Theis*, Der Einsatz automatischer und intelligenter Agenten im Finanzdienstleistungsbereich, Berlin 2021, p. 45 et seqq.; *Bianchi/Brière*, Robo-Advising (n. 7), 7 et seq.

13 Cf. more detailed *Linardatos*, Grundlagen (n. 5), marginal no. 17 et seqq.

14 See, e.g., *Theis*, Agenten (n. 12), p. 58 and the references contained therein.

15 Cf. *Better Finance*, Robo-advice: Automated? Yes. Intelligent? Not so much., Press Release 21 December 2021, 2; more detailed also *Better Finance*, Robo-Advisors (n. 6), 8.

16 *Bianchi/Brière*, Robo-Advising (n. 7), 14 discussing i.a. technological and knowledge as well as regulatory constraints (esp. fiduciary duties) as reasons why not more AI is built into robo-investing. Cf. also *Maume*, Robo-advisors (n. 5), 29: "rather simple procedures"; as well, *Linardatos*, Robo Advice (n. 6), marginal no. 6.

17 E.g., *Commission de Surveillance du Secteur Financier* (CSSF), White Paper Artificial Intelligence, December 2018, 41.

18 Cf., e.g., *F. Möslein*, Leitlinien für den Einsatz künstlicher Intelligenz und ihre Bedeutung für die Erbringung von Robo Advice, in: Linardatos (ed.), Robo Advice (n. 5), §3 marginal no. 2; also, *Better Finance*, Robo-Advisors (n. 6), 17: "highly possible in the future".

19 Cf., e.g., *Expert Group on Regulatory Obstacles to Financial Innovation (ROFIEG)*, 30 Recommendations on Regulation, Innovation and Finance – Final Report to the European Commission, December 2019, 38.

September 2021, the global standard setter for securities markets, the International Organization of Securities Commissions (IOSCO), published a report on the use of AI and machine learning (ML) by market intermediaries, including a Guidance with six (non-binding[20]) measures.[21] As regards the customer-side, Measure 5(a) stipulates that supervisors "should consider requiring firms to disclose *meaningful information* to customers and clients around their use of AI and ML that impact client outcomes".[22]

B. *Questions and scope*

Against this background, the aim of this paper is to explore the legal status quo around the disclosure of the use of AI[23] in the robo-investment context. In doing so, an attempt is made to analyse whether the current framework is requiring "meaningful information" to be disclosed or not. To answer these questions, I will structure the remainder of this article in three sections. In the next section, I will first briefly present potential transparency rationales (esp. in light of the use of innovative techniques), in order to build the foundations for the following discussions (B.). Subsequently, in the main section (C.), I will then assess the level of disclosure set out under the relevant EU financial law *acquis*, referring also to the national implementations in Germany and Austria, which have been the subject of some controversy. Lastly, I will end with a few brief remarks on the need for more information to stimulate further discussion (D.).

Before proceeding, however, it must be emphasised that there are other potentially applicable rules which are beyond the scope of this contribution. This concerns firstly the national private law framework, in particular

---

20 Nevertheless, national competent authorities (NCAs) such as the Austrian Financial Markets Authority *FMA* and the German Federal Financial Supervisory Authority *BaFin* are explicitly encouraged to consider the measures in light of their legal and regulatory frameworks.
21 *IOSCO*, The use of artificial intelligence and machine learning by market intermediaries and asset managers, Final Report, September 2021 available at https://www.fsb.org/2021/09/the-use-of-artificial-intelligence-ai-and-machine-learning-ml-by-market-intermediaries-and-asset-managers/ (last access: 18.10.2022).
22 *Ibid.*, p. 20 (emphasis added).
23 A note on terminology: although IOSCO stresses the use of "AI and ML techniques" in the Guidance, the two terms are used slightly differently in the following. This is because in the EU the proposed AI-Act refers to the notion of AI as the umbrella term; ML is (only) one technique and approach of AI. See Art. 3 no. 1 *juncto* Annex 1 of the Commission proposal, COM(2021) 206 final.

contractual information obligations arising from the relationship between service provider and investor. While the issue of private law enforcement will be picked up later, it seems justifiable to not place too much focus on the private law rules, because many scholars – at least in Austria and to some lesser extent also in Germany – agree that the interpretation of those obligations is subject to the *leges speciales* in the finance domain.[24] Something different is certainly true for the data protection regime, the General Data Protection Regulation (GDPR). Indeed, there is a discussion among scholars whether at least some aspects of the robo-investing process constitute automated decision making (with similarly significantly affects) as per Art. 22 GDPR[25] and, subsequently, whether service providers would need to comply with the granular information duties under Art. 13, 15 GDPR.[26] This issue, however, must be discussed elsewhere. Finally, the proposed "AI Act"[27] could be relevant in the future, although probably to a limited extent. This because requirements for so-called "high risk AI sys-

---

24 Cf., generally, e.g., *E. Brandl/P. Klausberger* in: E. Brandl/G. Saria (eds.), WAG 2018, 2nd ed., Wien 2018, § 47 marginal no. 10 et seqq.; also *K. Rothenhöfer* in: E. Schwark/D. Zimmer (eds.), KMRK, 5th ed., München 2020, Vor § 63 marginal no. 9 et seqq.; cf. in particular on the contractual duties *Linardatos*, Robo Advice (n. 6), marginal no. 72 et seq.; differing for Art. 25 MiFID II *R. Kulms*, Digital Financial Markets and (Europe's) Private Law – A Case for Regulatory Competition?, in: E. Avgouleas/H. Marjosola (eds.), Digital Finance in Europe: Law, Regulation, and Governance, Berlin/Boston 2021, p. 213 (229). For a monographic analysis see *F. Della Negra*, MiFID II and Private Law [:] Enforcing EU Conduct of Business Rules, London: Bloomsbury 2019.

25 Cf. *Maume*, Robo-advisors (n. 5), 25: likely; also, at least partially in favour *G. Spindler*, WpHG und Datenschutz, in: L. Klöhn/S. Mock (eds.), Festschrift 25 Jahre WpHG, Berlin/Boston 2020, 327 (335), but only for negative decisions (e.g., if not admitted to the service); generally against the application of Art. 22 GDPR *C. Hirsch/N. Y. Merlino*, Do Robots Rule Wealth Management? A Brief Legal Analysis of Robo-Advisors, SZW 2022, 33 (44), according to them Art. 22 would only apply if the amount invested represents more than 80% of the client's assets; also, *M. Henneman/K. Kumkar*, Robo Advice und automatisierte Entscheidungen im Einzelfall, in: Linardatos (ed.), Robo Advice (n. 5), § 13 marginal no. 17, even if not entering into a contract.

26 See generally for an interesting approach *H. Asghari/N. Birner/A. Burchardt/D. Dicks/J. Faßbender/N. Feldhus/F. Hewett/V. Hofmann/M. C. Kettemann/W. Schulz/J. Simon/J. Stolberg-Larsen/T. Züger*, What to explain when explaining is difficult? An interdisciplinary primer on XAI and meaningful information in automated decision-making, Alexander von Humboldt Institute for Internet and Society 2021, combining technical, social and legal aspect, available at https://graphite.page/explainable-ai-report/ (last access: 18.10.2022)

27 See reference *supra* n. 23.

tems" will only be applicable to a small number of financial service providers (not including the management of portfolios[28]); apart from that, the proposal contains rather rudimentary transparency rules.[29]

C. Potential rationales for informing clients around AI use

It is well known that disclosure is one of the primary regulatory techniques in the context of the provision of investment services.[30] The rationale behind this is first and foremost to enable clients to make informed decisions. More concretely, it is about the reduction of information asymmetries.[31] The relevance of this basic idea was also emphasised by IOSCO in its AI Guidance according to which the objective should be to disclose "sufficient" information to clients to enable them "to understand [1] the nature of, and key characteristics of the products and services that they are receiving, and [2] how they are impacted by the use of the technology."[32] On a more abstract level, enabling informed choices serves the overall goal of investor protection.[33]

Another aspect that is often mentioned as an additional reason for disclosure relates to the risk that a lack of transparency of AI processes could undermine the already low level of trust in the financial system and financial services.[34] For instance, in its 2020 Digital Finance Strategy the Commission stressed that customers would be fearing biases and exploitative profiling due to opaqueness and lack of understanding about how

---

28 It includes solely the use for credit scoring and insurance purposes – at least according to the presidency compromise text, see 2021/0106(COD).

29 See only Art. 52 of the proposal, which at least could have some relevance for the robo-onboarding process (arg. "interact"). Additionally, with respect to high-risk systems, this conclusion could be put into perspective by the fact that the AI Act, by mandating the provision of information to users in Art. 13, enables the user to fulfil its GDPR obligations. See *G. Mazzini/S. Scalzo*, The Proposal for the Artificial Intelligence Act: Considerations around Some Key Concepts, SSRN, 2 May 2022, 22.

30 Cf., e.g., *J. Armour/D. Awrey/P. Davies/L. Enriques/J. N. Gordon/C. Mayer/J. Payne*, Principles of financial regulation, Oxford 2016, p. 76.

31 Cf., e.g., *Maume*, Robo-advisors (n. 5), 22.

32 *IOSCO*, Report (n. 21), 20. Cf. also, e.g., *Organisation for Economic Co-operation and Development*, Artificial Intelligence, Machine Learning and Big Data in Finance, 11 August 2021, 45: disclosures should also allow customers to make the right choice between competing services and products.

33 *Armour/Awrey/Davies/Enriques/Gordon/ Mayer/Payne.*, Principles (n. 30), 76.

34 *Better Finance*, Robo-Advisors (n. 6), 45.

a particular outcome is obtained.[35] The underlying rationale corresponds to another building block of financial markets regulation, i.e. ensuring confidence of investors in markets and the services provided.

Finally, a last concern, sometimes stressed in connection with the trust issue and certainly also relevant from an investor protection perspective, is the difficulty of contesting ML-based outcomes.[36] Another plausible rationale for some transparency in relation to AI use could therefore be the need to have information to substantiate a claim when wrongdoing occurs,[37] and ultimately to enable self-advocacy.[38]

D. Analysis of the MiFID II transparency regime vis-à-vis clients

Considering the above, this section will assess the applicable disclosure requirements for the use of AI in the robo-investing context. The key legislation governing the provision of investment services in the EU is the Markets in Financial Instruments Directive (MiFID II).[39] As far as transparency towards clients is concerned, two provisions of MiFID II deserve particular attention: first, Art. 24, imposing requirements regarding "information to clients", and Art. 25, which regulates the "assessment of suitability". In the following, slightly deviating from the logic of the MiFID II, first any information requirements in the suitability assessment context will be analysed (I.); subsequently, the level of disclosure set out in Art. 24 will be scrutinised (II.). This approach can be explained, among other things, by the fact that in practise the disclosure required by the law is often provided at the end of the customer journey rather than at the beginning of it.[40]

---

35 *European Commission*, Digital Finance Strategy for the EU, COM(2020) 591 final, 11.
36 *Ibid.*
37 E.g., *H. Mueller/F. Ostmann*, AI transparency in financial services – why, what, who and when?, FCA Insights, 19 February 2020, mentioning an unfavourable loan decision; cf. also already *Maume*, Robo-advisors (n. 5), 40 et seq., noting the relevance for enforcement-actions, because only the disclosure of the algorithm would give a client a chance to prove his case in a potential lawsuit.
38 Cf., e.g., *Asghari/Birner/Burchardt/Dicks/Faßbender/Feldhus/Hewett/Hofmann/Kettemann/Schulz/Simon/Stolberg-Larsen/Züger*, XAI (n. 26), 13, providing an overview of transparency needs of different groups.
39 Directive 2014/65/EU, OJ L 173/349.
40 As the French financial markets authority *AMF* found in a digital mystery shopping exercise, the disclosures were made at a time when investors had already been confronted with a various different information, see *ESMA*, Final Report on

I. Disclosure in the suitability assessment and reporting to clients

As per Art. 25(2) MiFID II,[41] traditional as well as digital portfolio managers first have a duty to obtain certain information *from* the (potential) client to provide suitable services, covering knowledge and experience, financial situation (incl. loss-bearing capacity) and investment objectives (incl. risk tolerance). This information collection and assessment process is a cornerstone of the EU's investor protection regime[42] and also at the heart of robo-investing.[43] Here, the assessment is generally performed based on the information obtained from the customer via the online questionnaire, as described above.[44] In collecting the information on risk appetite etc., there is certainly an *implicit information element towards clients* because by answering these questions, a client will be already confronted with some information on the (robo-)investment process. In addition to implicit information in the customer profiling, the suitability assessment regime however also includes some *explicit information components*,[45] as will be explained below.

1. Information to clients about the purpose of the suitability assessment

Explicit information is not required by Art. 25 MiFID II, but at the so-called level 2[46] in Chapter III, Section 3 of the Commission Delegated Regu-

---

the European Commission mandate on certain aspects relating to retail investor protection, 29 April 2022, ESMA35–42–1227, para. 11. Furthermore, a similar approach has been taken by *Maume*, Robo-advisors (n. 5).

41 Transposed in Sec. 56(1) of the Austrian Securities Supervision Act (abbreviated "WAG 2018") and in Sec. 64 of the German Securities Trading Act (in short: "WpHG").

42 See, e.g., *E. Avgouleas/A. Seretakis*, Governing the Digital Finance Value-Chain in the EU: MIFID II, the Digital Package, and the Large Gaps between!, in: E. Avgouleas/H. Marjosola (eds.), Digital Finance in Europe: Law, Regulation, and Governance, Berlin/Boston 2021, p. 1 (24); explicitly *Maume*, Robo-advisors (n. 5), 28.

43 E.g., *Theis*, Agenten (n. 12), p. 185.

44 See Sec. A.

45 Cf. also *F. Mezzanotte*, An examination into the investor protection properties of robo-advisory services in Switzerland, Capital Markets Law Journal 2020, 489 (504).

46 See in general on this, e.g., *A. Schopper*, WAG 2018: Ausgewählte Neuerungen im Anlegerschutz, Zeitschrift für Verbraucherrecht 2018, 4.

lation (EU) 2017/565 (in the following: CDR).[47] According to Art. 54(1) subpara. 1 s. 2 CDR, it is specified that investment firms shall inform (potential) clients – clearly and simply – that the reason for assessing suitability is to enable the firm to act in the best interest of the client, thus optimise the recommendations.[48] While at first sight no robo-specific disclosure duties are mandated by Art. 54(1) CDR,[49] a different picture might follow in light of the next level of EU capital markets regulation.

Already back in 2018, the European Securities and Markets Authority (ESMA) issued a revised version of its "Guidelines on certain aspects of the MiFID II suitability requirements"[50] in the form of so-called "own-initiative guidelines"[51] under Art. 16 of the ESMA Regulation.[52] These quasi-regulatory rules[53] clarify different aspects of the suitability assessment process and have been specifically amended to take into account the phenomenon of robo-investing.[54] Although the Guidelines – as their title suggests – are primarily focused on the suitability assessment as per Art. 25 MiFID II,[55] they also contain certain disclosure considerations *vis-à-vis* customers in Guideline 1. Strikingly, these transparency aspects are under the hea-

---

47 OJ L 87/1.
48 Cf., e.g., *I. Koller* in: H.-D. Assmann/U. H. Schneider/P. O. Mülbert (eds.), Wertpapierhandelsrecht Kommentar, 7th ed., Köln 2019, WpHG, § 64 marginal no. 38.
49 It is however expressly recognised by Art. 54(1) subpara. 2 CDR that the ultimate responsibility for an appropriate suitability assessment lies with the investment firm if (semi-)automated systems are used for the suitability assessment, see, e.g., *Maume*, Robo-advisors (n. 5), 28; *Kulms*, Digital Financial Markets (n. 24), p. 229.
50 *ESMA*, Guidelines on certain aspects of the MiFID II suitability requirements, 6 November 2018, ESMA35–43–1163.
51 See *ESMA*, Guidelines (n. 50), para. 11; on the Art. 16 Guidelines in general see *N. Moloney*, The Age of ESMA: Governing EU Financial Markets, Oxford 2018, p. 145 et seqq. There are different views in the literature on the lawfulness of the guidelines. Against *Koller* (n. 48), § 64 marginal no. 38: without sufficient legal basis. Differently *C. Krönke*, Öffentliches Digitalwirtschaftsrecht [:] Grundlagen – Herausforderungen und Konzepte – Perspektiven, Tübingen 2020, p. 579: legitimate. The latter is further supported by the Case C-911/19, ECLI:EU:C:2021:599 and the legal nature of the guidelines. See on latter the text accompanying n. 66.
52 Regulation (EU) No 1095/2010, OJ L 331/84.
53 *Moloney*, ESMA (n. 51), p. 151.
54 Stressing this also *ESMA*, Final Report Retail Investor Protection (n. 40), para. 153. See for an overview of the guidelines *F. Möslein*, Regulating Robotic Conduct: On ESMA's New Guidelines and Beyond, in: N. Aggarwal/H. Eidenmüller/L. Enriques/J. Payne/K. Zwieten (eds.), Autonomous Systems and the Law, München/Baden-Baden 2019, p. 45 (47).
55 See also on the purpose *ESMA*, Guidelines (n. 50), para. 9.

ding "information to clients about the purpose of the suitability assessment", clearly referring to the duty under Art. 54(1) subpara. 1 CDR.[56]

A closer look at Guideline 1 shows that a distinction is made between a "general guideline" and "supporting guidelines". While "General guideline 1" only adds fairly generic information requirements with respect to Art. 54(1) subpara. 1 CDR,[57] specific aspects for robo-investing are put forward in the supporting guidelines to general guideline 1.[58] Especially, it is stated that firms "should" provide "a very clear explanation of the exact degree and extent of human involvement and if and how the client can ask for human interaction".[59] Moreover, "an explanation that the answers clients provide will have a direct impact in determining the suitability of the investment decisions recommended or undertaken on their behalf" should be given.[60] Finally, it also is set forth that a firm should offer "a description of the sources of information used to generate an investment advice or to provide the portfolio management service".[61]

The relevance of these supporting guidelines for algorithm/AI-related information has been discussed differently in the literature. On the one hand, it was noted by one scholar that the Guidelines would define the scope of the information to be provided to clients when using (semi-)automated procedures; by implication, a customer would not have a right to disclosure of the functioning or parameters of the algorithm used.[62] In stark contrast, according to other researchers, the Guidelines would actually mandate some information on the functioning (and purpose) of the systems.[63]

---

56 In addition, explicit reference is made to Art. 24(1), 24(4) and 24(5) of MiFID II as "relevant legislation". See *ESMA*, Guidelines (n. 50), before para. 15.

57 *ESMA*, Guidelines (n. 50), para. 15.

58 On this and the following also, e.g., *Krönke*, Digitalwirtschaftsrecht (n. 51), p. 579.

59 *ESMA*, Guidelines (n. 50), first point of para. 20.

60 *ESMA*, Guidelines (n. 50), second point of para. 20.

61 *ESMA*, Guidelines (n. 50), third point of para. 20.

62 Cf. *C. Herresthal*, Vertriebsbezogene Interessenkonflikte beim Robo Advisor – Der Vertrieb (konzern-)eigener Anlageprodukte sowie von Anlageprodukten verbundener Unternehmen, in: Linardatos (ed.), Robo Advice (n. 5), § 9 marginal no. 60, with explicit reference to the ESMA Guidelines, para. 20 and 21.

63 This was argued with reference to the ESMA Consultation Paper by *T. B. Madel*, Robo Advice [:] Aufsichtsrechtliche Qualifikation und Analyse der Verhaltens- und Organisationspflichten bei der digitalen Anlageberatung und Vermögensverwaltung, Baden-Baden 2019, p. 174. The Consultation Paper, however, was more detailed than the Final Guidelines, see n. 65. Presumably also assuming binding duties *Krönke*, Digitalwirtschaftsrecht (n. 51), p. 580, noting that these "informati-

As regards the latter view, it is highly questionable whether the supporting guidelines indeed demand such information on an AI system. ESMA itself was mindful to not create excessive information requirements vis-à-vis clients.[64] This is further supported by the fact that the Consultation Paper, leading to the adoption of the Guidelines, originally provided for more granular information to be provided to clients.[65] The above, however, should not lead to the opposite conclusion that the non-inclusion of algorithm/AI-related information is legally relevant in any way. This is because, as per para. 8 of the Guidelines, ESMA stressed that the revised suitability guidelines do not always reflect absolute obligations; rather, it was highlighted that if the word "should" is used, it would not constitute a MiFID II requirement.[66]

As a result, the specific disclosure aspects set forth by the supporting guidelines are merely recommendations by ESMA for "good" behaviour. For a firm intending to follow these suggestions, some conclusions can nevertheless be drawn for the use of AI/ML. While the guidelines were certainly drafted for "simple" rule-based systems at the time of their publication, looking at the wording of the first recommendation highlighted above, a service provider should communicate the use of AI. Secondly, if a firm emphasises the "direct impact" of client responses, it should not be possible that a potential customer can enter almost anything but change little. Finally, to be in line with the third recommendation mentioned, one should describe any additional input sources if a firm deploys a ML model not only using the responses from the customer, but learning on previous experiences etc.

In summary, due the nature of the supporting guidelines set out in the revised ESMA guidelines on suitability, no binding robo-specific information requirements arise as per Art. 25(2) MiFID II or Art. 54(1) CDR. Nonetheless, a "good" robot that uses AI should communicate about AI's pre-

---

on obligations" would require some basic information on the functioning of the systems, but no individual explanations.

64 *ESMA*, Final Report Guidelines (n. 8), 13.

65 See in detail *ESMA*, Consultation Paper Guidelines on certain aspects of the MiFID II suitability requirements, 13 July 2017, ESMA35–43–748, Annex III para. 21. Additional, more comprehensive "examples" for these draft guidelines were given in the background of the document, see para. 39. In the end, however, these draft disclosure requirements were not included in the final version of the (supporting) guidelines.

66 On the other side, the words "shall", "must" or "required to" would reflect a MiFID II obligation. See *ESMA*, Guidelines (n. 50), para. 8; highlighting this also, e.g., *Della Negra*, MiFID II (n. 24), p. 67.

sence and the type of sources a ML model or alike techniques are based in the profiling process.

2. *Ex-post and suitability reporting obligations*

Pursuant to Art. 25(6) MiFID II,[67] service providers are subject to two different reporting obligations, including (i) ex post reports as well as (ii) so-called suitability reports.[68] Art. 25(6) subpara. 1 specifies that a firm must give "adequate reports on the service provided [...] taking into account the type and the complexity of financial instruments involved and the nature of the service provided to the client", which is further fleshed out at level 2 (esp. Art. 60[2] CDR). Concerning the suitability of the service and specifically with respect to portfolio management, Art. 25(6) subpara. 4 adds that a firm has to periodically provide a report together with updated information on how an investment meets the client's preferences, objectives etc.[69] Additional details are set out in Art. 54(12) CDR.

At a first glance, one might assume that "adequate reports" would require some sort of AI/ML disclosure (esp. with reference to "the nature of the service provided") or that technology-related disclosures might be necessary in the suitability reports if AI is used in the onboarding. However, looking at the context as well as current understanding, the reporting framework does not seem to mandate such aspects.[70] Under the ex-post reporting requirement, the focus is more on providing an abstract review of the actions taken by the portfolio manager,[71] although some arguments put forward in the discussion around disclosure as per Art. 24(4) MiFID II,[72] could imply a different understanding.[73] Unlike Art. 24(4) *juncto* (5), which explicitly requires information about the service (and focuses on enabling informed choices), Art. 25(6) however only

---

67 Transposed with Sec. 60(1) and (4) WAG 2018 as well as Sec. 63(12) and 64(8) WpHG.
68 Cf., e.g., *Brandl/Klausberger*, WAG 2018 (n. 24), § 60 marginal no. 1.
69 On this in general, e.g., *Schopper*, WAG 2018 (n. 46), 8 et seq.
70 Presumably assuming this as well *Mezzanotte*, Investor protection properties (n. 45), 505 et seq.; *C. Müssig*, Aufsichts- und zivilrechtliche Anforderungen der digitalen Vermögensverwaltung bei einer Online-Abschlussmöglichkeit, in: Linardatos (ed.), Robo Advice (n. 5), § 5 marginal no. 71 et seqq. as well as 89 et seqq.; *Theis*, Agenten (n. 12), p. 199 et seq.
71 See in general, e.g., *Rothenhöfer*, KMRK (n. 24), § 63 marginal no. 378.
72 See *infra* Sec. II.1.
73 See the discussion at the text accompanying n. 82 et seqq. as well as n. 91 et seqq.

states that the nature of the service must be "taken into account". The suitability reporting requirement seems even less relevant; in order to comply with this obligation, one will indeed have to refer to the client's answers in the online questionnaire,[74] but not to the use of algorithms or ML.

As a result, Art. 25(6) appears not to require any information on AI use.

II. Overarching disclosure requirements to clients

After concluding that the suitability assessment regime merely provides for voluntary disclosure requirements, let us now turn to the actual information regulation pursuant to Art. 24 MiFID II, which has been the subject of controversy in the German literature.

1. Standardised information requirements

At the heart of the debate among scholars is Art. 24(4),[75] which obliges service providers to present a large amount of information to (potential) clients[76] and sets out the so-called "minimum content".[77] More precisely, it is stipulated that firms must provide "appropriate" information on several topics, including the firm itself and its services as well as the proposed investment strategies. What kind of information should be generally disclosed, is specified at level 2 in Chapter III, Section 1 of the CDR (relating i.a. to the firm and its services[78]). Para. 4 is further complemented by Art. 24(5), ac-

---

74 Stressing the latter *D. Linardatos*, Qualifizierung der Dienste von Robo Advisor im Kapitalanlagegeschäft und Wohlverhaltenspflichten, in: Linardatos (ed.), Robo Advice (n. 5), § 4 marginal no. 75; see, in general, e.g., *Brandl/Klausberger*, WAG 2018 (n. 24), § 60 marginal no. 85: the periodic reports will entail certain service-, investment- or client-related changes compared to the original suitability report.

75 This is transposed in Sec. 48(1) WAG 2018 and Sec. 63(7) WpHG.

76 Stressing this, in general *Ringe/Ruof*, Robo Advice (n. 5), p. 206 et seq.

77 For this distinction between "minimum content" and "minimum standard" see, e.g., *K. Rothenhöfer* in: P. O. Mülbert/A. Früh/T. Seyfried (eds.), Bankrecht und Kapitalmarktrecht, 6th ed., Köln 2022, marginal no. 13.24; calling it "general standardised information requirements" *P. Knobl*, Die Wohlverhaltensregeln unter dem WAG 2018, Österreichisches BankArchiv 2018, 460 (469); also *M. Brenncke* in: M. Lehmann/C. Kumpan (eds.), European Financial Services Law, Baden-Baden 2019, Art. 24 MiFID II marginal no. 19: overarching disclosure requirement.

78 See Art. 47 CDR, which will be discussed in more detail later in this contribution.

cording to which the objective of this information provision is that customers understand the nature and risks of the service and ultimately can make an informed investment decision. Lastly, Art. 24(4) and (5) also add some "procedural" clarifications: (i) the information needs to be provided "in good time", i.e. pre-contractually; (ii) firms have to do this a in a comprehensible form; and (iii), if a member state allows it (which is the case in Austria[79] and Germany[80]), it is also possible to deliver the information to clients in a standardised way (esp. in the terms and conditions).

The issue now is whether "appropriate" information on the firm, its services or investment strategies must contain disclosures on use of AI. While it is certainly true that there is no obligation to disclose the algorithm/ model or to give a detailed explanation,[81] it has been discussed whether some algo/AI-related information is required per Art. 24(4) *juncto* (5) MiFID II. Especially in Germany, the majority seems to be in favour of some (limited) algo/AI transparency. Generally speaking, it is argued that service providers have to disclose at least the use of an algorithmic/AI system[82] and/or describe the basic functioning of the system to meet the duties under Art. 24.[83] According to one scholar, a duty to disclose the basic parameters of the automated investment decision would also follow from the accompanying level 2 provisions in Art. 47(2) and (3) CDR.[84] Finally, one author also argued that firms would have to disclose the risks of error,[85] confirming this strong sentiment towards certain Algo/AI disclosure measures. On the other hand, there are only a few disagreeing voices

---

79 Sec. 48(3) s. 1 WAG 2018.

80 Sec. 63(7) s. 2 WpHG.

81 Cf. already *Maume*, Robo-advisors (n. 5), 40 et seq.; also in the suitability assessment context *ESMA*, Final Report Guidelines (n. 8), 13, noting "that it does not intend to require firms to disclose their algorithms in detail to clients".

82 Both for algorithms and AI *Theis*, Agenten (n. 12), p. 181; specifically for the use of AI and the respective, comparable Swiss rules *Hirsch/Merlino*, Robots (n. 25), 38 et seq., noting that one has to communicate the use of ML as well as "basic information on the functioning of these algorithms."

83 *Theis*, Agenten (n. 12), p. 181; *Linardatos*, Robo Advice (n. 6), marginal no. 53; cf. also with respect to AI and investment brokering ("Anlagevermittlung") *M. Denga*, KI bei Finanzdienstleistungen – Robo-Advice, in: M. Ebers/C. A. Heinze/T. Krügel/B. Steinrötter (eds.), Künstliche Intelligenz und Robotik, München 2020, § 15 marginal no. 44, emphasising the need to disclose the decision-making mechanism in a comprehensible manner.

84 Cf. *Krönke*, Digitalwirtschaftsrecht (n. 51), p. 578.

85 Cf. *Denga*, KI (n. 83), § 15 marginal no. 44, noting practical problems and calling for the necessity of weighing up the constitutionally guaranteed concerns (marginal no. 45).

in the literature. Contrary to the above-cited view, but also with reference to the specifications fleshed out in Art. 47 CDR, it was stressed by one researcher that there would be no duty for a traditional portfolio manager to inform a client in detail about the content of the investment strategy, the decision-making criteria, as well as the analytical instruments, which must also apply in the digital context.[86] In addition, there would be no basis for a higher standard for robo-investing[87] and no duty to disclose an algo or its core parameters.[88] Such an understanding was presumably shared by another voice in the literature.[89]

Interestingly, from an empirical perspective, the above-mentioned critical statements seem to be in line with a 2019 study of web-disclosed information of Swiss service providers finding that only a few them expressly mentioned the word "algorithm", and even less provided an explanation on their websites.[90] Especially the latter would also correspond to this author's impression, which of course raises the question whether some market participants are currently non-compliant or whether the alleged disclosure obligations (mentioned in the previous paragraph) are not as clear-cut as some voices suggest. Indeed, there seem to be still some open questions, which have only been partially addressed in the literature so far.[91] It concerns (i) the application of the level 2 rules, (ii) the technology neutrality of Art. 24(4) MiFID II as well as (iii) the overall purpose in light of Art. 24(5) MiFID II.

As far as the relevance of the level 2 provisions is concerned, there are two different aspects. First, as mentioned above, there seems to be some

---

86 Cf. *Herresthal*, Interessenkonflikte (n. 62), § 9 marginal no. 66, referring explicitly to Art. 47(2), (3) (c) as well as recital 94 and Art. 47(3) (d) and implicitly also to Art. 47(3) (a) and (e) CDR *juncto* the German transposition in Sec. 63(7) sentence 1 WpHG.

87 See *Herresthal*, Interessenkonflikte (n. 62), § 9 marginal no. 66: also, *de lege ferenda*.

88 Cf. *Herresthal*, Interessenkonflikte (n. 62), § 9 marginal no. 66 ("Kernparameter"). See also already marginal no. 65: no duty to explain the functioning of the algorithm, its limits or the underlying finance model.

89 See *Müssig*, Online-Abschlussmöglichkeit (n. 70), § 5 marginal no. 104, who raised the question whether algorithms should be disclosed, but concluded that it would (only) be sensible to describe them in abstract terms in a white paper and to make them available to clients on request, if necessary.

90 See in detail *Mezzanotte*, Investor protection properties (n. 45), 496 et seq.

91 Some aspects were already addressed in discussions around the ESMA suitability guidelines, to which references are made below. The replies are available at https://www.esma.europa.eu/press-news/consultations/consultation-guidelines-certain-aspects-mifid-ii-suitability-requirements (last access: 27.10.2022).

confusion whether the information duties pursuant to Art. 47 CDR, mandating i.a. to inform on "the management objectives, the level of risk to be reflected in the manager's exercise of discretion, and any specific constraints on that discretion",[92] would require some limited algorithmic transparency or not. In this regard, I believe it is more reasonable that a firm just has to inform very generally on the management objectives, but does not need to elaborate on the actual algorithmic implementation.[93] The second aspect that has not been conclusively clarified yet is the exact interplay between level 1 and 2. The researchers who have argued in favour of some disclosure appear to assume that level 2 information requirements are not exhaustive.[94] Looking at the legal basis (i.e. Art. 24[13] [b] MiFID II), it is stipulated that the Commission is empowered to specify the details about content of information to clients i.a. in relation to investment firms and their services. The purpose of this is "to ensure that investment firms comply with the principles set out in this Article when providing investment [...] services". Although this could indicate an exhaustive nature of relevant level 2 rules, a purposive interpretation of Art. 24(4) and (5) that additional information may need to be provided in certain cases in order to enable the customer to make an informed decision seems more convincing.[95] It therefore seems advisable to disclose at least whether or not the service is based on algorithms/AI in order to appropriately inform about the services.[96]

A second issue stressed in a few replies to ESMA's Consultation Paper on the draft suitability guidelines relates to the fact that not only "robots", but also some "traditional" service providers are using automated systems

---

92 Art. 47(3) (e) CDR.

93 Cf. in general on this *Rothenhöfer*, KMRK (n. 24), § 63 marginal no. 238; by the same token, I also do not believe that the details of the rebalancing/risk management process should be disclosed pursuant to Art. 47(3) (a), which requires "information on the method and frequency of valuation of the financial instruments in the client portfolio". From a contextual point of view, another argument against any AI disclosure pursuant to level 2 could be the fact that Art. 54(1) explicitly clarifies that the responsibility remains with the firm when a (semi-)automated system is used, whereas Art. 47 has not been modified.

94 See references at n. 82 et seqq.

95 Cf., in general, for a nuanced approach with regard to the German transposition *Rothenhöfer*, KMRK (n. 24), § 63 marginal no. 211, 228; see for the Austrian transposition and with references to German literature *Brandl/Klausberger*, WAG 2018 (n. 24), § 48 marginal no. 36.

96 Cf. the reply by the European Fund and Asset Management Association (EFAMA) available at n. 91.

for portfolio management or, put differently, quantitative processes.[97] This begs the question whether another standard for robo-investing is justified[98] or whether conventional portfolio managers using algorithms/AI also have to disclose the basic functioning etc.[99] On a more theoretical level, this question is linked to the principle of technology neutrality, according to which "[t]he same regulation must be applied to the same activity and the same risks", but "different rules should apply to different activities with different risks."[100] Precisely because of the wide reach of the algorithms (and in the future, presumably, AI) and the specific risks in the robo-context,[101] a technology-neutral interpretation of the information duties under Art. 24(4) will allow for some deviation from their previous understanding in relation to more traditional face-to-face services.

Finally, the last concern relates to the kind of information, which some authors seem to demand (especially the disclosure of some basic system capabilities and/or the risks). This could conflict with the overall goal of enabling an informed decision as per Art. 24(5). Already in the ESMA consultation it was stressed that it would be doubtful whether additional information will provide any value to customers.[102] Considering that firms have to disclose a vast amount of information to clients, further disclosures concerning the robo-investing process could actually have an adverse effect, leading to an "information overload",[103] an aspect that will be picked up in the conclusion. Nevertheless, also in my view, there are better arguments for some AI disclosure. This, however, will be limited — at least pursuant to Art. 24(4). Firms will have to inform that they are providing a digital service and/or using AI/ML. Further details, as well as how they are

---

97 Cf. the reply by the Association of Italian Financial Advisory Companies ASCOSIM. This was also highlighted by *ESMA*, Final Report Guidelines (n. 8), 13, however, without elaborating.

98 Critical *Herresthal*, see n. 87 in this contribution.

99 As far as can be seen no such requirement has been discussed previously.

100 On this and the following, cf. also *Zunzunegui*, Digital Finance Platform (n. 5), 295.

101 Highlighting this specific risk, e.g., *Madel*, Robo Advice (n. 63), p. 63; cf., in general, also *Maume*, Robo-Advice (n. 2), 646 et seq.; as well as *ROFIEG*, 30 Recommendations (n. 19), 39.

102 Cf., e.g., the reply by the European Association of Co-operative Banks available at n. 91.

103 As already mentioned, because of this, in the suitability context, some draft disclosure requirements did not find their way into the final version of the guidelines. See *ESMA*, Final Report Guidelines (n. 8), 13, in response to comments made in the consultation and specifically the reply by EFAMA at n. 91.

communicated (e.g., on the website)[104] will be in the discretion of the firm due to principle-based nature of the level 1 rules.

2. *Requirements for the way in which information is provided*

Having established that Art. 24(4) MiFID II does mandate some, albeit limited information on AI, it remains to examine Art. 24(3) MiFID II.[105] In addition to the above, para. 3 clarifies the "minimum standard" for providing information.[106] To be precise, it is set out that all information provided to (potential) clients shall be fair, clear and not misleading. This standard is not only applicable to the required information pursuant to Art. 24(4) MiFID II, but also to any other voluntary information provided to customers.[107]

Also here, the concrete scope has already been the subject of some discussions, although not as extensive as under para. 4. On the one hand, according to some scholars, there would be a duty to disclose some (limited) information on the system in place.[108] From one point of view, it would not require a "comprehensive disclosure" of the functioning or of the parameters of the algorithm, but would necessitate a simple explanation of the functioning, the limitations of the algorithm as well as the underlying finance model.[109] On the other hand, according to another researcher, no such an obligation would exist. Rather, it was argued that Art. 24(3) MiFID II would only outline the general standard that a firm

---

104 Cf. in other context, the discussion whether information not specified by the CDR, must be provided on a durable medium or not *Rothenhöfer*, KMRK (n. 24), § 63 marginal no. 225.

105 This corresponds to Sec. 49 WAG 2018 and Sec. 63(6) WpHG.

106 See for the distinction "minimum content" vs. "minimum standard" already n. 77. In other literature, the provision is also discussed as "General transparency requirement" (cf. *Knobl*, Wohlverhaltensregeln [n. 77], 469) or as "Fair Treatment Clause" (see *Della Negra*, MiFID II [n. 24], p. 66).

107 Cf. for Germany *Koller*, Wertpapierhandelsrecht Kommentar (n. 48), § 63 marginal no. 55.

108 For the German transposition of Art. 24(3) *Linardatos*, Qualifizierung (n. 74), § 4 marginal no. 87, with special emphasis on a circular of BaFin on minimum Requirements for the Compliance Function and Additional Requirements Governing Rules of Conduct, Organisation and Transparency, better known as "MaComp". Also, referring to the German equivalent of para. 3 (as well as para. 4) *Krönke*, Digitalwirtschaftsrecht (n. 51), p. 578.

109 See *Linardatos*, Qualifizierung (n. 74), § 4 marginal no. 87.

must meet when providing any information and not a duty to explain how an algorithm works, its limitations and the model used.[110]

Even if Art. 24(3), also in my view, does not stipulate any obligation to provide information,[111] this does not necessarily preclude the conclusion that some algo-transparency is required *de iure*. In fact, taking a closer look at this issue, it seems quite possible to align these (only at first sight) opposing views. This is because in any communication related to robo-investing, a firm most certainly will need to present some information about the capabilities of the system (and specifically about the use of AI, if this is the case) in order to be fair, clear, and not misleading. More precisely, with respect to the use of AI, caution needs to be taken if a firm claims to use such innovative technologies without explaining what kind of technique is used; otherwise, there seems to be a high chance that the information is too superficial, leading to problems with respect to its clarity.[112] Information is generally clear, if essential information is not left unmentioned.[113] Additional requirements follow from Art. 44(2) CDR[114] providing i.a. that information must always give "a fair and prominent indication of any relevant risks when referencing any potential benefits of an investment service"[115] and that it "does not disguise, diminish or obscure important items, statements or warnings".[116] Thus, particular attention has to be paid to cases where a firm highlights the benefits of ML use, without disclosing all the relevant risks.[117] In this context, it may be difficult to reconcile the

---

110 Cf. again with respect to the German transposition *Herresthal*, Interessenkonflikte (n. 62), § 9 marginal no. 65, calling it a "structurally unsuitable" legal basis.
111 Also, e.g., *Koller*, Wertpapierhandelsrecht Kommentar (n. 48), § 63 marginal no. 55.
112 Cf. generally *Maume*, Robo-advisors (n. 5), 39, noting that many clients do not even have a sound idea of what the term "robo-advisor" means, which is why there is a particular need for explanation and clarification.
113 Cf. *D. Poelzig* in: C. H. Seibt/P. Buck-Heeb/R. Harnos (eds.), BeckOK Wertpapierhandelsrecht, 4th. Ed., München 2022, § 63 marginal no. 134.
114 Similar to the discussion above at the text accompanying n. 94 et seq., one might question whether the level 2 rules provide an exhaustive list or not. See in favour for Art. 44 CDR *Brenncke*, European Financial Services Law (n. 77), Art. 24 marginal no. 16; against *Rothenhöfer*, KMRK (n. 24), § 63 marginal no. 181. Again, I assume a non-exhaustive character, although it seems less relevant because of the openness of the level 2 rules (e.g., "fair").
115 Art. 44(2) (b) as well as recital 67 CDR.
116 Art. 44(2) (e) CDR.
117 Cf. generally *Maume*, Robo-advisors (n. 5), 39, stressing that firms seem to overstate the potential benefits while giving far less priority to the risks involved; cf. in general also *Brenncke*, European Financial Services Law (n. 77), Art. 24 margi-

assumed information standard with the duty that any information should be provided in an understandable way for the average investor, which is also required by the same provision.[118] While I do recognize the challenges in balancing the necessary information on the system-use on the one hand and the comprehensibility of the information on the other hand, I do think that certain information on AI use incl. risks will be necessary. This is also supported by the general literature, according to which one can assume that the average investor has the time to read some documents.[119]

All in all, it seems reasonable that a firm stating to use AI etc. will need to disclose some information on the applied technique to comply with the requirement under Art. 24(5). Otherwise, the information provided to (potential) customers is likely unclear. Similar concerns arise with respect to highlighting benefits of ML and alike approaches while failing to disclose related risks.

E. Concluding comments

This contribution attempted to evaluate whether existing EU financial law requires "meaningful information" around AI use in the robo-investing context. Except for the recommendations included in the supporting guidelines concerning the suitability assessment, no specific provisions mandate the disclosure of information relating to the use of algorithms etc. This, however, does not mean that there is no legal basis for some transparency. Firms providing algorithm-based financial services are subject to the very general information obligations under MiFID II which apply also to the use of ML and other techniques. Taken together, there is some but limited transparency pursuant to Art. 24(3) to (5), which could prompt the question whether we need new requirements for more detailed information.

To answer this, let us briefly come back to the rationales for customer transparency outlined in Sec. C. First, as regards facilitating informed decision making, it has already been stressed that too much information

---

nal no. 17, stressing that "risks" is to be understood broadly; cf. in detail also *Rothenhöfer*, KMRK (n. 24), § 63 marginal no. 183.

118 Art. 44(2) (d) CDR.

119 This is because the law is based on the normative figure of a reasonable and average-educated customer, see, e.g., *Brandl/Klausberger*, WAG 2018 (n. 24), § 48 marginal no. 55 et seq.

could actually lead to an information overload.[120] With respect to ensuring confidence/trust in services and markets, too much disclosure about AI and specifically related risks might also have a detrimental effect, increasing the reluctance of retail investors to engage with capital markets[121] and undermining the meta-goal of a true capital markets union. Last but not least, as regards the private enforcement of investor rights, there might be other preferred options. As already highlighted in the literature, consideration could be given to fine-tuning the civil procedure rules.[122] A similar approach was recently taken in the proposed AI Liability Directive,[123] which, however, would not apply to contractual relationships.[124] In the short term, therefore, it may be more practical to place greater emphasis on the responsibility of NCAs to monitor the soundness of robo-models[125] and to link supervisory findings to subsequent private enforcement in the case of investor losses.

---

120 See on this the text accompanying n. 102.
121 Cf. on the issue of "algorithm aversion", by mere reference, *Bianchi/Brière*, Robo-Advising (n. 7), 18 et seq.
122 See especially *Maume*, Robo-advisors (n. 5), 30 et seq. and 41, discussing a reversal of burden of proof, expressly due to the opacity; in general on the challenges in this regard A. *Schopper*, Haftung für Veranlagungsentscheidungen bei Portfolioverwaltung auf Einzelkundenbasis, Österreichisches BankArchiv 2013, 17 (25).
123 See COM(2022) 496 final, which provides i.a. for the "disclosure of evidence and rebuttable presumption of non-compliance" (Art. 3) and a rebuttable presumption of causality in the case of fault (Art. 4).
124 Pursuant to Art. 1(2) of the proposal, the directive would only cover "non-contractual fault-based civil law claims for damages".
125 The need for supervisory involvement was also emphasised to varying degrees in the responses to the ESMA Consultation (available at n. 91), i.a. by EFAMA, AMUNDI and the French Financial Companies Association ASF. See further on this issue, P. *Raschner*, Supervisory Oversight of the Use of AI and ML by Financial Market Participants, in: L. Böffel/J. Schürger (eds.), Digitalisation, Sustainability and the Banking and Capital Markets Union. EBI Studies in Banking and Capital Markets Law, forthcoming 2023.

List of Authors

Marco Billi
PhD Student at the Department of Legal Studies and Research fellow at the Centro Interdipartimentale Alma Mater Research Institute for Human-Centered Artificial Intelligence – (Alma AI), Department of Law, University of Bologna.
marco.billi3@unibo.it

Dr. Jonas Botta
Postdoctoral Researcher at the German Research Institute for Public Administration, Speyer.
botta@unifoev-speyer.de

Dr. Gordian Konstantin Ebner
Research Assistant at the Chair „European and International Information and Data Law" (Prof. Dr. Moritz Hennemann, M.Jur.), University of Passau.
gordian.ebner@uni-passau.de

Jun.-Prof. Dr. Elena Freisinger
Junior Professor for Innovation Management at the Department of Economic Science and Media, Ilmenau University of Technology.
elena.freisinger@tu-ilmenau.de

Joris Krijger
PhD Candidate at Erasmus School of Philosophy, Rotterdam.
krijger@esphil.eur.nl

Paul Nolan
Barrister-at-Law, Sessional Academic, Macquarie University, Sydney.
paulnolan@barristerchambers.com.au

Dr. Tobias Mast
Head of the Research Programme "Regulatory Structures and the Emergence of Rules in Online Spaces" at the Leibniz Institute for Media Research | Hans-Bredow-Institut (HBI).
t.mast@leibniz-hbi.de

Jun.-Prof. Dr. Juliane Mendelsohn
Junior Professor for Law and Economics of Digitization at the Department of Economic Science and Media, Ilmenau University of Technology.
juliane.mendelsohn@tu-ilmenau.de

Alessandro Parenti
PhD Student at the Department of Legal Studies, Department of Law, University of Bologna.
alessandro.parenti3@unibo.it

Kostina Prifti
PhD Candidate Erasmus School of Law | Erasmus Graduate School of Law, Rotterdam.
prifti@law.eur.nl

Dr. Patrick Raschner
Postdoctoral Researcher at the Chair of Banking and Financial Market Law, University of Liechtenstein. Until September 2022 teaching and research associate (prae-doc) at the Institute of Business and Tax Law (Department of Business Law), University of Innsbruck.
patrick.raschner@uni.li

Dr. Christopher Rennig
Postdoctoral Researcher at the Institute for the Law of Digitalization, University of Marburg.
christopher.rennig@jura.uni-marburg.de

David Schneeberger
Research Assistant at the Institute for Constitutional and Administrative Law, Medical Law Department (Prof. Dr. Karl Stöger, M.Jur.), University of Vienna.
david.schneeberger@univie.ac.at

Prof. Dr. Evert Stamhuis
Full professor at Erasmus School of Law, Rotterdam.
stamhuis@law.eur.nl

Tamara Thuis
PhD Candidate at Rotterdam School of Management, Department of Technology and Operations Management.
thuis@rsm.nl

Prof. Dr. Thomas Wischmeyer
Professor for Public Law and Digital Law, University of Bielefeld.
thomas.wischmeyer@uni-bielefeld.de

List of Editors

Dr. Simone Kuhlmann
Postdoctoral Researcher and Coordinator of the Project 'The Law and its Teaching in Digital Transformation' at the Centre for Law in the Digital Transformation (ZeRdiT), University of Hamburg.

Fabrizio De Gregorio
PhD Student at the Albrecht Mendelssohn Bartholdy Graduate School of Law, University of Hamburg.

Martin Fertmann
PhD Student at the Centre for Law in the Digital Transformation (ZeRdiT), University of Hamburg and Junior Researcher at the Leibniz Institute for Media Research | Hans-Bredow-Institut (HBI).

Hannah Ofterdinger
PhD Candidate with Prof. Dr. Dr. Milan Kuhli and Research Assistant at the Chair for Criminal Law and Criminal Procedure Law including their international and historical References (Prof. Dr. Dr. Milan Kuhli) and the Chair for Criminal Law with International Criminal Law (Prof. Dr. Kai Cornelius), University of Hamburg.

Anton Sefkow
PhD Student at the Centre for Law in the Digital Transformation (ZeRdiT), University of Hamburg.